GW00502901

a *resilient* spirit

a *resilient* spirit

CATHERINE JOHNS

Lothian
BOOKS

Thomas C. Lothian Pty Ltd
11 Munro Street, Port Melbourne, Victoria 3207

Copyright © Catherine Johns 2000
First published 2000

All rights reserved. No part of this publication may be reproduced,
stored in a retrieval system or transmitted in any form by any means
without the prior permission of the copyright owner. Enquiries
should be made to the publisher.

The publication of this title was assisted by the South Australian
Government through Arts SA.

National Library of Australia
Cataloguing-in-Publication data:

Johns, Catherine, 1949–.
   A resilient spirit.

   ISBN 0 7344 0090 X

   1. Johns, Catherine, 1949–. 2. Children – Australia –
   Biography. 3. Country life – Australia – Biography.
   4. Australia – Rural conditions – Biography. I. Title.

994.092

Edited by Gwenda Smyth
Central front cover photograph by Floortje Costain
Background photographs from author's collection
Back cover photographs by Janet Cashmore
All internal photographs from author's collection except
photographs on pages 157, 170 which are courtesy
the Estate of E. S. Gee, and photo page 296 by Floortje Costain.
Cover design by Kim Roberts Design & Illustration
Typeset by J & M Typesetting Pty Ltd
Printed by Griffin Press Pty Limited

Dedication

A friend once said, 'Take good care of your friends, for lovers come and go but friends can be there forever.' My friends are part of the tapestry of my life; they give it colour and texture, and I value each of them in their own unique beauty. This book is dedicated to them:

Anastasia (and Enya, the beautiful red border collie), Jean Lilly, Kathy H., Joy, Jayne, Lilith, Irene, Lynne, Denise, Lesley, Clare, Heiko, Jane C., Lin and Roxie, and the truly wonderful friendships in my communities; you all know who you are. I honour and thank you.

My thanks to the parent who bestowed on me that greatest gift for a Romany child: my godfather, a blind violinist.

To all the horses I have shared time with and for those I still share my life with: Espirit, Tigger, Ebony and Missy, and, Chloe the donkey too! And to those friends who share their life with horses, you all inspire me with your love of horses. To you all:

> And to create the Mare, God spoke to the south wind; 'I will create from you a being which will be a happiness to the good and a misfortune to the bad. Happiness shall be on its fore-head, bounty on its back and joy in the possessor.' (Arab legend)

'Horses, horses, horses, that's all I ever hear from you,' yelled my father.

'Okay,' I replied. 'I'll do what all the other girls are doing and chase boys!'

'You'll stay with the bloody horses!' He instantly responded.

Contents

The horse has her heart

Dogs were always there. I can't remember a time without them. But I do remember seeing my first horse — beauty, the presence, the eye, the movement and grace, the colour and smell. That very special horse smell — a perfume like no other, only attainable by patting or hugging a horse. It is still my favourite perfume and I drink in horse smells from my clothes long after I've come inside for the night. When I was a child I hated washing my clothes or body, ridding them of that special smell. I can stand for ages, my arms around a horse, or just leaning against that warm body, soaking up the smell. Horse breath is sweet. It smells of sunshine and grass.

'Look at that body, that muscle, that beauty,' my father would comment. 'All that grown on grass.'

And the warm breath that comes rippling through the nostrils. The feel of hot horse breath as it ruffles my hair or tickles my face is as important as the tender touch of a lover — the awareness as a horse blows and sniffs, exploring my scent, knowing who I am through its breath.

When I saw my first horse I fell deeply and respectfully in love forever. A love that began forty-eight years ago just before I was two years of age.

My nana, mother and father had decided to attend a race meeting. My nana was somehow related to one of the jockeys;

my mother thought race tracks were 'all the go', because where else (perhaps only at the football or in the armed services) were there so many men; and my father was a man of horses. Horses had been his life until he returned from the war to find them all replaced by petrol-driven farm vehicles and cars. He did get another horse when I was young but we only had him a couple of years before he was sold. My father loved horses but he was not overtly sentimental about them as I was. Am. So to the race-track we all went.

Before each race the horses were paraded so the spectators could 'cast their eyes over a horse' before placing a bet, or — once having placed a bet — have a look at what was riding on their money.

My nana chose by the look of the horse. 'That one,' she would say, pointing. 'That one is beautiful. I like the colour.'

'You don't go on looks,' my father would say. 'You go on form. On breeding.'

'I'll go on what I like,' my Nana would reply, 'and what I like is what I see. It's a feeling in my guts and behind my eyes.'

If the horse didn't win my father would say to my nana, 'See, Mary, it's about breeding.'

'Oh, that horse will win,' my nana would reply. 'Not today. It isn't his day. But he'll win.'

My mother went by the sound of the horse's name or by the look of the jockey. She was very keen on any horse whose name had anything to do with alcohol or Ireland, like 'Empty Cellar' or 'Paddy's Choice'.

'You don't go by the name,' my father would say. 'That's not the way to place a bet. Study its form.'

My mother studied horses' forms by their jockeys. 'I don't like that one, he's got a tight pinched face', or 'That one's got a skinny arse and a face worth smacking.'

My father would go for a beer at that point. He'd return more ready to listen to the whims of the women of the family. 'Now which one?' he'd ask.

'That one. Because I like the name,' my mother would say tightly.

'Okay, okay. One bets on the way the horse looks and the other bets on the name. Give me your money and I'll place the bets and meet you in the bar.'

The first time they took me no one met in the bar. I was in love and I disrupted all their plans.

While they were talking I had stood up in my pusher, seen the beauty behind the wire and fallen besottedly in love. I had wedged my fingers and toes into the wire mesh and there I clung like a monkey all afternoon, screaming blue murder if my nana or either parent tried to remove me. I attracted so much attention that my mother stormed off, embarrassed. My father gave chase, trying to console her but I had ruined her day. My nana sat with me all day and every other time we attended a race meeting from then on. My father kept her wet with stout.

'She's been awakened,' he said. 'Been bitten with the love of horses. We can't do anything.'

'She's been touched by their beauty,' a friend of his replied. 'The horse has her heart. No man will ever move her heart, missus, not like a horse will.'

'She's a goner, mate,' said a big man in a checked shirt. 'Bring her around after the races and let her pat the buggers.'

I fell in love with race meetings because of the horses. I loved the colour and the excitement of the day but it was the beauty and pride of the horses that captured me. Not the race itself. For years I was tied to racetracks. Attending meetings with my father and then going by myself to be with the horses. Offering to brush horses, walk horses, wash horses. Anything just to be near them. Then I worked in trotting stables, training the harness racers, and for a time the track became my second home.

I can still recall the excitement of my first visit to the stables. It is an excitement of the heart and soul. I relive that experience whenever I visit new stables: the flaring nostrils, the deep ancient eyes and the veins that stand out on the face of each horse; the individual movements of each horse — head movements, tail movements, the way the feet move and the neck arches — all so expressive in a language as powerful as words; mouths that search pockets or bite, and the individuality of each neigh. I still hold my hands or face against a neighing horse and feel the vibrations as the sounds rise into the throat and explode into the air. Or the soft whicker of response that melts my heart.

Then there is the colour. Bay, black, brown, chestnut, pinto, paint, grey (white), spotted, patched, palomino and more. A feast for my eyes, every colour and point individual. No two horses are ever the same, at least to my eyes. The colours are varied and, like a rich tapestry, so beautiful.

That first time in the stables the colours flashed before my eyes and the dancing black hooves were a motion from an ancient past that rang with myth and glory; the silk colours of the jockeys, a circus in themselves. My nana and I wandered along row after row of beauty; I patted each nose. Men laughed and warned, 'Watch that one, Missus, he bites.' Not one bit me. I patted and kissed without fear but with the respect that still remains.

My father returned without my mother. He shrugged. My nana became all stiff and cold. She handed me to my father, her shoulders suddenly falling as though she felt old and saggy. 'It's not your fault,' she said to my father. He walked away and I did not protest. My eyes were full of the stars of horses; I couldn't have cared if my mother never returned. I would not let my father wash me for days.

The only horses I saw for the next two years were at the race-track. I would plead with my father to take me to the races.

My Aunt Julie was troubled and shocked. 'She'll grow up a betting woman and have nothing, nothing.'

'She wants to go for the horses.'

'It's wrong and you should be reported taking a child that young to the races.'

'We go for the horses.'

So my nana took me to a circus, to see the horses. I sat in the front row, besotted. I didn't like the clowns, I didn't like the trapeze acts and I wept at the way the lions were treated. But I loved the horses. The way they danced around the ring. For years I dreamed of running away with a circus. I would attend every circus I found—usually by climbing under the canvas and sitting under the seats. Circus patrons used to drop their soft-drink bottles under the seats and I would collect these bottles and buy apples and sugar to feed the horses.

Often I would work unpaid at a local circus, brushing the horses, watering them and picking up their droppings. For me the circus held only the delight of horses and I kept well away from any of the caged animals and the shackled elephants because I would start to cry and then someone always made me feel a fool for displaying what I felt in my heart.

Over the years I would skip school if there was a circus in town. My father always threatened me, 'If you ever run away with a circus I'll never speak to you again.' So I kept to the horses and myself. I couldn't bear to lose my father. I desperately wanted to run off with a circus but it was only for the horses. I spoke with the horse handlers and trainers but if anyone else spoke to me I'd look at the ground and not reply. The adults frightened me and I was scared witless of the clowns and all the yelling and screaming. At times, it was as bad as home.

When I was around four years of age my mother and father began to leave me with my nana in suburban Adelaide. My bed was in one of her front rooms. I remember awakening to the sound of clop, clop, clop. Hooves on the bitumen. I was out of bed in a flash. Horses!

There in the pink and grey of the morning came a giant of a horse. A magnificent sight of big chest, big body, long, long mane and white hair all the way down his legs, spilling across the ground like two big fluffy slippers. It was the time before the bright light of day when all the world was silent except for the milkman and his horse. I couldn't get out of the house fast enough. I dragged a chair up to the front door, had it opened and was outside by the time the giant pulled to a stop in front of my nana's place. I wet myself with excitement. The milkman handed me the cold bottles.

'Good morning, Nipper. Where's your dressing gown?'

I put the bottles down and headed for the beauty at the curb. Nothing else existed. That huge head bent down and hot air explored and warmed me. He moved on. In a daze, I followed along the footpath behind. The next moment my nana was beside me, hauling me home. Into a bath I was dumped unceremoniously while she gave me a tongue-lashing about letting myself out of the house, peeing myself and following the horse. I heard her words many, many times from then on. I was a disgrace, uncontrollable ... what would the neighbours say ... think? People would think I was mad. I'd inherited it all from my father. It came from his side of the family. They should never have taken me to that racetrack. I was touched. It was all in my Irish background and she'd have to take me to the priest. I'd get into serious trouble over all this horse business. I had to stop this nonsense and be like normal people.

My nana had a wonderful repertoire that came from her own history of being persecuted. It was like water off a duck's back to me. I heard but took no notice. Every morning I would be out that front door and at the front fence waiting with a piece of bread for my hero. When she barred the door I pushed out the wire screen from my window and climbed out. One morning I was waiting in the cold winter rain, soaked to the skin, when she came looking for me.

'Why can't you wait on the verandah?' she asked.

'I need to see if he's got his raincoat on.' Shivering I waited and worried. Down the road clopped the giant, a huge rug of hessian over his back. I was happy.

It wasn't just at dawn that I had the opportunity to admire and fall in love with the giant horses. Later in the morning the streets echoed to the coming of the bread man.

Clop, clop, clop came the horse. Always the same route for 'Dobbin' or 'Nugget' or 'Bluey'. No fancy names for these big workhorses and if one were out of action for a day it was one hell of a job to get a replacement horse because each horse had its own route and just did not like to change routine. Brakes would smell hot and the baker would yell to some kid or mum to 'Come and hold the horse, will ya, for a moment. The bugger wants to go home. Old Blue is off today and Ned here just thinks he's bloody Phar Lap!' Like warhorses with their chariots they came, the bread man going from house to house, leaping fences and gates like an Olympic athlete. From garden to garden, dodging roses, beds of flowers and yapping dogs. Like a ballet dancer he wove patterns, swinging his basket and whistling his songs. The horse slowly plodded along until the baker returned to fill his basket or yelled a command to stop.

The bread man was a gossip. He could hear a story and pass one on in seconds while delivering the bread and change. He was a link between the women in the community. Often they were women who only knew each other through his stories. He related who was ill, or dying; who was getting married or divorced; who was having an affair and with whom. He knew who was having babies, what the babies were named and their genealogy. He knew who was in financial trouble, who was the victim of their man's fists and who was 'on the grog'.

'You know Joan, who's married to Jack, who was married to Anne. Well, their second girl, Daisy — you know the one — that one with the long dark hair who got caught up with that bloke who was married. Well...' And so it went on.

Women talked to him. He listened. He gave back. He was a part of their life.

The horse would jingle and jangle along, with a bevy of fans all under five years of age wetting themselves in anticipation of his arrival as they waited in homage, carrots or apples held expectantly in their hands.

The giant would spot a child, stop, and his head would descend for the offering. Hands would jerk, fingers tremble, and the brave would offer their gifts while the faint-hearted would drop the gift into the gutter as the giant's hot breath tickled their hands. The giant would patiently vacuum the gutter. We only came up to the giant's knee. When he stopped we were beside that great hairy leg; the heavy head would be lowered, the moustache would come into our view and the deep, knowing eyes of magic would penetrate our dreams and fill us with love.

I'd walk the length of the street just to be in the presence of such wonder. The bread man might call, 'Whoa!' My hero would lumber to a stop and search my body for titbits. I'd stand very still and let that warm breath tickle my body. In my nana's street the horse might stop three times as a woman made decisions over bread or there was a long piece of gossip exchanged.

When I patted a horse my hand became precious and was not washed until my nana forced me to do so. The smell of the horse would be sniffed over and over again. The day the bread man put me up on the wide back of his horse was the day my heart was dedicated in love for evermore. I sat there and felt how the horse was alive — the warmth of his body, the beating of his heart and the strength of his presence. I lay flat out on him and soaked in the essence of horse that still remains forty-five years later my favourite smell. From the beauty of that giant came a reverence for all living things. From that moment I could no longer be impressed by any form of technology.

The bread man would throw me onto the giant's back and tease my nana, 'Look at her, missus! A ring-in, that one, or did ya daughter really go down inta the woods with that gypsy fella? You got a gypsy child there!' I would glow with pride. I loved all animals and if that's what being a gypsy child meant then I was proud. Besides, one of my aunt's neighbours always called me 'the gypsy kid'. My aunt would mutter, 'Well, it must be on her father's side because we've got none of that in our family.' We only had my mother and her millions of boyfriends whom I had to call 'uncle'. My father wasn't really in the family; he was the outsider. The gypsy.

My nana would become cross and order me to climb down from the horse. 'By the living God,' she would mutter, 'I may die trying but I'll make a lady out of you yet.'

Then she would send me inside to get a shovel and to collect the horse's poo from the road. Hot, steaming poo that smelt of rich green grass. The mountain of shit the giant left behind was a coveted gift and it was pounced upon by all the rose growers in the street. My nana often had me follow the horses up the street, dragging a shovel behind me.

The day the bread man told my Nana that the horses were all being replaced by motorisation he lifted me up onto that big broad back. I sat without breathing. This beauty. This alive, warm, breathing horse was to be replaced by a smelly van with no heart, no character and a new bread man who had no time for gossiping. Bread tins were to be placed on verandahs and the bread man would have a schedule to run to. Time was now money, not people, living and horses. I put my arms around that big neck and sobbed. My nana was embarrassed. The bread man gave me a big horseshoe. I carried it with me for years.

My nana and the other women stopped waiting for the bread man. They left the correct money and an impersonal note in the roll-fronted green metal bread tin on the front verandah. The bread came sliced, wrapped tightly in waxed green paper. The gossip link was broken and the women moved in the shadows cast by their venetian blinds.

When I started school my nana kept the waxed paper to wrap my lunch in. I used to sniff at it, longing for familiar smells but the smells had changed too. Other kids would tease me about my wrapped lunch.

'Can't you afford lunch paper?'

'Lunch paper is just waxed paper like this,' I'd reply.

'Your lunch is wrapped in second-hand paper,' they would tease.

We had second-hand everything; new stuff just didn't seem to impress me the way it did other kids. I was taken to other kids' places to visit their new fridge or television or carpet. I learnt to make some sort of appropriate noise but it was never enough and I'd overhear parents mutter, 'She's a strange kid, that one!'

At my nana's house we were also visited by a man with a huge old tired horse; he collected all our bottles and papers and anything else my nana wanted to throw out. His flat cart was piled high. He didn't come very often but he always yelled at me, 'Don't touch the horse. He bites!'

I always patted the horse and gave him an apple. He never bit me. I think it was the junk man who bit. He was the kind of man my father despised. He smelt really bad and I was sorry for his once beautiful horse that had lost the fire from his eyes. The junk man took a swipe at me once when I was patting his horse and sneaking sugar into its mouth. 'Get away, ya little bastard.'

My nana had him up against that cart so quickly it was

frightening. She cursed him high and low and threatened to 'tack his bloody knackers up on the wall'.

Some time later the bread man told us that the junk man died in a knife fight and my nana replied, 'Good bloody riddance. I hope that poor horse got a real good home.'

Once a short man in a brightly coloured waistcoat turned up at the door, looking for bits and pieces of furniture that the woman of the house might have for sale. He had a big black moustache the same colour as his magnificent Clydesdale. The magnificent presence of that horse stopped my heart for a moment. I was in awe of him. I stood with my mouth open as my nana sold the man some chairs. I touched that beautiful face as it lowered itself to my eye level. I fed him all my nana's apples and she yelled at me later because she had wanted them for the apple pie. This horse oozed pride and gentleness. I could only whisper how beautiful I thought he was. The small rotund man of colour laughed. 'Gentle, gentle, see, see, and still a stallion.' My nana gave an embarrassed laugh but I looked under to where the man was pointing. There hung a set of testicles in all their glory, a source of pride for horse and man.

I couldn't get enough of horses.

In those days when the bread still came by cart I knew that the bread horses were kept in a paddock a few streets away. They would be turned out there, after being washed, brushed and fed. One day I'd followed the bread man and discovered this secret — just a few blocks away. I stood up on the fence rails, delighted. The heavy hand of my nana came down on my back and I was dragged home with every threat of punishment she could think of. I was locked in the back yard. I climbed over the fence and headed for the horses. My nana locked me in the house. I climbed out of the window. If she took her eyes off me for a second I was off. No amount of threatening had any effect.

'I can't cope any longer with this child,' my nana told my Aunt Julie.

'Then send her back. She's their child. Or put her back into that home.'

My nana sat down with a bang in utter distress. She probably didn't know where my mother or father were. Or if they were together.

When I was little my mother would leave me at the orphanage and go off with some new man. They would contact my nana and she'd claim me. Sometimes my father would collect me from my nana. Sometimes he left me with her. She was my holding station. As I grew older my mother's usual pattern was simply to wake me up and say, 'I'm leaving with so-and-so,' and go. Then I'd be alone somewhere with my dog and would go to other adults for help or catch a train or bus to my nana's. Once my aunt suggested she adopt me. The shit really hit the fan. My mother blew up and threatened my aunt with all sorts of consequences. My aunt knew never to suggest that one again. From that day on she never said one kind word about my mother. Nevertheless she would often relieve my nana of me, to give her a break, though I was far too wild for my aunt. I hated dresses, and she tried to curl my straight hair and turn me into her doll. I rebelled. Back to my nana I'd be marched.

'She's got a foul mouth too,' said my aunt. 'This one is like her parents and she'll come to no good.'

I loved my immaculate aunt with her pristine home and my tall, quietly spoken uncle. They lived a perfect, suburban, quiet life. I'd dream of living with them in that clean, clean house and having three meals a day and playing bowls on the carpet. The dream would fade in a day and I'd long to get outside. There were no horses visiting and the front and back doors were always locked. Within two days I'd be fretting for the open air.

'Make no ripples,' Aunt Julie would say to me.

My poor aunt and uncle who wanted life to be without a ripple, adopted a little girl who turned out to love horses, then boys, then alcohol, then gambling.

I exasperated Aunt Julie beyond belief. She wore my nana down. My nana decided to try and wear me down.

'No more horses. Do you understand me, child? No more horses or I'll tie you up!' Horses were more important to me than anything except dogs. I ached for horses. My nana gave in.

'You will go down to the horse yards and stay there. You will come home at lunchtime. It's called a compromise.' Looking at my face, she amended her order. 'Then be home either in the morning or the afternoon.' I agreed. She put a dog collar around my neck with a tag on it giving my name and telephone number.

'Now when you go down to the horses people will know you are not lost. Okay?' I nodded. 'And take the dog.' I think we both sighed with relief.

'But —' with adults, there is always a but — 'one or the other. Morning or afternoon.'

I liked the afternoon. All the horses were there. The afternoon was longer. I still saw the bread man's horse and had a fresh roll for lunch. My nana liked to lie down in the afternoon for a rest. I hated to rest.

Up the street the dog and I would toddle. I'd be careful not to step on the cracks in the pavement and I'd play in the chalk hopscotch games that were drawn on the concrete. Every walk was an adventure. I'd peer over fences and pat dogs. I'd talk to cats and old people. No one bothered to question my dog collar or me. They either recognised my determination or knew who I was. I'd look at each house, smell it as I went past. The smell of houses gives clues to who lives there. So do gardens and garments hanging on the clothes lines. I'd look at the blinds or curtains hanging in the windows. 'Wash your windows whenever the season changes,' my nana would say. 'Clean the eyes of the house. Be proud of where you live. It's your home.' My father and nana always talked of being poor but proud.

I read houses and gardens, smells and animals. Every walk was a tour of discovery and I'd arrive at the paddocks no matter what the weather.

I'd sit on the fence all afternoon talking to the horses and watching them. The men came to know me. They'd hand me a brush and encourage a horse to stand next to the fence, enticed by hay, while I'd brush the bits I could reach. Sometimes the men would sit me on the back of those gentle giants and let the horse amble around with me.

'Like a little bloody mosquito,' said one.

'More like a pimple on a pumpkin,' said another.

They laughed about my dog collar, but they all recognised my love. I just loved to sit and admire those horses. It was enough to be in the light of their beauty. My dog Tex would sleep away the day until suddenly he'd stand and bark. Home we would amble — just before the kids came out of school. I had learnt that I had to get back to my nana's before that happened or well after school kids were home. I hated being teased and school kids love to tease. Tex's teeth and growl kept them from touching me but words still hurt.

My father found me at the horse yards. He sat beside me on the rail. 'Their time is nearly over, mate.' My eyes filled with tears. 'Oh shit. Oh well, kid, better the truth. They cost too much.'

'Do they really?'

'No. No, they don't, but companies have to become modern and use vans. It's a different world.' He looked at me. 'You'll never really understand that, will you? You will never understand a world in which riches are measured by money and possessions. What's this?' he asked, pointing to my collar.

'It's so I won't get lost.'

My father laughed and laughed. He then pulled from the inside of his coat a beautiful black and white puppy. He took the collar from my neck and placed it around the neck of the border collie. 'There, he can wear it now.'

The puppy was mine. My very own dog. We had another border collie dog and a couple of beautiful greyhounds and Tex, but they were all my father's dogs. Tex was a special dog and he came with me but he preferred my father. I loved one of the brindle greyhounds called Tiger, but my father wouldn't let Tiger come to the city with me because of the prejudice of town people. 'People have funny ideas about greyhounds,' he'd tell me. 'They think they'll rip up their cats and kids.' Then he'd laugh. 'They have funny ideas about us too. You'd better take Tex. He'll look after you.' It was Tex who protected me against bullying kids.

Now I had my very own dog. I hugged the wiggling, licking puppy to me and named him Tip for the white tip on his tail.

'Are we going away or are you visiting?' I asked my father.

'We're going.'

'Then I'll just say goodbye to the horses and tell them I'll be back.'

My father patiently waited until I had completed my rounds, farewelling each giant with a pat and a kiss. I yelled to my watching father the history of each horse. 'And this one here is a bugger. They call him Hercules and they reckon they should have given him another name that wasn't so tough because he thinks he can pull a train. He has to stay on the same round all the time because he's used to it and he likes his round. If they try to put him on another round he just heads off back to the round he knows. Tom reckons he's burnt out every brake they've put on him.' On and on I would ramble until my father knew all about each horse.

'You've learnt new words,' he said.

'I know. I've had a few rows too.'

'I know. Your aunt's at your nana's place. She still wants you to live with her.'

'Mum said Aunt Julie would adopt me over her dead body.' My father roared with laughter. My mother didn't particularly want me but she was damn sure that her older sister wasn't going to get me. Fourteen years later she asked the same sister to adopt the child growing in her belly — the child of her punch-drunk lover, but my aunt refused.

'Your aunt really does want you. She can't have kids.'

'Why not?'

'Well, some people just can't have kids. You know that dog we had that never had puppies even though the boy dogs got her?' I nodded. 'Well, it's like that for some people too. No babies. So they adopt unwanted babies.'

'But I'm not unwanted.'

'No. I want you and your nana wants you, but your aunt wants you too. Do you want to live in the nice home with your aunt?'

That nice home was tempting but it strangled me. 'No.'

'I'd go on seeing you but you'd belong to them. They want to give you a proper home.'

'What about Tip?'

'Well, your aunt says you can have him.'

We sat in silence for a while staring at the horses.

'Tip will not be allowed inside, though,' my father said, breaking into the silence and my tumbling thoughts.

'She won't let me find horses.'

'No. She wants you to be a girl. All that normal stuff — you know.'

'No, I don't know.' I knew my aunt wanted me but strictly on her terms. No travelling and no horses. I'd die. She'd prune and train me and I'd either have to continually fight or succumb. I wasn't old enough to keep up the fight and I'd choke to death on all that pristine cleanliness and being moulded into a proper little girl. That much I recognised, young as I was. I might be small but I overheard everything and was, as my father would say, 'a little pitcher with long ears'. I looked at him. 'I don't want to go.'

'I don't want to give you up but you should have the choice. She has got a nice house.'

'But she follows me around with the brush and the broom!' We both laughed.

I came and went from my nana's. Tip grew into his collar. Each time I visited the horses there would be one less. I grew tall enough to stand on a box and brush them. I had also graduated to trotting around the paddocks on their broad backs. I kissed and brushed and talked my adoration into the ears of each horse. My father always knew where to find me.

'Treat them well,' he told me, 'like your best friend. There is no way we could do anything with a horse if it decided not to let us. It's bigger and stronger than us. The way to get a horse to do what you want is to treat it with kindness and understanding. Never, never break the spirit of a horse or starve it into submission. The people who do that are cruel and have no understanding of horses. If you are cruel to a horse you will be cruel to everybody and everything in the world and you have no right then to keep animals. Bullies are bullies. Avoid them.'

He told me this over and over until he had hammered it into my head.

'People who have deep respect for horses and dogs also have respect for themselves. If you mistreat an animal or child you are the lowest of the low. The war taught me that humans are less than animals.' He'd sit with his head in his hands and I'd lean beside him, feeling his grief.

I had seen my father in heated arguments over the way some men treated their animals. He taught me that animals were the others with whom we shared the earth. He thought humans were animals. 'Learn to hear the others,' he would tell me. 'Watch them and learn how they speak, for we may not fully understand them but we do share this earth with them and they were here long before us. Treat them with kindness.'

My mother was another story. His private pain. She invited the violence he abhorred. He tried to blame the war and the booze for the pain but it lay deeper than that and she fed on it.

He was caught in a dilemma of his own — a violence he could not fully understand or blame on alcohol. There was a fourteen-year age gap between him and my mother. She was tall and beautiful and needed to live her life to the full. Usually without my father, but surrounded by men. My father was short, thickset and a wanderer. He loved my mother with such a passion that he would beat her. Opposed to violence towards animals and children, he'd use his fists on her and other men. He was caught in a violence he hated and couldn't control. Often she would set up scenarios that led to violence or goad him into hitting her. She would never stay with us long but as my Aunt Hilda remarked to my nana, 'She has him dangling. One word from her and he's running after her.' My Aunt Julie called her 'a bitch in heat'. My nana would shake her head and say, 'She's my daughter.'

There was no dilemma in my father's respect for animals. He would have agreed with the words of George Bernard Shaw who said that one can tell the spirituality of a person or a nation by the way they treated animals.

One day I visited my beloved horses and there were none to be seen. The paddocks were empty. I stood there in disbelief. I knew it was happening but I didn't want to know. All had gone, for the meat market. I sat and cried. I visited once more in hope

— just hoping one horse might be there. But the trees and fencing had all gone. Ugly houses were being built on the land.

Despite my father's respect and compassion for animals, he had no misgivings about killing them for food. When I turned six my father gave me a single-shot twenty-two rifle. He taught me gun lore. One bullet, one death, how to carry, break and clean the gun. I shot hundreds of tins to pieces until he allowed me to shoot a bird. On his instruction I shot a bird.

'Look, and look well. It's dead and you took its life. Now what are you going to do about that? You've killed it.'

I stood and stared at the dead bird.

'Nothing will bring it back. It's dead. Can you eat it?'

'You told me to shoot it.'

'And you took its life. Now what can you do with that bird? It's your responsibility. What if she had young? You've killed them too.' He took the gun and walked away.

I cried and cried. I begged the bird's soul for forgiveness. I talked with the spirits but they turned their back. I yelled at him that it just wasn't fair because he told me to shoot the bird. I cried myself sick. The dogs cuddled around me.

The lesson bit in deep, never to be forgotten. I buried the bird under a tree, left it flowers and songs.

A week later my father handed me the gun again. 'Go and get dinner for us and the dogs.'

I sat above a rabbit warren. I watched the rabbits. I felt sick and cold. Two bullets, two rabbits. I had to skin and clean them. The skin would be stretched inside-out over a loop of wire to dry. Once dry it would be added to our pile. My father sold fox and rabbit skins.

'I hate traps,' he'd rage upon finding one — usually with a decomposing body caught by a leg. Sometimes only a leg remained, the animal having gnawed itself free.

'Don't ever use bloody traps. It's not a clean death — it's torture.' Away he'd go leaving me sick and crying. I'd crawl into a pile of dogs and whimper to the spirits.

He hammered the lessons in. He tried to teach me to kill a
sheep and a pig, using a knife to the throat. The eyes watched.
I'd run crying from the scene but I always had to return and help
him with the dead animal.

He taught me to skin and dress animals, not wasting one
drop of blood. 'You only waste the oink,' he'd say, about killing
a pig.

I couldn't eat what he did — the tongue, liver, kidneys, feet,
brains, lungs. Tripe, the stomach, his favourite. He made
sausages with offal, and pickled head. He talked of feeding me
testicles to make me strong! I could only eat the flesh.

'Kill a male if you have to or an old girl, and thank them
before you kill them. Don't ever kill a young female. Wrong
thing to do,' and he'd shake his head.

'I can't tell what sex the rabbits are,' I'd protest.

'Look for their balls then.' He'd roar with laughter.

Disgusted, I'd stalk off, but I always said a silent thank you
to the rabbit as I lined it up in my sights, hoping it wasn't female.

My nana too would use all the parts of any bird she killed.
What humans couldn't eat, the dogs and cats did. She even kept
the feathers of her slaughtered poultry. She would lay the
feathers out in the sun and dry them off for stuffing — pillows,
cushions, toys.

'Waste not, want not,' she would tell me as I distastefully
helped to clean the feathers.

I hated the smell of wet, gutted chook. I'd gag and she'd
push me out to sit in the sun and pull feathers from a dead duck.

My nana gave up keeping geese and ducks but she still
insisted on buying freshly killed and feathered birds. So I still had
to help with the plucking. 'Don't think you can get out of it,'
she'd yell. 'Not like your uncle.' My uncle, so the story goes,
once placed all my nana's chooks in a bucket of disinfectant! I
never found out if he did it deliberately to get out of such a
macabre job or whether, because he had no sense of smell, he
simply didn't know the water had phenol in it! My nana gave me
no such chance!

The chickens she killed herself. Chook head on the block, one hand holding the axe, one foot on the bird to hold it down and the other hand over the chook's eyes! She liked to hide the watching eyes. Chop. The head would fall to the ground. My nana would hold the chicken until it stopped convulsing.

'Give it a bit of dignity in death, not like those other buggers.'

Those other buggers were people who chopped off the head and let the headless chicken run around the yard spraying blood and setting children and women screaming. I saw countless headless chickens pumping their life blood across tin sheds, corrugated iron fences and screaming humans. Someone always thought it funny. Usually the man with the axe.

A friend told me the story of how all the neighbouring kids had gathered to watch the killing of a rooster. Chop. Off came the head and away went the rooster, turning all the kids into shrieking banshees. The rooster died, staggering against its death. The men cheered. The rooster was taken to the laundry by the women while the men retired to wash down the excitement with beer. Kids gathered around the chopping block. Congealed blood upon the block and axe fascinated.

Why not try this game? thought one. They turned and wordlessly selected a victim. He was chased, caught and his head placed on the block. A kid grabbed the axe and mimicked the father. Dragging the axe around, looking all-important, he'd stop, spit on his hands, rub them together, run his thumb along the edge of the axe.

The audience gathered. The yard became silent. Too silent. Warning bells rang in some mother's ears. She looked out of the laundry door and screamed. Little so-and-so was trying to hoist the axe over his friend's head while others held the 'chook' down.

Adults exploded from the house, screaming. Kids were belted and dragged away howling — even 'the chook'!

When we were short on rabbits my father would suddenly have a taste for pigeon. I wouldn't eat them and I hated helping him in this deed. He'd choose a shed full of grey cooing balls of feathers. Into the darkness of the shed we would tiptoe, my father whispering, 'Quiet, quiet. It's as dark as the inside of a cow's bum in here.'

The shed would smell of hay. Sometimes hay and horses, or hay and sheep. The gentle 'coo-coo' of the birds would upset me and I'd refuse to climb.

'But you're lighter,' my father would hiss. 'Get up on those bloody rafters.'

'No,' I'd hiss back.

'It's food. Bloody food, damn you.'

I would close my ears to him. Some food I could do without.

'Waste' was a dirty word to my father. I'd just shake my head. 'Oh bugger it,' he'd hiss and begin to climb. He would edge along the rafter towards the pigeons. One pigeon after another would have its neck wrung and be dropped to me below. I'd gather them up into a hessian bag. Slowly and quietly, not even disturbing the air, he'd kill them until he had enough. No fuss. The human fox.

I wouldn't help him dress, cook or eat them. I'd sit outside and listen to his loud appreciative noises. 'You don't know what you're missing,' he'd yell through the door. He didn't understand, just as he didn't understand when I started to give up eating meat. But he did teach me to respect the life taken, to eat only when hungry and to be aware of each mouthful of food, be it meat or cabbage.

'I grew that cabbage,' he'd proudly say when we lived somewhere long enough to have a vegetable garden. 'Be proud to grow food for it keeps you alive.'

Years later, in a remote New Guinea village, I asked the headman about human flesh eating. He grinned down at me and, smacking his lips and feeling the flesh on my arm, he replied, 'Not you skinny little white woman. I like big, pink, fat missionaries!' He roared with laughter. 'You all called "long pig". Taste like pork when cooked.' His belly shook and he ushered me into his home to view his collection of shrunken heads. The sight reminded me of my father's taste in offal and how I would watch him eat what he termed a 'delicacy' while I gagged and thought of other things.

Boarders

My nana took in boarders. It's how she made a living. Before boarders she ran a pub for thirty years on Kangaroo Island but sold it to follow her children to the mainland. I loved the island. Nana loved the island.

'Why did you leave?' I once asked my mother, knowing that my father left the place he loved because she had left vowing never to return.

'I couldn't get away fast enough,' replied my mother bitterly. 'Every day until I was eighteen I stood on that bloody wharf and thought if it wasn't for the sharks I could swim across the sea to Adelaide.'

I looked at my mother, trying to see her from a perspective other than the fashion plate that she presented. 'You could swim?'

'Like a bloody fish. And dive too. I was once engaged to a fella and we had this big row, so I broke it off and threw his ring off the end of the wharf.'

'Did you ever speak to him again?'

'No, but I spent hours diving off the end of the jetty trying to find that bloody ring.'

None of my nana's children wanted to stay on the island and they never returned once they left and so she moved to be near them. She was used to caring for people and she liked to have company about.

Mrs Rogers, Mrs Simpson and Mrs Wilson 'took in' boarders. The people who lived in their houses were all connected in some way with the church. They were all very serious boarders. Their landladies were all very pious — 'up their bum' was the expression my father used, and 'they wouldn't say shit to save themselves'. Mrs Barns also 'took in' boarders. The Barns family lived in what had once been a very big double-storeyed hotel. It seemed to me a 'true' boarding house and not just a home that rented out rooms. It sat crouched on a road junction, a big red brick building that still seemed to sway to drunken brawls and smelt of men's piss and beer. Even after Mrs Barns threw bucketfuls of disinfectant and water over verandahs and along stone passages the old place would quickly recover and return to its old familiar smell. The upstairs verandah had a wrought iron balcony rail — twisted leaves and flowers in rusty metal. There were sections boarded off to make more bedrooms, which were called sleep-outs.

The Barns children slept in the sleep-outs. Some boarders' windows opened directly into the children's rooms. No man was allowed window access to a girl's bedroom. The floorboards of the verandah bounced as feet trod them, and they were deadly on bare feet, throwing splinters into the tender part of the feet. Running along the verandah was hazardous as, not only did the floor buckle, but boards would break with the weight of a running body pounding on them.

Three of us girls were sitting outside a sleep-out one day when Mrs Barns's brother Wally came yelling along the verandah, his six-year-old namesake out in front, heading for us.

'Stand still, you little bastard, so I can belt you,' roared Wally.

Little Walter raced past us into the nearest sleep-out and through the window to safety. Big Walter in his rage was not watching where he was going. He stood on two rotten boards that we all customarily avoided. Down he went — both legs through the verandah, his bum at floor level. He roared. We ran. Through the window and down the stairs. He yelled and cursed. He called us all many, many names. We stood under the verandah watching his legs hanging down, as his wrath stung the air. Mrs

Barns came out. 'Jesus, Mary and Joseph,' she yelled, looking up. 'What in God's name are you doing, Wally?' Oaths floated over the balcony.

Mrs Barns roared with laughter. 'Oh, I'm going to piss myself, I am.' She sat down and rocked from side to side, tears streaming down her face. When she finally composed herself she went for help and Wally was lifted from his stocks. Still yelling and swearing he stomped off towards the pub, shouting at all the kids to 'Bugger off, youse little bastards! Go laugh at something else. Bugger off!' Mrs Barns watched Wally stomp off — laughing and lighting up another cigarette. She always lit one cigarette from another.

'One day she'll bloody well burn us all up,' John, one of the boarders, would inform us. 'She goes to bed smoking. We can smell it when she singes the blankets. Sometimes she singes her hair too, and as for her yellow and brown fingers — ugh!'

My mother smoked heavily too. In fact, most women I knew did. I worried about my mother smoking in bed but never at the state of her long fingers as she kept them clean and free of tar with a pumice stone. 'Ugly,' she'd declaim. 'Ugly to have fag stains. Scrub them off.' It was a 'ladies' thing to do. She didn't mind nicotine-stained hands on men, but not on women. She also disliked women who 'rolled their own'. Tailor-made cigarettes were for women and she smoked filter tips. 'Rollies' were for men. And women never, never smoked while walking on the street because that was 'cheap'. She carried a packet of 'Life Saver' mints to suck after she had been smoking. I hated her lollies because they were always handed out stuck with purse fluff and smelling of perfume. Mrs Barns didn't suck lollies. Her breath smelt like an old, unwashed ashtray.

Mr Barns had been taken away screaming about purple devils climbing the walls.

That's when the pub became a boarding house. I asked my nana about Mr Barns.

'It's the DTs,' she said.

'What's that ?'

'Booze madness. It comes from drinking too much. They go crazy and begin to see things.'

'Dad sees things sometimes but it's usually the Japs, or he hears planes that are coming over to drop bombs.'

'That's not the DTs; that's war sickness. All men suffer war sickness after they've been in a war. Some just stew it all up inside and others rant and rave. They all have to face their demons.' My nana looked hard at me. 'Your father screams because he remembers the pain. And, being scared, he drinks to forget.'

'So why does mum drink?' I asked.

'Because she likes it.' My nana stomped off. I had to be very careful talking about 'the drink' with any adults. My father was probably the easiest to talk to but even then I had to be careful. Talking as a child about 'the piss' to an adult was like walking on eggs. Among other kids we knew that we experienced similar alcoholic scenarios; we just knew that the adults 'drank'. It was a matter of fact. When a kid said, 'Dad's off,' or 'Dad's sick,' we usually knew the 'sickness' was alcohol-related. We didn't talk about 'the piss' or the violence because we all knew and shared similar experiences.

I asked my Auntie Julie about the DTs.

'They deserve it. The whole rotten, drunken lot. Comes from drinking all the time.' I knew she didn't mean water.

My mother was a 'drinking' woman.

'Will Mum get the DTs?' I asked my nana.

'Of course not,' her voice quiet and hard.

I didn't tell her that my father had two kinds of fits. His war fits were very different from his drinking fits. His war fits left him yellow and shaking, the aftermath of malaria.

My parents were disgusted that Mrs Barns had not renewed the lease on the pub and had let it 'run dry'.

'That bastard drank all the profit,' Mrs Barns would tell anyone. 'So I fixed him. No booze, just boarders. Then he just had to have that last God Almighty fling. Well, they've got him now and only Jesus knows what's gunna happen to him.'

'That woman will kill herself,' said my nana. 'Too many Bex.'

I thought my nana was wrong about the Bex but right about Mrs Barns killing herself. By fire! Lots of the women my mother knew, including my nana, 'took' Bex . It was an aspirin powder wrapped in paper. There were many powders in a box and I'd often watch women sharing out their powders. My mother's powders all smelt of lipstick and face powder, perfume and cigarette butts. Everything that came out of her handbag carried that smell.

My father never indulged in Bex. He would occasionally take an Aspro tablet if the hangover was bad but usually 'a hair of the dog' kept the hangover at bay. At least for the weekend. Monday and Tuesday were 'bad' days; Wednesday he was 'clearing', and Thursday was the beginning of the weekend 'run'.

'It won't be the Bex that kills Mavis Barns,' my father would comment. 'It will be all those bloody kids.'

Mrs Barns gave birth fifteen times. Ten children lived and they all slept in sleep-outs along the verandah. The sleep-outs were adjoining and so no one was private, except for the two rooms at either end of the verandah and even they had a tenant's window staring in. The hotel windows along the verandah were ideal escape routes and not one locked, so the kids could open them in seconds.

'I just bloody well hate living on that bloody verandah,' said my best friend Pam. 'Everyone can see us for miles around. We're the bloody local picture show. There's not even a bloody tree for Christ's sake. I can't wait to leave this dump. And I'll never, never have bloody boarders. I hate them!'

'Yeah,' said Brian, her brother. 'I have to always be polite and the boarders are not even related!' We were taught always to be respectful to adults — even if we didn't like them. Anyone older was 'Auntie' or 'Uncle' and if this was forgotten a slap behind the ear reminded us.

When all the lights were on in the old place it was lit up like a Christmas tree. At night the old pub was a puppet show of moving shapes. Pam and I would sit across the road in the paddock and watch the shapes in their piece of night theatre. 'See, see,' she'd giggle. 'Ronnie is having a ciggie. Mum will kill him.'

We could clearly see Ronnie's silhouette smoking. A light behind cotton curtains gave us a great show — so did candlelight; but, when a blind was drawn, as they were on the boarders' rooms, nothing could be seen.

'I bet he pinched them from old Emma,' giggled Pam. Old Emma was the cook and she was related to Mrs Barns. Left over from the pub days, she cooked solid food: meat and three veg, tuna casserole on Fridays, roast on Sundays. Her desserts were mountains of thick, bright yellow custard, rice puddings you could slice and tins of fruit salad — the cheap kind — full of pale tasteless cherries and pears. As in all the homes I knew, there was always plenty of bread.

Old Emma smoked after each meal, always with a cup of tea. 'It's pure enjoyment,' she'd say, blowing smoke, sipping tea and closing her eyes. She used to show us girls the huge knotted purple veins that highwayed her legs. 'They kill me, they really do,' she'd say. She'd soak her feet in a big tub of water and salt, sighing as she did so.

'She's always going on about her veins,' said James Barns one night when being chastised about being rude to old Emma.

'Well, she's old,' said Mrs Barns, 'and she's in pain. She was in the war too. A nurse. She's worked hard all her life — it won't hurt you to just listen.' She was always telling us to 'just listen'.

I'd listen to their dance of life and I'd tell it in detail to my father when we had nights of sitting beside a camp fire.

I taught the Barns kids how to build and light a fire. Fireplaces in the old pub had long been boarded over and electric heaters had replaced wood. One year we built a fire for Guy Fawkes Day.

Guy Fawkes Day, on 5 November, used to be celebrated all over the country until it was decided to ban the unlicensed use of fireworks. Too many accidents, too many fires, too much noise! We loved the thrill and the scare of Guy Fawkes night. All the pretty sky rockets and fountains. The fright of crackers and big bangers. Dogs were all locked inside where they howled their frustration out at all the noise. That Guy Fawkes night the sky was full of magic, the air of smoke. Flagons were passed as men, women and children danced around the fire. Songs were sung to clapping hands. In the firelight passion raged and the blood sang. Children ran wild until they dropped. They either slept where they fell or some adult dragged them inside and covered them with a rug.

I awoke in a kitchen of sleeping bodies. Crawling over them I stood up outside. More bodies. I fanned a smoking ember into a fire and placed a billy full of water to boil. I revisited the kitchen, performing a ballet to get back out of the door with tea, cups, sugar, milk and a spoon between my teeth. No one even changed their breathing and it was the same in the yard until the smell of hot water hitting tea was like a switch, and bodies sat up groaning.

All day people came and went from the fire. Into a large pot went the ingredients for a stew, people added potatoes to the pot or wood to the fire. Children woke, ate and listened; played, ate, listened, slept. Adults told stories — fairytales, myths, legends and the stories of their lives. I sat and listened until the last of the poetry had nodded into sleep and the fire was a soft glow.

'Do the ghosts in the pub worry you?' I asked Pam.

'Nope, they're okay. They don't bother us and the boarders get used to them or leave.' We paused to watch the fire for a time.

'Some spirits are really wicked,' I commented, 'but I don't know too much about ghosts. They just seem to crop up in some places.'

'The kids tell really scary ghost stories.'

'So do I.'

We laughed and laughed. Ghosts were a normal part of life for many of us. Lots of old places seemed to have their share. My father taught me never to be afraid of a ghost, just to accept it and ask it what it wanted or ask it to leave. It could only stay where it was welcome. Ghosts were easy to banish and my father had great respect for them. 'They are souls trapped in some place. They stay and can't let go. They are sorrowful.'

My nana thought ghosts should be respected and, like offerings to her Catholic god, on certain nights she left out food and milk for them. My mother thought ghosts were there as fun, like people under a sheet. Or so she tried to convince herself.

Once, when I was living with my parents on the Duttons' property, a new maid came to work for old Mrs Dutton. My mother and Mrs Dutton's cook arranged a 'ghosting' for the new girl. My mother fizzed the poor girl up on ghost stories, then dressed herself in a sheet. When the maid came into the library after dark, out stepped my mother, going 'Woo, woo, woo'. The maid turned and screamed off down the hall. My mother, hysterical with laughter, removed the sheet and came face to face with the real ghost! My mother galloped past that maid and out into the courtyard, yelling. Never again did she play a ghost.

That ghost was really friendly. It was the only one I ever saw in that huge old manor house.

Mrs Dutton told me the ghost was her friend. I told Pam about it; she told me about the boarders' reaction to the ghosts in the pub, and we talked until pink shredded the grey.

My last visit to the pub was just before we were to hit the road again. I'd stayed for tea and told them all we were off the next day.

We were eating in the dining room. Oval-framed pictures of old heavily whiskered men and severe-faced women in bonnets stared down at us. I was looking up at them when Mrs Barns said, 'We came from a long line of Salvos. Born and bred for Christ.'

She reached behind her, rummaged around in the old dresser and pulled out a battered tambourine. She held us all silent as she removed her cigarette and lifted the tambourine above her head. To a stunned audience she then sang 'Onward Christian Soldiers', banging out the rhythm on the tambourine. A younger woman shone from her face, her voice filled the room, and a band of ghostly musicians filled the space. Suddenly it was over. Mrs Barns bowed and threw the tambourine back into the cupboard, slamming the door. 'Bugger!' she exclaimed as she retrieved her dead cigarette. She looked at the silent room. We all held our breath. Lizzie farted with nervousness. The room erupted in roars and shrieks. Lizzie blushed and hid her face. Mrs Barns banged on the table, roaring with laughter.

Living was not always easy. The adults always worried about money, even as they spent it.

'Today we live well,' my father would say as all his pay went on alcohol and his mates. He would work tomorrow, or we would make do. Somehow.

Nomads

For a few years my father and I moved from place to place by hitchhiking, train or shanks's pony. I'd walk behind him along the dusty roads, on my back my small swag containing a book, pen and paper, a change of clothes and my sleeping gear. My father had the larger version plus our cooking gear. Sometimes he'd walk slowly, at my pace, and I'd talk, talk and talk, 'Why, why, why?' Then he would tire of the chatter coming from beneath him and he'd stride away so that I had to hurry after him, yelling, 'Wait for me, Daddy, wait for me.' When my father refused to talk to me, worn out from all my questions and observations, he'd yell, 'Why, why, why. Because "why" is a bloody crooked letter and you can't make it straight. Now shut up!' Then I'd simply talk to the dogs.

Hour after hour we walked the dusty roads, sleeping under the stars and living from what my father shot and, of course, potatoes. My father would often procure a cabbage. Then it was cabbage day after day until I'd grizzle and groan and the cabbage would be replaced by cauliflower. Rabbit was the main meat of our lives while we were on the road. By the age of six I could shoot with precision and use the single-shot walnut-butted twenty-two he gave me. My father shot 'bunnies' for the dogs and us. He'd skin the rabbit and place the skin over wire to dry. When he had a bundle of skins they'd be sold and we'd have chops or a liver instead of rabbit. Stew was his speciality. We also lived on yabbies that I caught.

If we were camped near a town my father would leave me at the camp and walk into town for 'a few snorts'. Off he'd go to the pub carrying rabbit and fox skins, Tiger and Tex at his heels. With the other dogs and my special friend Tip, I would go yabbying, rabbiting or exploring. At dusk I'd shoot rabbits, feed the dog and place a billy of rabbit stew over the fire. The pubs closed at 6 p.m. Unless my father found a 'mate' and they went on somewhere to drink, he'd return to camp at dusk. Always with a Cherry Ripe or Polly Waffle for me. He'd stand outside the firelight and throw in his hat. Then he would wait in the dark until I picked it up, and only then come into the circle of light and sit while I made him a cup of tea. Sometimes he'd not return until the stars were fading into dawn and I'd find him asleep with the dogs under a tree, collapsed in a drunken heap. He'd be sheepish for days if I'd found him outside camp, sodden.

The only time I really hated the pubs was when I'd have to go into a bar to remind him that I was waiting on the verandah and that it had been 'hours!' Men would yell, 'Hey, whose nipper?' and 'Someone's pup (bluey, joey, kid, handle) is at me feet.' Legs like tree trunks and boots caked in mud. I'd look straight up into beery, red, whiskered faces leering down at me. My face level with their crotch, I'd have to look up or down at the butt-slopped floor or I'd be staring at zippers and half-undone buttons. My father would lift me high up on his shoulders, pick up his hat and say, 'Hoo-roo, we're off.' I always banged my head on the door, forgetting to duck. Then I'd be crying and grizzling with him telling me to just shut up. 'Why the hell couldn't you have stayed out on the verandah like you were told to? Jesus Christ, a man can have no peace. I'd got you a lemonade too. Now shut up. You make a man look a bloody mug.' He'd drag me weeping and wailing behind him. 'Will ya shut up for Christsake! You got the whole bloody place watching us. Next it will be the bloody coppers! Now stop waking the friggin' dead!'

We were often picked up in farm trucks or utes and given lifts to the nearest town. My father preferred walking. 'Don't depend on any bastard,' he'd say over and over. He accepted lifts depending on distance, the weather and my level of tiredness. Sometimes my father would be offered work on a farm or station and we'd live in the shearers' quarters until the job was done. Dogs were no problem. A man on the land, one who worked with sheep and cattle, was expected to have dogs.

I knew to keep out of the way of the owners, managers and nosey parkers. I'd go bush with the dogs, sit under the trees and be with the day. Every place had different spirits, different smells, different stories. I'd sit and feel them all unfold in the same way that I watched people and animals, weaving their stories into the tapestry of my life.

I'd watch horses being broken in. I didn't like the cruel way in which they were taught to accept a rider and harness. Very few men were kind or patient and when I'd question the cowboys they always answered, 'The old ways are the best,' or 'I was taught by one of the best — he was hard but good.' Very few made friends with the horses and a brush was only used to remove heavy sweat or because if it wasn't brushed clean the horse would chafe. Horses screamed and some arenas were like rodeo rings. I felt the pain of being broken in and couldn't bear to watch. Foals would be taken from mares too early, stallions would be gelded without anaesthetic, then branded and if it was a working horse the tail would be docked. Blood, pain and terror. Not a nice way to introduce a horse to living with humans.

There were a couple of places where my father was hired during winter to chop wood and keep the manor fires burning. At one such squattocracy holding we lived with the groomsmen and stablehands in their quarters and at the other place we were given a dark airless room behind the kitchen. I used to annoy the cook because it was winter and I'd be in our room with the light on, reading.

'Get out here, you, and string these beans. Reading will do you no good and the master can't afford you to have that light burning all day. Get out here and make yourself useful.' We knew our place on those properties and we were clearly reminded of our status. When I tried to visit the stables the head groomsman in both establishments told me to 'piss off'. Both places had beautiful horses for hunting and polo. Horses that came from paintings. When I tried to get to the stables, my father was the one who received severe censure about my behaviour.

'She loves horses,' he explained. 'Just give her a brush and she'll be all right.'

'The stables are out of bounds to the workers' children. She is in the way.'

'This is not her place. You are the woodcutter.'

'These stables are not for you people. What if the master's children should come down?'

We left and moved on.

'I'm sorry, Dad. I lost you the job.'

'No, you didn't. They just lost a good worker, mate. You.'

At one place where my father worked I saw a hunt. Before dawn the stables were buzzing. Horses were arriving and cars were full of dogs barking to get free. I climbed up on the barn roof to get a really good look. Men, women and children arrived at the stables, dressed in red, black or tweed jackets, black hats, black long boots, brown short boots and jodhpurs of various sombre colours. The master of the hunt wore white pants. Servants moved among the mob with glasses of red or gold liquor. Everyone was talking, handlers held dogs straining on leashes and horses pranced and snorted their excitement. Then someone blew a bugle note and in a flash all were mounted and the hunt was on! I stood up to get a better view.

Horses galloped across a green paddock, following the hounds. Over the hedge and away into the distance went the hunt. I followed them with my ears, listening to the noise of galloping horses and baying dogs. Every now and again a bugle would sound and the wind brought the notes back to me. For an instant I'd see a terrified fox streaking across the landscape — a blur of red terror.

I expected the hunt to return but in the cool of the evening the horses were brought home in warm trucks.

'Where's the hunt?' I asked my father.

'At the pub. They have this big chase and then end up at the pub where they all sit down and eat and get too pissed to ride their horses home. Then they have a sleep, eat again and have this big do called a hunt ball. They get pissed again.' He bent down and looked into my eyes. 'It's not a nice sport, mate. A man called Oscar Wilde once said it was "the unspeakable in pursuit of the inedible".

'But you shoot foxes.'

'I do. I get money for those skins and the farmers are rid of a pest. One shot, one fox. I don't chase it to death and then pull it to pieces.'

At the other home of the landed gentry where my father worked I sat up on a shed roof and watched a polo match. It was played in a field surrounded with elegant cars and beautiful people eating from large picnic hampers and drinking wine from beautiful glasses. I nearly fell off that roof in excitement as I watched my first polo match. Back and forth galloped the horses, weaving and turning, propping and backing, all with the speed and skill that kept my heart in my mouth. The riders' skill took my breath away. Silently I cheered my chosen favourite.

'Don't bloody well let them see you up on the roof or all hell will break loose,' said my father. Then, smiling, he'd add, 'Not likely they'll look up, those people — they only see what's directly in front of their noses. But be careful and for Christ sake don't bloody well fall off or I'll just leave you there. Hear me?' I nodded. I learnt to climb roofs with my boots skidding sideways.

My father was the only person who never said of anyone that they had too many animals! We always had plenty of dogs and I'd gather injured animals like some people do money. My mother complained, and so did my aunt, my nana. Later, friends and of course lovers would always eventually exclaim, 'You just have too many animals!'

I've always replied, 'What's too many?' That criticism, spoken unkindly, has always puzzled and amazed me. I've heard it but never understood, and when I read the books of Gerald Durrell and Joy Adamson I felt I had friends at last. People to whom animals were as essential as breathing. They became my heroes, though I didn't discover them until I was in my late teens. Until then my reading consisted of comics and books about horses. Like most horse-besotted children, I loved *Black Beauty* and *Fury*.

My father in his own fashion taught me to ride. He threw me up on a warm mountain of a horse, handed me the reins, showed me how to hold them and yelled, 'Hold on'. Then he slapped the horse on the rump. 'Ride, ride,' he yelled. At first I bounced all over the back of strange horses but I held on with my legs, knees and sheer determination. I hated hitting the ground. I certainly learnt to hold on! Years later when I bought my first saddle I had to learn to use other muscles to hang on. I then learnt to ride feeling the horse through leather! It leaves a different smell on my clothes. Riding was certainly not the shock that learning to swim was.

One day my father and I were standing on the edge of a large dam throwing sticks into the water for the dogs to retrieve.

'See the way the dogs swim?' he said.

'Yeah.'

'Well, watch carefully.' I did. I stared hard at the dogs from under my oversized hat. 'You got that?' I nodded. He picked me up and threw me into the dam. I hit that ice-cold water and sank.

Water is not one of my elements. I came to the surface with his voice in my ears, 'For the love of Christ, bloody stupid, stupid kid, swim! Swim, you bloody stupid kid, swim!' I dog paddled. I swam. It was easier than drowning. When I crawled up onto the bank he looked down at me and said, 'Now you can swim so you need never drown,' and walked away.

Then back to my nana for a time. When my father came for me a couple of weeks later he was very excited. He'd 'done a deal' in a pub and had a surprise for me.

We hitched a ride in a truck to a small rural town called Gawler. At the back of the pub stood 'the deal'. A very, very old carthorse called 'Nugget'. He was black with a white blaze and white feet. His lower lip hung down but his eyes were bright and he called out to us when we arrived.

'He's gorgeous,' I cried.

He came with a tattered set of harness, more wire and string than leather, and an old wooden flat cart that gave me splinters in the hands, knees and bum, but it was better than walking, even though we could have crawled faster than Nugget walked. It didn't matter because he was ours and I loved him immediately. My father went to the pub to celebrate and I brushed the new member of our family.

The dogs loved to ride on the cart and barked with excitement, running back and forth if a car passed us and snapping at trucks. My father generally preferred to walk beside the cart. 'I can walk faster and I'm not trampled by those bloody stupid dogs.'

I loved being outside and moving slowly so I had the chance to look at everything and ask my father questions. Sometimes he'd sit on the back of the cart, his legs dangling over the back, and he'd whistle, curse the dogs, tell me to shut up, and smoke. He rolled his own cigarettes from a tin of rich-smelling tobacco and whenever we met other travellers he'd hand them the tin and stop to 'boil the billy'.

Outside has a special smell, especially away from people, towns and car fumes. The smell of freshly wet earth, eucalyptus trees in the heat, Cootamundra wattle in full bloom and the smell and taste of an impending storm. And Vicks! The smell of Vicks VapoRub will never leave me, and the feel of my father's rough hands as he'd rub my chest and back. A jar of Vicks was his remedy for every cold and sniffle. If I coughed, and I always have because of my acute sense of smell, out would come the jar. I didn't mind the Vicks at night but I hated to have it on my body if I had to go to school because even the smelliest of kids would wrinkle their nose at me and comment, 'Phew, you smell!'

When we camped at night it was now my job to clean the harness, water and feed Nugget and the dogs and collect firewood. If it looked like rain my father would make a shelter from canvas and we'd huddle underneath trying to keep warm and dry while he'd yell at the dogs. 'Bloody well get out of here, you stupid buggers, all wet and you smell like a bunch of chooks.

Gorn, getoutahere! Get under the bloody cart.' Dogs would be pushed and shoved out into the rain and they'd stay there just long enough to get wet and then come slinking back under the canvas for a good shake. My father would rant and rave, but eventually he'd let them stay and he'd smoke 'to take the smell of the buggers outa me nostrils'.

If a pub were close, he'd go to 'wet the whistle and give myself some air'. I'd stay under the canvas with the dogs, watching the rain.

I brushed that old horse until he shone and I'd cut sweet grass and add it to his feed at night. That old horse pulled us from job to job, pub to pub, hangover to hangover.

Then we arrived at 'Anlaby', a squattocracy holding owned by the Dutton family. A model English farm: a manor house, young Mr and Mrs Dutton's home, the manager's house, white-washed cottages for the workers, big draughthorse stables, cobbled courtyard and the other stables. Church, school, blacksmith's shop, dairy, sheds and tennis court, it was a village all of its own and the lord of the manor was a lady, old Mrs Emily Dutton.

Mrs Dutton lived in the beautiful mansion surrounded by a diverse and beautiful garden, truly a 'secret' garden with croquet lawn, water tower, running water, fountains and places to hide and read or to sit and be with the garden spirits. The draught-horse stables still had the brass nameplate of every horse attached to the stall walls. I loved the big garden and Mrs Dutton gave me free range to enjoy her space. We both loved horses.

I loved living at 'Anlaby' and we went to and from the station many times, my father always being welcomed back because he was such a hard worker.

When the time came for me to start school we were living at 'Anlaby'. My father and I were living in the old grooms' quarters, where I awoke each morning looking into a cobbled courtyard to hear the ghosts of a time gone by.

'Now, you have to go to school,' explained my father.

'Yes.'

'You got that? You got what that means?'

'Yes.'

'You have to stay there all day. You got that?'

'Yes.'

'You have to learn stuff.'

'What stuff?'

'To read and write.'

'I can do that.'

'Well you have to go to school. That's the law. You have to go. And, you have to stay there. All day.'

'All day!'

'I'll be in trouble with the police if you don't go. So go. And stay. All right?'

'Yes.'

My father gave me an old leather satchel, paper, ruler and pens. He made me a thick Vegemite sandwich.

'Do I get a cup of tea at school?'

'No. Kids don't drink tea.'

I looked at him in amazement.

'You get milk to drink. They give you milk.'

'Then I'll take the billy.'

'No. No. You have to drink milk.'

'But I don't like milk.'

'Then drink water.'

'No. I'll just boil the billy.'

'You can't boil the bloody billy, you're at school for Christsake.'

I just looked at him blankly.

'Look. It's like this. You have to go to school 'cause that's the law. They give you a break in the morning, for lunch and in the afternoon, and you take your lunch and you drink milk or water.'

'Am I locked up in a room all day?'

'No. You're not locked up but you have to stay there. You'll like it. Lots of other kids.'

I looked at him in horror and disbelief. This school business sounded as bad as my mother's threats of 'If you don't behave I'll have you locked up until you're eighteen.'

He hoisted me up on the back of old Nugget. I rode to the local schoolhouse, Tip following. Nugget was placed in the paddock next to the school, his bridle hung on the fence, where Tip was instructed to stay and guard. He sat and waited. His manners were very good and he knew not to come near or into certain places if I gave him something to 'guard.' There were other horses in the paddock and saddles on the fence.

I entered the one-room schoolhouse. Every eye turned to watch me. The teacher sat me at a desk and asked my name. She wrote it in a big book. All the kids stared at me. Some giggled, others whispered.

I arrived home at lunchtime.

'Jeeeee-sus, blooody Christ, what are you doing back here? I told you that you have to stay at bloody school.'

'I'm not staying there. I'm not staying in a room all day. Besides they can't even read and write.'

'You're going back. Tomorrow.'

Each day my father would make me a bread-and-Vegemite sandwich, or two bush biscuits welded together with butter, and I'd amble off to school. I'd stay until my name was marked on the roll and then ask to 'please be excused' (go to the toilet), or I would disappear at recess time. Nugget, Tip and I would go exploring. We went yabbying at dams or we followed dry creek beds and explored the country, making sure we were at the opposite end of where my father would be. We'd stop for lunch and I'd share it with my two companions. Sometimes the old horse would lie down and I'd lean on him in the sun, drinking in his presence to warm my soul.

I made friends with old people I met who asked me why I wasn't at school, and I told them the lie that I was ill and could not go. I met men who walked the road carrying their swags upon their backs and those who lived on the road travelling like us from place to place to work. There were fruit pickers and shearers, drunks and down-and-outs. I'd talk to them all.

I had always read and asked questions. My father taught me, and I'd read aloud to him — everything: boxes, packets, signs, books, papers and stacks of comics.

He encouraged me to talk and read until my questions drove him crazy.

'This child should be a lawyer,' said my nana. 'She can talk her way out of a brown paper bag.'

'I don't want to be a lawyer. I want to be a vet.'

'Well, you can forget that,' replied my aunt. 'We haven't got that sort of money.'

'If I found some money, would you be a lawyer?' asked my nana.

'No, I want to be a vet. Couldn't you give me the money for that?'

'With your mouth, it has to be the law,' replied my nana.

'But I want to be a vet.'

One day this argument culminated in a huge fight, a clash of wills, my nana telling me she would only be willing to 'run herself into debt' if I became what she wanted and nothing else.

I stormed out the back door, yelling at my nana about her unfairness and slammed it with all my might. It crashed into the frame and shuddered. The top half of that door held a beautiful pattern of coloured leadlight glass. It buckled and shattered before my horrified eyes. I stood staring through the door at the shock on my nana's face. Never again did we talk about my being a vet or a lawyer.

My father bought me books and comics: *Bobbsey Twins*, *Famous Five*, *Secret Seven*, *Fury*, *Champion*, *Black Beauty* and other kids' books he found at the tip or in second-hand stores. My mother only read *The Truth* newspaper so my knowledge of murders and sex crimes was exceptional. Reading opened worlds for me.

The school teacher did not follow up on my noted absences. That harassed teacher was far too busy to keep a roll check. Most teachers were, and roll monitors could be bribed.

While we were living at 'Anlaby' my mother came; my mother left with one of the station hands. She returned battered and bruised. Flagons of alcohol decorated our kitchen table. The fights and the violence became worse.

Men came and went to and from the drinking parties and I took to shooting rabbits to feed myself and the dogs. I knew to hide from her, to always wait and see, hear and feel her moods. I avoided her as much as possible.

One afternoon I came home early, fed Nugget and went towards the house garden. I stopped at the gate — I could hear my mother swearing and so I hid in the bushes to check the lie of the land. My mother came from the house carrying a shotgun. She was dishevelled and agitated, dressed only in a pink nylon nightie, her feet bare and her eyes wild. Standing over six feet, she was an imposing figure. I watched her stalking the yard, pointing at things with the gun and muttering to herself. 'Where are you, you little bastard? Come out! Where are you? Catherine! Bastard. Bastard.'

I was terrified. I had seen her drunk. I had watched her being beaten and I had found her beaten. I had experienced her gaiety, her flirting with men, her viciousness and her rejection of me. I had seen her raging and wild, but I had never seen her this mad. This broken. She yelled and swore and pointed the gun, swinging it round and round.

Could she see me? Was she finally going to kill me? She had certainly threatened it many times. I was petrified and shaking. Surely she could hear my body shaking and my teeth chattering as I crawled under the boxthorn hedge and flattened myself into the ground, hardly daring to breathe. I willed myself to be invisible. I had shut the dogs out of the house yard and I was aware of them sitting and panting near the gate. I willed them to be invisible too.

My mother went around the side of the house, yelling, and I bolted. Out from under that bush and into Nugget's paddock. I had that bridle on in seconds and that poor old horse was banged into a canter so fast he didn't have time to refuse. He knew the urgency of what I asked. I expected to feel the bullets hit my back. The dogs chased me, barking. I cantered into the vehicle shed area where my father and several other men were working.

'Steady down, steady down, you'll give the old boy a heart attack.' The men all looked up and laughed. I fell from the horse, yelling, 'Mum's got a gun and she's going to kill me!'

My father turned white and within seconds all the men were in the buckboard and gunning it down the road. I stood on the running board, hanging on for grim life. The old wooden-spoked wheels of the buckboard had never gone so fast. We banged into the yard as my mother came around the house with the gun up at her shoulder.

'Jesus Christ,' said someone and all the men flattened themselves inside the cabin or on the back of the ute. One man pulled me into the cabin and pushed me down on the floor. I could hear my father's voice. When I finally managed to get my head and eyes up to dashboard level I saw my father holding my sobbing mother and the shotgun lying some distance away.

I was taken to a neighbour's place where I stayed for a few days until my father collected me and we returned to the grooms' quarters. My mother had gone.

The incident was never mentioned. I overheard 'nervous break-down' but it was years before I understood what that implied.

One evening I went to feed and brush Nugget and he was gone. I was hysterical. My father had sold him. I sulked and raged and cried for days. I refused to go to school. I was ill. I wouldn't eat.

'Where is he?'

'God only knows where he has gone. Gone to work.'

'Tell me where he is.'

'I dunno.' My father's lips were sealed.

I thought he'd been sent to the knackery. I went into silence and refused to talk to my father.

'I dunno what's worse, you blabbering on or this bloody nothing,' exploded my father.

The ice was finally broken after I took all of young Mrs Dutton's dachshunds (Fritz dogs, my father called them) rabbiting. I figured they were the ideal dog to flush the bunnies out of their warrens. All fifteen were as keen as mustard and down the holes they went. None returned. They all wedged themselves down the holes and would not back out. All stuck. I had to talk to my father. He swore and cursed, took a long-handled shovel and dug each dog out. I had never heard so many expressions — all gathered from his time spent in the Middle East.

'Bloody twisted bowel of a pig's arse,' he muttered, and 'Maggoty arsehole, may the worms eat out your intestines slowly and painfully.'

Old Mrs Dutton understood my grief over losing Nugget. Her passion was to rescue broken-down racehorses.

'Look at him,' she'd say to me. 'That beauty made someone very rich and now he's to be made into glue. That's immoral; they deserve better than that.'

We'd take huge bags of jelly beans and go out to her beloved horses where we'd talk to them, pat them and feed them the glucose lollies. I kept the red and black ones for myself.

They were all old, big, sway-backed horses. Once elegant and admired, like old men they roamed around their paddocks lost in memories of former glory. Many were scarred, with damaged legs and knees. All had long faces with soft eyes. Their feet were broken and some wheezed with broken wind. I'd brush prickles from their manes, count their ribs and sing to them. Old Mrs Dutton was patient with me and would sit in her Rolls waiting.

I loved to spend time with her, and her library in 'the big house' captivated me. I'd never seen so many books and I'd sit with clean hands and turn over pages of enchantment. I loved the big home — each guest bedroom with a wall of books, the servants' quarters, the big bathrooms, the cellar where mush- rooms grew and the huge painting that hung in the hall. That painting fascinated me. It was old Mrs Dutton as a young woman and she was so beautiful and so regal, like a woman from another time that I had no memory of.

The small schoolhouse was closed down and all the station kids and others who attended that little one-room school with its big clanging bell were now picked up by a small bus and taken to a large road junction where we were transferred to a big bright yellow bus full of bullies. We had to go to an area school. I had to wear a grey woollen box-pleated uniform, which I hated. My father had hemmed it up for me, so I could grow into it, letting the hem down as I grew. The skirt was double thickness; it steamed in the heat and in winter smelt like a cross between a wet sheep and a drowned chook.

I couldn't escape from that school. The big yellow bus delivered us to the door. We were watched. The yard was patrolled.

I spent a lot of the time being 'sick', with unknown stomach wogs. I'd be in the sick bay reading. I hated the closed-in stuffy classrooms; the perfumed sickly smell of the teachers; the wet-wool smell of the other kids and the smell of the school itself — decay, chalk, disinfectant, and milk sitting curdling in the sun. We were forced to drink this hot bottled coagulation as it was supposedly good for us and it was free! I still can't drink milk without being sick and even the smell of hot milk makes me gag.

The teachers were strict, ruler-wielding tyrants. I couldn't breathe in school. I missed the horse and the dogs and I fretted for my freedom. The other kids called me names. I fought them and ripped their clothes.

I spent hours looking out of the window daydreaming. I wanted to learn on my own terms. I loved learning but, held in a classroom by threat — ('I will go to jail if you don't attend'; 'You will go into a home if you don't attend'; 'The police will get you if you don't go to school') — made me restless and anxious to be outside. I could not learn on those terms. I was labelled a talker, disruptive and hard to control. I asked continual questions until the exasperated teacher would send me to 'the office'. My continuous questioning was viewed as 'trouble'. My hands were tied behind me and I was made to sit on them to stop me talking.

It was harder to skip school when I was forced to catch a bus, but I'd often take off at recess or lunchtime and head for the nearest creek or find horses to be with. I'd be back in time to catch the bus home.

It was time to hit the road once again and Eudunda Area School became just another school experience. I moaned and groaned for ages. I missed Nugget. I'd stop at every horse we passed and pat it. My father knew he was being paid out and so he'd sit in the shade of a tree and roll a smoke. Then on we'd go. If I took too long he'd call, 'Come on, Skeeter, let's go!' (He called me Skeeter, short for 'mosquito', because I was a pest.)

We walked everywhere. From farm to farm, town to town. Whenever we settled for a while, I'd be enrolled in another school. I'd spend long enough to be registered — sometimes a few days, a week, a month. It all depended on where my father could get work. Or if he were too drunk for us to travel. Or if the Welfare were breathing down our necks.

All schools had compulsory religious instruction. I became bored. I tried to get out of these classes at several schools but such a protest seemed to bring on an uncontrollable fit in teachers and headmasters; they would rant and rave at me and call me ungodly and a sinner who was going to burn in hell.

'Write me a note,' I begged my father. 'If you tell them I'm a Jew then I don't have to attend religious instruction.'

'But you were baptised Church of England and even given a godfather.'

'Bugger my godfather. I hate all that religious bullshit. So tell them I'm a Jew.'

My father explained who the Jewish people were and why he couldn't tell such a lie.

'You're a bloody pagan.'

'I tried that too but they get really angry and red-faced when I say that.'

He explained some of the differing religious beliefs to me and told me to go and listen to different religious views before making up my mind or condemning other beliefs.

'Don't be ignorant,' he'd often say. 'It breeds contempt.'

So in every school I attended I was a different religion. (I learnt a great deal about God and even more about those lay-teachers of religion.)

I attended all manner of churches. I went to the Catholic mass with my nana. I liked the Catholic ceremonies with all the theatre and wonderful music. I horrified my nana by boldly taking Communion. I wasn't going to be left out and I wanted to taste the wine. My nana was a 'good' Catholic. She even gave away her cockatoo because my father taught it to swear and to call the Catholic Father foul names! It seemed to wait until the priest arrived at my nana's door and then the swearing would begin. Those priests that came to visit my nana all had limp handshakes and soft, wet faces with voices that reminded me of chalk scraping up and down a blackboard.

'For Christsake keep your mother away from the bloody priests,' my father would warn when she and I were at my nana's. 'I don't know who likes the piss more, your mother or the man of God.'

It was a Catholic Father who started my mother drinking alcohol. When she was a long-legged teenager the priest and my mother would sit on the cliffs overlooking the sea and knock back a few bottles of communal wine.

But it was the Salvos that I really loved. Because of their music. I'd walk along the streets with them, roaring at the top of my voice. My father put a stop to my career in the Salvation Army when he caught me trailing along in and out of the pubs, begging for money and selling their newspaper to drunken returned soldiers. Those weeping war veterans were easy pickings — especially for a kid who told lies about her dead father who had gone to God. My father seriously threatened me over that incident.

The Church of England had great hymns but none of the pomp and theatre of the Catholics, even though they tried hard. I gave them up. The Lutherans, Methodists and Presbyterians were serious and mournful, they lacked joy; their churches were ugly and their preachers humourless. In high school I joined the Mormons so I could have free dinners and that often saved me from hunger. I let them dunk me in slimy green water and do their baptising ritual just so I could be fed. Besides, I'd been baptised heaps by then, all to my own advantage. I recognised only one baptising though — the Anglican rite when I was a baby and was given a godfather. The rest were just convenient and led to my enjoying many a meal in a variety of homes. I was always hungry, growing fast, and religious belief, for the moment, provided food. I learnt a great deal about people and table manners this way!

The Mormons were very white-skinned, white-hearted, white-belief-based. People of colour were considered 'lower'. I enjoyed meeting the young, well-scrubbed, pimply-faced American boys in their white-on-white shirts and dark ties. I used to steal their bikes and go riding while they were door-knocking for God. I wasn't interested in their God — just their food. Our neighbours were from Scotland and they were Mormon. Their dinner table groaned with the weight of food. I loved them.

My mother carted me off to spiritualist churches where people spoke in tongues and fell on the ground screaming and tearing at themselves. They would foam at the mouth and dance in the aisles.

My 'Aunty' Bea took me to revivalist meetings where everyone sang and clapped and rocked the foundations with their weeping and wailing.

The business of worship fascinated me once I got going. I was told to 'stay pure ... do good, be good,' and yet, observing many within the churches, I saw the hypocrisy and the 'talking from the side of the mouth'. I was taught religion by zealots and madmen. I was taught that each religion was 'right' and that any other was the work of the devil. I was taught that the devil had horns, tail and a long cold member. (I had to ask my father what a 'frigid member' was. He relayed that question for weeks, accompanied by bouts of hysterical laughter.)

I was taught that God was kind, compassionate, mad, violent and vengeful.

At one school the teacher asked all the students to write a story on what we would all do with a million pounds. We had to read out what we would do. The students gave themselves big cars, clothes, material goods or became famous. I opened a lost dogs' home and an orphanage. The class and the teacher roared with laughter. My face burned. The teacher said I told the funniest story. She told me I couldn't think like that. I told her what I thought of her and the class. As she was screaming at me to 'go to the headmaster's office' I walked out. It was months before I returned to school and then only because I was stuck yet again in the orphanage, waiting on my nana to claim me.

Walking with my father from town to town I'd be a horse. Whenever there were no horses I'd become a horse — neighing, trotting, cantering, galloping. I was every horse in the world galloping free. When it became too much my father would shout, 'For Christsake be a human for a moment. The wind will change and you'll stay like that — half horse, half human. Now cut it out, you're giving me the shits. And stop talking to the bloody spirits for a while 'cause it's giving me the willies.'

I'd search for a place to camp near horses and then I'd be off. Talking to them, making friends, occasionally taking an illegal ride around a paddock. Sometimes those rides would turn into a mad gallop with me flattened along the horse's back, absorbed in the whole experience, yelling or trying to breathe into the wind; feeling the freedom of flight and always aware that what was under me was a living, breathing beauty with a big heart. I'd cry at the beauty of horses.

I came off frequently, hitting the earth and trying to perfect a soft roll when landing; it never worked. I had permanent scabs on my hands, knees and nose. I was okay if the horse kept straight or turned a wide circle, but propping or sharp turns or even a buck would send me sailing. It also took me a long time to teach the dogs to sit at a fence and wait for me. They loved a wild ride across a paddock but in their exuberance they'd stir up the horse or horses into a frenzy of bucking. Having horses overexcited, kicking and bucking, squealing and wheeling, was not, and is not, my idea of fun unless I can watch their performance from a safe distance. The dogs would sit at the fence line, whining.

My father liked a campsite near water, from which he could

walk into town, to the 'rubberty' or, to use the full rhyming slang, the 'rubberty dub'.

'Just going to the rubberty for a snort.'

Off he'd go, whistling, a couple of dogs always following him. Old Tex the terrier was always torn between going with my father and taking care of me. Tiger the greyhound was glue against my father's leg, and Tip was loyal to me although he worked well for my father. At this time we were down to three dogs, as he'd given Lady, the beautiful chocolate kelpie, to one of the men at 'Anlaby'. 'She's too good a dog not to work,' he'd explained. 'She loves it and we can always get one of her pups.' Lady did truly love to work. She'd round up the chickens if sheep, pigs, cattle or kids were absent.

'See ya later, I'm off to wet the whistle. I'll bring back some chops for tea so you boil the spuds, and put salt in them! You gotta have some salt or you'll get scurvy. Don't like salt, don't like milk, don't like fruit … I dunno.'

'I eat fruit. Well, what we pinch anyhow. But I'm sick of tough grapes. Why can't you buy some nice ones?'

'We're in the bloody Barossa Valley; the vines are full. For Christsake stop your moaning and help yourself. Look at them. Green, black, purple — you've got God's acre to choose from and you're moaning. I'll bring you back a Polly Waffle. You're a dragon, kid!' Then he'd laugh. He often called me a dragon — 'one that loved chocolate'. I did, do, love chocolate. I'd ache for chocolate as I pressed my sticky face against shop windows, or I'd wander around shops, longing for that dark smooth taste in my mouth. I only stole a block of chocolate once and I felt so guilty that I gave it to the dogs, not even having one lick of my passion.

He knew the way to my heart, and I knew every pub visit brought a chocolate bar of some kind. My father loved liquorice. He'd eat a full bag at a sitting, with me helping him. Then we'd both have the shits for days.

'Even me bloody farts smell like liquorice.'

'Well, that's a change because they mostly smell like Vegemite or bloody horses,' he'd reply. 'You know, you're gunna turn into a horse.' And he'd laugh.

My father always made for the pub in any town. It's where he heard about what work was available in the area — chopping wood, clearing, shearing, fencing, shooting. 'Never be proud,' he used to say. 'Every job has a purpose and some are more necessary than others. The most important man in your life is the one who takes away your shit and garbage. What is the most important question you can ask about that?'

'Where does my shit and garbage go?'

'Good, because you might just be eating or drinking it!'

When he was just wobbly drunk he'd arrive back at camp around dusk or in the early dark. If he was 'shickered', or 'pissed as a fart' because he had gone on a bender with 'mates', he might not be back until the next day. Occasionally he was jailed for being 'drunk and disorderly'. I'd just wait or go looking in the local drunks' hangout or at the local police station. I had a fear of the police and hated going to the lockup to look for my father.

The police often hassled us, coming into our camp or home — all very polite and all very inquiring.

'Is she at school?'

'Yeah.'

'You working?'

'Yeah.'

'How long you gunna be in this area?'

Dad would shrug his shoulders.

'Keep moving.'

Those huge people in pressed blue clothes — they reeked of authority and power. Towering above my father and me, they seemed like giants.

'They are giants,' I barely whispered as they left.

'No, mate, they're not giants, they don't have any magic. They just think they're giants because they have this power called Law and they know we all have to bow to that power. It's not a good thing to have too much power all because of a piece of paper and a badge. Keep out of their way, mate, just keep out of their way.'

My father taught me that giants once lived on earth and there were many places where we could still find traces of them.

'When the giants died they became hills and mountains. They lay down and the land covered them. You can still see giants' burial places if you look closely at the land. Look around and you will see the shapes of giants. It was easy for them to walk the world and they left their special magic behind.' I looked for that special magic and found it in rock faces, cliffs, hills, mountains and rivers. The Kimberleys are alive with rock people. Faces stare out of the stone from a world long gone but the images are a reminder of a magic that still flickers for those who search.

I'd point out faces in rocks to my father.

'That one… Jesus Christ, it's uglier than me, mate.'

'That one… looks like a dog,' or 'I had a mate who looked like that.'

I searched the landscape for giants. Many female giants once died in the Adelaide Hills and their shapes can be quite clearly seen. Today I have a beautiful buried giant across from my front gate. Female. So easy to see with her two large breasts, full belly and legs pointing towards my gate. She was a magnificent woman. I greet her with great respect, feel privileged to have her in my life and thank my father for showing me landscape and the magic it holds if only we look.

When I was ten years old I had a period of to-ing and fro-ing. From mother to father to nana, aunt, orphanage. From road to house, and then to another house. I'd start school in some local town. I'd try to make friends with the kids who had horses but we had very little in common. They were the wealthy kids; usually belonging to the local pony and hunt clubs, they had status within a society to which I didn't belong. I'd beg for rides that were refused. 'Oh, you can be our groom.' I'd spit at their feet. Their parents would be up to the school in a flash and I'd be caned for rudeness. My father would not sympathise. 'Keep away from them. They're not your sort.'

I still hung around the horses, watched pony club events and local races. So many of my father's 'mates' had a trotting horse or two that I could keep busy brushing and talking to what I called 'my chariot horses'.

I found a book on an English rider called Pat Smythe. She jumped horses, worked with horses and was an Olympic rider. That was it. I wanted to be like her and ride in the Olympic Games. I bored my father with my dreams.

'Ahhh, shut up. Just shut up. Dream it all but for Christsake stop talkin' to me! I'm fed up to the back teeth with the bloody Olympics. Talk, talk, talk, you'd talk the leg off an iron pot!'

Bush biscuits

I was always hungry. My father usually had a supply of bush biscuits. Always two for a penny. Stuck together with a slab of butter as thick as cheese.

I was a child in the time of pounds, shillings and pence; a time when two bush biscuits were viewed as a substantial lunch. Bush biscuits were thick, heavy and square, the size of a bread-and-butter plate. You paid for them with a penny. Never a three-pence or a sixpence — always a penny rubbed shiny by my fingers turning it over and over as I savoured my wealth.

I was always told by my nana never to put money in my mouth because 'you never know where it's been!' It could choke you too. She had a wealth of horror stories of children who had suffocated or nearly suffocated, changing colour from red to blue to white. 'Then you knew they were gone,' she would say as she swept or dusted or banged flour from her hands. 'Gone just like that. All because they swallowed a penny. Now keep the money out of your mouth!'

Once in an act of rebellion (something that happened about once a day) I told her that I had never heard of anyone dying that way. Then I was told all the names of those poor unfortunates who had nearly choked to death. If she didn't personally know the offenders (it was after all their fault, they had all been warned), then she knew someone who did. She finished, 'and

52

what if some dirty old wino had had that penny? He probably sucked it in hunger, but more likely to help hold off the cramps and shudders until his next drop of wine. You never know where a penny's been.' She'd bang her floured hands together, white powder emphasising her point.

When I handle money as an adult I often wonder where it has been, what hands have held the money, what it has been exchanged for and what dreams rested on it. It often feels as though a great sigh comes from money, a great sadness.

My nana was an expert on winos and drinkers because she once ran a pub on Kangaroo Island. The story goes that she kept a bottle of gin on the counter and whenever someone offered to buy her a drink she would graciously accept and pour a gin and tonic for herself, but the gin was water. She seldom drank. She was against 'drinking all the profits'. Profit was what she aspired to. To be successful. So her lover was the local copper — that way she could sell 'grog' on a Sunday and after hours.

'Your nana was cunning,' one old local told me. 'She had the local policeman just where she wanted him. He even rolled out the barrels for her. No missing the Sunday tourist trade for her. She'd be up all Saturday night making pasties to sell the next day. On Sundays all the tourists would come over and there'd be Mary. She was the first on the island to own a fur coat!'

My nana would indulge in a small glass of stout or brandy with my mother and she sometimes liked a 'lady's drink', a small sherry or port. She had several ritual brandies when making the Christmas puddings! She used to put threepences in the pudding — they didn't leave the sharp metallic taste that pennies did.

My nana never had bush biscuits. She made Anzac biscuits and sultana cake.

The malt-flavoured bush biscuits were my school lunch on and off for years, depending on the financial state of my parents. I often swapped them for two Weetbix held together with butter and jam.

Sometimes we had jam, usually plum, but if the finances stretched a little there would be apricot; and the big sloppy apricot pieces would slide from between the bush biscuits down onto my box-pleated uniform and into my lap. My jam spill was hardly noticed as others rescued pie droppings of scalding gristle and sauce, splattered milk and enough crumbs to feed an aviary of birds. We sucked the spills from our clothes, picked our noses and our knee scabs and yelled to be heard amid the endless screeching of kids at play.

Each school I attended had a different-coloured summer uniform. Because I attended so many schools a summer uniform would have been a waste of money, so I sweltered the summers away locked in my woollen tunic, looking like a well-cooked lobster. Deodorants hadn't yet come into fashion, so powder and scent were used to mask body smell. Scent (now known as perfume) was usually bought from Coles. We reeked of scented chemicals. Those in fashion bought 'Rose' or '4711'. They stank like old lace handkerchiefs that were stored in a drawer. The heady sweetness of Helena Rubinstein or Revlon indicated the wearer had stolen from her mother's collection. We slathered ourselves in Ponds products. It was bold and an offence to wear perfume to school. One would be 'called up' to the headmaster's office if even a whiff of perfume lingered from the weekend. Scent was worn when one was 'going out', usually to the 'pictures'. The boys wore Californian Poppy oil in their hair which was slicked back, oil dribbling down their necks. They looked like pop-eyed, sleek seals with pimples.

Clean on Monday morning, after the weekend bath, we'd smell of Palmolive or Cashmere Bouquet soap, a sweet all-pervading aroma in a time when soap was important. Or at least the brand was. Velvet was popular, used to wash the dishes, the floor, the laundry, the body and the dog! Anything green or white was a luxury, and I once gazed at a rich brown slab of Pears with greed! My mother caught me washing my border collie dog in the bath with me. She yelled and screamed about me getting some disease. I couldn't understand all the fuss. I washed the dog when he needed it and the logical place was in the bath with me. That way he also smelt nice, of whatever soap we used. My father had never made a fuss, even if I used his towel to wipe the dog.

I sniff in those soap smells when I come across them today in strange bathrooms or wafting about some stranger. Smells awaken memories, and I visualise those other kids in all those schools I attended and wonder if we would recognise each other now. Every once in a while a familiar name pops up with an adult attached.

One name became a beauty queen in her teens. That was no surprise because she was chocolate-box beautiful. In primary school she lounged against the fence while the boys whistled and cat-called after her. A select group of us were her friends.

She decided she wanted her hair permed. Not in the cork-screw style of the mothers but in the blonde fly-away fashion of Marilyn Monroe. We were recruited to help her. We had no perming lotion but we set her hair in curlers and painted the hair liberally with sugar and water. Then we blow-dried the lot. The hair crackled as we removed the rollers and sprang back into sug-ared tightness. No soft waves. Our Marilyn Monroe screamed as we tried to brush the hair into waving loveliness. Her hair broke, snapping like straw. She yelled and the mob vanished; I stayed. We washed and washed her hair. The end result was frizzed as if shot through by a thousand volts of electricity. Unfortunately, the 'Afro' was not yet in fashion. My friend and her mother didn't appreciate our version of the Monroe hairstyle. A week later she returned to school with a new and expensive hairstyle.

One Christmas years later there sat the young Marilyn before me — a beauty queen in an ermine-bordered coat, a soft perm wrapped around her head, all shimmering loveliness. The crown glittered, the gloved hand waved. I smiled and waved back, catching her eyes. She frowned and turned to stare at me, recalling another time. I walked away, not wanting to be the mirror of her painful past. The pain of the hair fiasco was nothing to what she endured from the male members of her family. Her friends knew and we kept the secret. We always knew who was being bashed, tormented, raped. These were experiences many of us shared. The 'normalcy' of violence. One friend at ten years old had no teeth — knocked out by his father, while another's legs were always black and blue from the belt. One friend became a mechanic, another a radio personality, one a wife and mother, another a nurse to climb the ladder to a position as hospital matron. One boy became a murderer, chopped the body into pieces and scattered them along the Nullarbor Plain. But to get back to where I began. We all ate bush biscuits!

Bush biscuits cemented together with Vegemite. Vegemite; a thick, black tar-like substance that, once tasted, becomes addiction. (Just listen to all those Australian tourist stories about how a jar of Vegemite had to be flown across the world to them, through sleet and fire, just so they could have their morning fix on toast.)

My mother made me addicted to Vegemite soup. A big teaspoon of Vegemite into a cup of boiling water, add pieces of white bread until all the liquid is absorbed; stir and eat!

Vegemite added to everything to give it flavour. When my mother was not adding Vegemite she added curry powder. Sometimes she added both.

> *We're happy little Vegemites as bright as bright can be,*
> *We all enjoy our Vegemite for breakfast, lunch and tea...*

The Vegemite jingle. Along with the Sorbent toilet song and the Aeroplane Jelly ditty, we sang it lustily as we played hopscotch, skipped ropes and pounded each other's hands in slapping games. Advertisement songs were part of the playground culture. We had a large imported repertoire ('Oranges and Lemons', 'Ring-a-Rosy', 'London Bridge') but we also embraced the advertisements with high exhilaration. Jingles ricocheted across the bubbling, liquorice tarmac that was affectionately termed 'the playground'. The noise died somewhere in suburbia where adults muttered about the shrillness of screechy little girls.

Summer in South Australia is dry — mouth-blisteringly dry. The land is burnt; orange dust seeps into tightly shuttered houses, misting every surface with fine grit, while outside the air shimmers in expectation of a bushfire.

School playgrounds, of concrete or tar, were usually reserved for the girls. The concrete playgrounds shimmered and burnt;

the tar playgrounds bubbled and stuck to the soles of our shoes. There was a corrugated iron shed, blazing hot even to touch. Girls huddled in the shade of the school buildings or fought for ownership of scarce tree shade. Gangs were formed to guard territory. The boys had unlimited use of space while the girls were not allowed on the boys' domain — that patch of green termed 'The Oval'. It was for cricket, football and boys' talk. The only times we could set foot on that precious piece of turf were during sport lessons or on interschool sport days. The oval was an oasis of mowed green, a few hot gum trees around the edges to offer panting boys shade.

In winter the playgrounds were deadly with ice water or thick with mud. They added another dimension to the kid smell. Whatever surface we played on, most of us had bloodied elbows and knees. Lovely for picking scabs from! The school nurse was always sadistic — she'd paint all injuries with iodine. Our games nearly always hurt and involved pain, blood and bruises.

Brandy was a favourite ball game. When you were 'it', you had possession of the ball and, chasing other players, you attempted to 'brand' them with it. Not too gently either. When playing with the girls I only hit them in the arm or leg, but the boys I would hit anywhere, as long as I hit hard. It was permissible payback.

Skipping was another 'girls' game'. Fast and furious the 'pepper' ropes would burn the playground and our ankles. Hopscotch was never played at school. The squares perfectly painted for us were never used. We preferred to chalk the grid on the concrete driveways of our homes or on the footpath. A walk around the block would become a dance of skipping and turning on the concrete squares. One foot up, hop, hop, two feet down, hop, hop, turn. Always the hopscotch was drawn with pilfered pieces of chalk, the most prized pieces being those the teacher threw at you. Hopscotch was considered by the adults to be a suitable game for girls who could therefore enjoy it while 'dressed up' in shiny shoes and bows.

One day to my delight I discovered that adults also, thinking themselves unobserved, would merrily play the game if they came across it sketched on the footpath. I would sit in a tree and stifle my giggles as I watched women stop, remember, look around to see if they were being watched, then quickly hop and skip across the grid — old ladies with big bags, mothers with prams and once a man in a dark suit carrying an umbrella. The game of watching became more fun than playing the game itself!

The game I excelled in was knucklebones. Mine were real bones — knuckles my father cleaned for me. Sometimes I'd paint them with Silverfrost — the only paint we ever seemed to have plenty of. It covered everything. My father painted the iron of the sheds, the house, fences, gates and my bike. Everything shone as if wrapped in foil.

I won and lost bags of knucklebones. I won from the other kids and lost to the teachers. When bored in class I would practise under the desk and become so absorbed that I frequently caught the attention of the teacher.

The best place to practise was on a pub verandah waiting for my father. After the Cherry Ripe was finished, the last drop of raspberry-and-lemonade licked from the glass and the comic read for the third time, out would come the knucklebones.

We sat there, lines of kids waiting for their fathers. Sometimes we'd talk and play together, mostly we just waited patiently, passing the time with whatever we could find. Some kids just sat and stared. Kids and fathers came and went. Occasionally an adult would stop and say, 'G'day,' but only if there were a heap of us crowding the verandah and he'd have to step over us to reach the door leading to the bar.

If you were to park a couple of kids on a pub verandah today while the old man was inside, drinking, talking and listening to the races, the Welfare would be alerted to the situation, calling it 'neglect'. We were not neglected and I never felt unsafe, even when drunken men would lean down to peer at me and ramble on with some boozy tirade. The drunks were soon moved on, either by other adults or by a mouthful from some annoyed kid. If some kid yelled out, a head usually appeared around the door to check out the scene. If a kid had ever yelled 'Help', the whole bar would have stampeded through the door.

I considered kids who were left waiting in cars to be 'poor buggers'. They would press their noses up against the windows, watching us. Occasionally there would be a woman in a car along with the kids, and once a woman sat by herself in a car, smoking and watching the bar door like a hungry tiger. Too long in the car with whingeing kids and the woman might send a kid in after the father or begin to blow the horn. Men seemed to know the sound of their own horn. The horn blowing brought one of two reactions. Out he would come with a tray of drinks, soft for the kids and mild for her. All smiles, he'd hand the drinks around and be back in that bar before I could cough. Her drink had to stretch a long way! Or out he would come, murder on his face, slam into the car, roar at everyone, and drive away in a shower of spun stones. We'd grin at each other. If kids who'd been left in a car hooted the horn, the reaction from the father was very different. Out he'd come, bang a few heads together and storm back into the pub.

One evening my father toppled out of the pub and fell down the steps. Not a kid moved a muscle. My father stood, swayed and staggered to the car. He pulled himself into the driving seat and slumped against the wheel. I stood, brushed down my clothes and went to the car. The other kids sat quiet. I pulled my father into a sitting position behind the wheel and sat in his lap. I closed the driver's door and turned the ignition, giving the car life. My father's foot went down on the clutch, I changed gear; his foot went down slowly on the accelerator and we cruised away from the pub. We drove home in second gear, me steering.

Before we reached home I had to put the lights on. I peered through the windscreen and battled with the steering wheel. Up the dirt drive to the house and in through the gate. 'Brake, brake,' I yelled. My father stomped on the brake and we stalled.

My mother was living with us at the time and she came out of the front door like a hurricane. I opened the driver's door and as my mother reached the car my father fell out. I was still holding the steering wheel.

'You bastard,' yelled my mother and, picking up a length of pipe from the driveway, she crashed it against my father's skull. Red stained the earth. I looked at her in horror.

'Where's my bloody drink?' she screamed and went back inside the house, banging the door. I ran to the nearest neighbour, a mile away; they called the ambulance and left me to walk home alone. 'We can't interfere,' they said as they shut their front door. My father was gone when I arrived home.

Next day I walked five miles to the hospital. He was sitting up in bed, his head bandaged and his cheeky grin spread across the ward. 'Bring me my bike,' he said. 'I'm in here for a couple of days.'

The following day I rode his bike to the hospital and walked home. Two days later he was still not home. I walked to the hospital. He'd left the day before. I was heading back home when I saw him — walking down the road, pushing his bike, swigging from a brown paper bag. I ran to catch him. 'Where've you been?'

He laughed. 'Oh, they let me out and I stopped in for a short snort. Would you believe it, the bloody coppers picked me up.' He laughed again. 'Riding a bike while pissed! "Under the influence", they called it. I tried to tell them it was the bang on my head made me shaky but the bastards wouldn't listen and so I spent the night at her majesty's hotel!'

'Mum's gone,' I replied.

'Yeah, I expected that.'

'You were riding your bike drunk,' I yelled at him. 'And you drive the car drunk, too.'

He just laughed. 'We'll have to stretch your legs, kid, so you can reach the pedals. Here.' He threw me a bag of marbles.

I learnt to play marbles. Few girls ever played. The game was dominated by boys who were very sure of themselves. I loved beating them but I was never the whiz with marbles that I was with knucklebones. Cowboys-and-Indians was my favourite game. Girls were always the Indians. That was okay by me because I saw the Indians as fighting for what was theirs against the cowboys who were the really bad guys, despite what the Saturday films told us. Besides, the Indians loved their horses and I was horse-besotted. I had made a bow and a set of arrows that flew — a few paces. But, more importantly, I was an Indian with a gun! Not a stick or a rusted piece of metal but a big shiny cap gun. I had begged and begged my father for a silver gun.

Every year there were Christmas parties for kids. These were usually organised by the father's place of work or by his chapter of the RSL. There would be a keg out the back, trestle tables filled with food, a large decorated pine tree (the floor beneath groaning with presents) and a half-tanked-up red-nosed Father Christmas. He would stagger around in his red suit and white wool whiskers, handing out presents and patting the kids as though they were beautiful lost puppies. If Father Christmas belonged to Kate or Brian or Dawn then all the kids would groan because those fathers liked the gift recipients to kiss them on the cheek as he handed over the gift. As if he had really brought all this stuff from the North Pole, when we all knew it was our parents who had supplied it. We were bored by the adults' antics and dress-ups. We just wanted to grab our gifts and rip into them. But the charade was not quite over. We had to show our parents what 'Father Christmas' had brought us.

Each Christmas during my Cowboys-and-Indians years my father promised he'd get me the coveted cap gun. I begged and begged and tried to behave myself in the way that he thought was 'good'. He told me that such a present was not suitable for a girl. I screamed at him that I was not a girl — I was an Indian. Besides, from the age of six I had had my own rabbit gun — a single-shot twenty-two. Now all I wanted was a play gun and he wouldn't let me have one.

'I will not let you shoot people, even in play,' he said.

'I'll shoot over their heads,' I yelled.

'No.'

'You shot people in the war.'

'That's why I'll not let you have one in play.'

He bought me a cowboy suit — all fringes, but no gun. I swapped it with Ronny for his new, silver, chamber-rolling cap gun. My father was furious. I loved it. I could bang away at those bloody cowboys. Bang! The cowboys would drop dead after a few bloodcurdling screams and some spectacular death throes, then come back to life. The Indians, the girls, if caught, were shot dead and scalped. Not me. Not being particularly fleet of foot, I became an expert on hiding, wriggling like a snake along the ground or standing to make myself invisible. These kids couldn't track to save a life! I would sit up in trees, on the sides of sheds, high in the hay bales. There I learnt that not only kids but adults too did not look up. They were not good searchers. The Aboriginal kids I had played with could find me no matter how careful I was. They taught me to hide, to track and to watch and listen.

No cowboy was ever going to catch me, especially after what they did to Julie Young.

Julie had the misfortune to be caught, tied up and forgotten during one auspicious raid. Hours later her mother found her, all cried out and well past the hysterical stage, bound to a tennis court post. Mrs Young went what we termed 'ape shit'. Her kids were grounded and the rest of us warned that if we ever tied anyone up again we would be tied up and hung by the ankles from the hay shed roof! The Indians pleaded not guilty but Mrs Young was beyond listening and threatened to bloody well kill us all.

Amazing how many times we were threatened with death! Death threats by parents and other adults were a part of our life. My mother constantly threatened me verbally and she threw anything she could reach at me as well. My ball practice taught me to catch, and my reflexes were such that even forty years on I can weave and duck a thrown missile. (Once she learnt that I could catch and return airborne objects she stopped throwing things!)

We rode ghost horses and galloped as fast as our legs could carry us, clicking our tongues at the top of our mouths as an added touch of realism. We played Cowboys-and-Indians on the horses within ourselves rather than giving chase on the heavy farm horses. We did use them for our circus performances though.

Once, on a station, we rode bales of hay down the side of the huge haystack. You sat astride a bale and let some kid give it a shove into space. Out you would fly into the air and then ride the bale to the ground, screaming with excitement. Back up the haystack we'd climb, ready for another go. Bales of hay flew in all directions and one kid broke her arm in a fall. We all received beltings because of the number of bales we rode ecstatically into ruination.

We were screamed at for riding the poddy calves and the merino rams, enticing the big Hereford bull to bellow and chase us, and for using the heavy horses as we thought knights used to do. When we were banned for jousting from their backs we used our bikes instead and battered each other into the hard tennis court.

Kids came and went in my life. We moved. They moved. My mother came and went, depending on what men were available, and always the women clucked and talked about her. It was always easy to tell when my mother was being discussed. The adults would fall silent when I entered a room and give me those dreadful long pitying looks that they reserve for kids they think are neglected.

I became tough and 'big-mouthed'. 'It's all right,' I'd reply. 'You can keep talking. We all know she's gone off with so-and-so. I dunno why you blame her though; he's been screwing her for ages.'

Often he was someone's husband and I fully knew the reaction my comments would bring. I brought it all out into the open and refused to allow her to carry all the blame. Men were always sniffing around my mother. She made them feel good. When men were around, it was as if all the lights were on and flashing; she was like a Christmas tree offering gifts and happiness. When men weren't around, the lights were off, though they would come up to 'dim' for my father.

Seldom was the kitchen empty of some man's presence.

My father bottled up his resentment. I'd watch for signs of the explosion that would inevitably come, and I'd hide food in my cubby. The dog and I could last for days out there. Until the dust settled at least.

Bread was the favourite food to hoard. I love bread as I did then — homemade or shop bought, thin, flat or thick: bread. Spread with a slab of butter and tarred with Vegemite. Treacle was also a favourite, dripping thick from the bread edges — great dollops of gold.

At one farm where we lived I had to walk down to the mailbox each day to collect the post and bread. The post was always bills; the bread was always warm. The bread was in the shape of a baking tin with a piece of greaseproof paper wrapped around the middle, but it was the smell that lured me into a small pick at the crust. That warm crusty smell of yeast filled my nostrils with sweet delight. Many a time my mother chased me with a strap, or broom, or mop because I came home with the bread mutilated. She never really understood the temptation. I would 'just tidy the bread up', was my excuse. Make it all neat. If it were half a loaf then just peel off the raised front layer where the loaf had been split. I would arrive home and be totally baffled by the huge hole that had appeared in the centre of the loaf. When my father brought home the bread I'd hang around like a vulture, slobbering with the thought of the crust which I coveted, but so did he.

I had a great-aunt who sat on her verandah and watched the world change around her. She saw the horses and carts of the bread man and the milkman replaced by motorised matchboxes on wheels, then by the local milkbar, and finally by trips to the supermarket.

She lived on Glen Osmond Road in Adelaide. A road that led to the city, it snaked its way from the hills, and now is lined with garages, restaurants, motels and glass-and-steel monoliths that bounce the sun's glare into motorists' eyes. Nearly all the old stone homes with character have gone. One or two have hung on, disguised as businesses. The road has widened and a blue exhaust film settles within the corridor of tarmac.

My great-aunt had worn a bum-smooth saucer into the wooden chair on the front verandah. From her vantage point she watched the world and her street modernise. When my mother took me to visit her she still had her ice block delivered and placed in her mesh ice chest.

'See, the ice keeps the butter real hard,' she said, showing me a slab of thick, homemade, yellow butter that tasted of salt.

It seemed that each time we visited this old aunt the ice man would arrive with his big block of ice. In his leather apron, with muscles like ripe oranges bursting through his skin, he smelled of man sweat. He scared me with his big ice-holding pincers; like claws on the end of his hands, they would snap shut as he released the ice from his grip. His boots were heavy but his voice was gentle.

My mother, the chameleon, had a man within her focus and her whole demeanour changed from a tall, strong woman into a small, fluttery forgetful one. All eyelashes and sighs, she exuded promise. Later I heard people say that her promise was like being hit with a Mack truck, but when the ice man was in our lives I just thought, 'Here she goes again being friendly!'

My mother would push my old aunt and myself out into the back garden where we would sit until she called us. Then I would have a pee, kiss my old aunt on her papery skin and we'd depart. My mother always left a couple of ten-bob notes on the table. 'Helps her out with the pension. Don't tell your father.'

We also met an 'Uncle Kevin' at my old aunt's. He was a sailor and dressed in bell-bottom pants. My mother told me he was a 'cousin', but I never knew who to. I couldn't tell my father about him either. My mother must have liked Kevin because I found a photograph of him in a large box of photos of people who were mostly unknown to me.

My old aunt and I would be banned from the house while my mother 'talked business' with her men friends. Under the aged pepper tree we would sit sucking our coffee and making appreciative noises. It was the only place I had coffee until I was a teenager. It came as syrup, thick and black, from a bottle that read, 'Coffee and Chicory'. My aunt added cold milk and heaps of sugar. Looking at the bottles on a supermarket shelf today, I see the old aunt's face with that secret smile she had and her way of conspiring with my mother in some huge joke that I was not quite a part of — a small piece, but not an acknowledged part.

The men who scared me most were not my mother's friends but the rabbit man and the dunny-cart men (toilet waste collectors).

At my nana's, the dunny man would crunch up the drive once a week, just after breakfast time, when I was always 'hanging out' for a shit, but — knowing it was a Tuesday — I'd hang on and hang on until the old tin was removed and a clean tin placed under the seat through a trapdoor at the back of the dunny. By the end of the week the toilet smelt bad. The tin would be full and the odour of phenol would mingle in a heavy oppression of sludge-like vapour that made breathing with the door shut impossible. I was always worried that I'd be sitting on the toilet when the dunny man arrived with a fresh tin, and there I'd be, bum exposed. His cart was called 'the night cart' but ours arrived some time on Tuesday morning and by the time it did I had a stomach ache from delaying. I wondered how the dunny man could carry a full tin of piss, shit and paper on his shoulder and never spill a drop! I would fantasise about what I would tell people if my father did such a job. 'Oh, he's your shit collector,' I would nonchalantly say. Ha! In truth I'd probably invent some other job for him. Trish, one of my schoolmates, hated the fact that her father was a garbo — not even the dunny man! She was particularly embarrassed because he was really proud of his work and, when the truck passed by the school, he'd honk the horn and wave at her. There she'd be, under the desk or heading for the girls' toilets, her face aflame.

It was the rabbit man though who was the bogeyman. Luckily we didn't get to see him very often and then, after a while, my nana began to buy rabbits from the butcher because she reckoned it was healthier. It certainly was for me because the rabbit man looked to me like a character out of an Edgar Allan Poe story. A ferret of a man with yellow pointed teeth that had brown stains running down each one. His face was wrinkled and yellow and his hair was white with nicotine-yellow streaks in the front. His eyes swam in pools of broken veins, and dirty stubble hung like green moss on his face. His thick red fingers were knotty and tobacco-stained with the fingernails black and broken. His pants were held up on his hips with green haybale twine, and my nana described his arms as 'chickens' insteps'! His horse was not a chariot giant but a skinny, overworked old pacer with a droopy bottom lip and a ferocious bite if any human came within striking distance. Snake-like, the neck would whip out and those long yellow teeth would fasten onto any flesh they could reach. He made me sad even though he was mean. The shine was long gone from his coat; his feet were cracked and his harness brittle with dirt. I'd roll apples along the gutter towards him and he'd crunch them in a single snap of his long teeth.

'Don't touch him,' would shriek the rabbit man, 'He'll bloody well bite!'

This didn't stop me rolling apples to the horse, and when the rabbit man was busy talking to my nana I'd look under the wet hessian bags in his cart at the macabre sight of naked, pink rabbits stacked in boxes of crushed ice. Other boxes held pet food — rabbit paws or heads, their glassy eyes shocked in death.

The rabbit man, the bread man, the ice man, the 'Hellooooo, grocerr' man, the milkman — all transformed into one person behind a counter, far too rushed to share gossip and to link a neighbourhood of women into a pattern of life that is now watched in exaggerated forms on daytime soapies. The cats' diet changed from rabbit heads and fish bits to tinned food. The beer bottles were left for the garbage man. Milk came in cartons, ice in eskies that someone's father would bring to 'keep the tinnies cold' and bread came unrecognisable.

I scrounged for soft drink bottles that returned cash which I exchanged for a little white bag full of lollies.

'Did you buy them here?' the shopkeeper always asked.

'Of course,' would be my polite reply, though we both knew that I'd scrounged the bottles from every possible source. I'd be thinking, 'What does it matter? I'm spending the money here on lollies!' But deep inside was the niggle of dishonest guilt, as when the paper boy or the milk boy would arrive for their payment and I'd hide inside, under the window, so when they looked inside they couldn't see anyone. They all knew we were home!

When my parents were playing the game 'Let's try one more time to live together', I often had to play the 'Let's pretend we're not home' game. It wasn't just played with debt collectors but with men friends, women yelling outside the house, the police and the school authorities. And once we hid while watching a woman smashing up our letterbox with a lump of iron and screaming that she was 'Gunna do it to your bloody head when I get you! Now leave my bloody man alone!'

I looked at my mother in horror but she just lit another cigarette, shrugged her shoulders and left the room.

If one of the debt collectors caught me in the yard I'd say, 'They'll fix it up later.' It was embarrassing because we both knew the truth. The petty debt collector was some pimply youth aged between seven and seventeen and usually known to me. Those young men were like the Hitler youth or the prefects of every school I ever attended. The law protectors! They probably went on to be evangelists; they possessed a vocal power that would stun a bull at twenty paces. But the serious debt collectors just handed me a summons.

There were so many lies, so many hidden truths. Well hidden. Like the amount of alcohol drinking. Like the violence. The sound of flesh upon flesh. The sound of flesh hitting walls. The splattering of blood. The screaming. The wretched crying. Her crying. My silent crying. His crying — the next day. Saving face. Whose face? Her battered face.

'My mother's not well.'

'My mother fell.'

At these times, I was always in for a long stretch of bush biscuits.

Yabbying

Yabbies are big business. Small fresh-water crayfish found in dams. Grey-blue in colour, red when cooked. A thick fleshy tail, small bulging eyes, long waving eyelash and wicked snapping claws.

Yabbies appear on menus under a variety of fancy names. Their meat is prepared in a variety of fancy sauces. For the bold and brave the yabby turns up on the plate complete with shell, cooked of course. Bodies are broken open for the succulent sweet white meat, and claws are vigorously sucked. Some establishments tart up the name 'yabby' with Gothic or mediaeval calligraphy. The humble yabby is now farmed for restaurants — a connoisseur's delight.

I spent hours catching yabbies from dams. Every dam seemed to have an abundance of them.

'I bloody well don't know how they got there,' one old farmer told me. 'Millions of the buggers. I swear some mug musta put 'em in. No one says they did but that was a new dam a couple of seasons ago.'

I've heard all sorts of theories about the yabby. That the yabby falls from the sky in the rain. That they follow a water line underground. That they smell water and can travel across the land to find it. That they arrive with floodwaters. How they arrive in dams seems to be a mystery, at least to the white settlers in this land of the Dreamtime. My father would say, in a tone that indicated a dam wasn't real unless it had yabbies, 'It's a rare dam without yabbies. Very rare indeed.'

Mostly it was us kids who did the yabbying. It was fun and it was a meal. When the adults came it was still fun, but more noise, more fuss, more yelling at 'all those bloody kids and dogs'. When we went with the adults it was a different experience and dogs would bark themselves into excitement, chase anything and constantly fall into the dam. Someone's father would be shouting, 'Tie those bloody dogs up!' or 'Shut up that bloody barking and for Christsake get out of the bloody water — you're scaring the bloody yabbies!'

When I went with other kids it would be just two or three of us, sitting quietly beside our lines or together under the shade of a gum, talking. But that depended on the kids one yabbied with. Most couldn't keep quiet or sit still. Townies lasted about five minutes before they were bored. I'd head off before some parent would collar me and whine, 'Here, take so-and-so yabbying with you. They're stayin' with us for a holiday.' Sometimes so-and-so would be okay and full of information. I'd been taking Jim and Molly yabbying every Saturday for weeks before they told me why they were coming out to the farm every weekend with their father.

'Oh, he bribes us. We get extra pocket money to tell Mum that we all go yabbying. That's why we ask you for extra yabbies. He plays cards down in the shearing shed, and Mum won't let him play cards.'

I started to take an interest in the visiting kids for a while. John's father came because he was besotted with young Mrs Price, and Mr Price was away shearing. John and I watched them through the window once and I was amazed at the length of John's father's balls. Amanda's dad came to drink with my father while Paul's dad came to visit my mother — when my father was out.

But mostly the townies were on school holidays and I was supposed to amuse them. I preferred to go yabbying just with the dogs. They knew when I was going and they'd follow with great enthusiasm. Once at the dam they would have a swim and then leave the dam to me. They would sit patiently panting under a gum tree. We had an understanding. They would have another swim before we left.

Yabbying was an art, not a production line. It was the ideal occupation. It gave us food, cleaned out the dam, gave us something to do, and was a wonderful way to have a picnic. I also enjoyed yabbying with my father when we were on the road. Sometimes, camped outside a town, he would leave me 'to get dinner while I wander down and pick a couple of bottles. Get yabbies — I'm sick of rabbit.' Yabbies would be caught and cooked. The billy would be over the fire and the day dropping her skirts when I'd hear him whistling his way back.

Sometimes we caught yabbies and sold them to the townies. Usually he'd swap the yabbies at the local pub for a couple of bottles or a flagon. If he returned with just the alcohol in exchange I'd yell at him.

'I caught most of the bloody yabbies and you're drinking the bloody profits,' angry that all the money had been spent on alcohol and that there wasn't enough for a Cherry Ripe or even a bottle of lemonade. I'd refuse to catch yabbies for days and only shoot a rabbit for the dog. My father would then take rabbit and fox skins and sell them. He'd remember the lemonade and also bring me back a comic to say sorry. Comics were precious to me; they could be exchanged over and over again. My father and I both liked *Phantom*.

There were a couple of ways to catch yabbies. One way was to have a loop of strong wire attached to a broomstick, then cover the circle with fine wire to make a net. Then you needed string or baling twine with a piece of meat attached to the end or long strings of meat to be thrown in at spots along the side of the dam. When a yabby was busy eating, the line would be gently and carefully pulled in, the net placed ready in the water. Scoop — the yabby would be swept into the air and dropped into a waiting bucket of water.

The other method was to place the meat in the middle of the wire net, then pull up net and yabby. I sometimes used the dogs' meat; that way it served two purposes — the dogs just had water-logged meat that night.

I liked to yabby; it gave me time with myself. And the dogs. I'd jam my father's old slouch hat on my head, call the dogs, grab my yabby gear and take off. Especially if my mother was living with us. It gave us both space and she considered that I was 'doing something other than riding those bloody horses'.

My mother considered horses to be something she placed bets on. She called them 'neddies' and 'gee-gees'. She was as interested in the trainers and jockeys as she was in the horses.

My father and I loved horses because they were horses. 'Humans don't "break in" a horse,' he'd say. '"Break in", what bloody arrogance! Oh yes, we can break their spirit and soul all right. Beat them into subservience or train them like we train people to be car salesmen or bloody war heroes. They *let* us do that to them. Do you hear me? They let us! If a horse decides not to let us, then we turn them into dog meat and tell everyone what a mean bastard that horse was. You treat them as a friend — a friend that needs education to live in this bloody world of our making. Don't ever let me hear you say you're "breaking in" a horse. The horse was here long before we bloody well were. Have respect for them.' He'd go on and on about the respect for animals. 'It's bloody humans you can't trust,' he'd yell as he'd bang around the house threatening to kill my mother when he found her.

Away I'd fly, calling the dogs — Tip, the black-and-white border collie; Tiger, the brindle greyhound and Tex, a small hairy dog that my father called a 'bitsa' (he was bits of this and that). The dogs would bark and cavort around as we headed towards a dam. For them there were rabbits to chase and smells to trail. I'd walk across the sun-stubble of wheat to a far-off dam, well away from any living area. Old storytelling gums would circle the dam and singing bees would shimmer the stillness of air. Always a swim first, naked. I revel in the freedom of swimming in my skin, always hating bathers. Those hateful flannel suits and later the two-piece that became a bikini. I preferred shorts if I had to wear clothes, or not to swim at all. The dam water was hot, warm and cold, depending on what part of the dam I swam in. Sometimes the water would be warm on top while my legs would be going blue with cold beneath. The dogs and I would play, my imagination supplying stories of other places, other magics, other landscapes. The sun would dry my skin pink as I sat under my father's war hat. Once dry and warm, I'd move to the shade of a tree because my skin burned easily. I wanted to be brown; I remained red. Under the tree I'd eat the middle out of my sandwiches, sharing the crusts with the dogs.

In the heat I'd doze and dream, watch the spirits of fire and the slow-moving fat lizards. Occasionally a snake would bake in the sun or a lizard cook across a rock.

As the shadows began to stretch their long fingers across the dam I'd wake and begin to yabby. When darkness fell it would be time to drag a heavy bucket of yabbies home. A large pan of water would be set to boil. Bread would be buttered, salt and vinegar placed on the table. The yabbies, drained of water and mud, would be dropped to their death in the boiling water. I hated to hear their claws scrabbling on the sides of the pot as they died and I'd cover my ears. 'They die instantly,' my father tried to reassure me, but I felt bad. Not bad enough to refuse them though. Hot, sweet, fleshy tails and succulent claws. We threw the shells onto the newspaper-covered table. We belched and sighed after such a feast. I didn't have to say 'Excuse me' even if I farted.

When the adults decided to come yabbying, the day would take on an entirely different flavour. A party was happening! We would all gather at a particular point and the men would discuss the weather, the football and which dam to go to. If someone had a new car then more time would be wasted while the men fondled the engine and gear stick. Patiently the women would wait — talking, catching up, wondering where my mother was, and counting the men to make sure their husbands were in the crowd. Sometimes my mother came — usually when we were new in the community, when she was still getting to know the men — and the women envied her for her looks and vitality. Before they had come to resent her and keep their hands on their husband's or son's arm, or private bits!

It was easier on me and my father when she'd leave with her latest man. My father and I would get sympathy unless it was one of the community, and then we'd also leave to hit the road or find another place to live. Inevitably she'd find us. For her, yabbying was a chance to watch the men. All the kids watched the adults. And had fun. We'd scream around the cars, impatient to be on our way. Finally someone's father would order us to 'Get on board'. Our old ute would be stacked with rugs, picnic baskets, dogs and kids — by the women. Amid the nets, buckets and meat some kid sat on guard, fighting off the dogs. The men would load the beer, flagons of wine and themselves. The men drove out; the women drove back while the men sat in the back of the utes and roared old war songs into the night. Mothers slapped sunscreen onto our faces. We needed a trowel to get it off! Other mothers jammed hats on heads, oblivious of the protests that the kid had ears.

At one stage, when my mother was living with us, we had a buckboard — an old, high-cabin flat-tray truck with wooden-spoke wheels and a steering wheel that was so enormous it took up most of the window space. I couldn't turn that wheel and my father would curse when pulling with both hands to get the 'old girl' around a corner. When sitting on a cushion in the driver's seat I had to peer between the spokes to see through the wind-screen. Even sitting on my father's lap I couldn't see over the wheel. I hated driving that buckboard, though I often had to drive or steer it home when my father was too drunk to do so. He made up two big blocks of wood that I could tie to the brake and clutch so my feet could reach the pedals. It was like a team of draught horses. My father called that big old buckboard many names, the kindest being 'that old girl'. Cars were always women to my father. 'Blasted temperamental old bitch,' he'd yell at them when they broke down. They always broke down.

'Give me a horse any day,' he'd yell at the hot boiling heap of metal. But I remembered that he had sold the horse and cart because, 'it's just too slow, mate, and this is a bloody big country to find work in. We have to get places quicker.' We often had to find my mother quicker!

She never travelled in the horse and cart but at least she would sometimes go places in the car. She would never camp out and when my father suggested we did she'd ask to be left at the local pub and be gone in the morning.

'Why isn't there any money for us to stay at the pub too?' I once shouted at him. The rain was pouring outside the tent and I was cold and hungry.

'She never has to pay! Now bloody well SHUT UP!'

He called that buckboard all the names I'd heard him call my mother, and then some. Especially when he'd be cranking it into life and it would backfire, sending the heavy crank handle smacking into his knuckles or across his shins. He'd roar obscenities into the wind, and the dogs' ears would go up and down like air signal batons. I hated sitting in the middle of that buckboard's seat because my legs would be belted with the gear stick. I'd sit like a bird perched up on the seat, peering through the window. There were no shock absorbers on the 'old girl' and being in the cabin was equivalent to being in a concrete mixer. Standing or sitting on the tray was far preferable since my body could sway with the bounce and motion. I sat with my back against the cabin or on the side of the tray, legs dangling towards the dirt. Two large rocks sat like warty frogs at the end of the tray. These were to help with braking. When we stopped I'd fly out and jam the rocks under the back wheels.

When a gate loomed into view my father would pump the brakes, crunch the gears and slow down to a crawl. 'Go, go, go!' he'd shout. I'd leap from the back, race up the track, grab the gate, swing it open, wave the car through, shut the gate and run to catch up. We seemed to do this with all the cars we had. Perhaps because they were all really old, all had radiators that boiled and faulty brakes!

Sometimes the gate would be one of the old wire and strainer post jobs. I'd struggle to release the wire, my small hands getting raked in the process. Swearing, I'd pull the gate aside. I always had trouble closing that sort of gate and I'd have to run hard and long to catch up to the vehicle, swallowing dust and cursing all the way. If my father had to stop to help with the gate, then the 'old girl' would shudder and grind to a halt. I'd whack the rocks under the tyres and hope she wouldn't boil. If she boiled then my father would yell, 'Close the bloody gate, can't you!' and turn off the engine. The car, ute or truck would be left to cool down. The dogs and I would sit under one tree, my father under another. He'd roll a smoke and sit. After the smoke he'd fill a metal cup with water from the water bag that we always carried on the front of the car, and bring it over to me. I'd share it with the dogs.

'Let me drive it through the gates,' I'd beg.

'No. You're the gate opener. That's what you're good for, opening bloody gates.'

'I'm sick of bloody gates.'

I whooped with joy when gateways had metal grids across the ground instead of gates.

One time when my mother was living with us, we were driving home from the local town in the buckboard and my father was driving. 'Open the gate, open the bloody gate!' he yelled. I had been dozing in the front seat leaning on my mother.

'She's asleep,' retorted my mother. 'Don't be so bloody lazy. Stop the car and open the bloody gate yourself.' My father stopped the vehicle and raced to swing the gate open. 'Bastard,' my mother muttered. 'Bloody dictatorial bastard.' She slid across the seat under the steering wheel. 'Let's teach him a lesson. This can't be hard to drive.'

I was suddenly awake and on full alert. Before I could shout for my father or bail out we were off. Through the gate, past my open-mouthed father and down the hill we went. The road curved at the bottom of the hill. We went through two fences before we stopped, my mother shrieking into the night like a banshee woman let loose. We climbed from the cabin and laughed and shrieked. My father panted up red-faced and furious. My mother belted him to the ground and there he lay.

'Got him,' she yelled. 'Got him before he got me.'

We walked home through the dark bush, laughing and giggling like free spirits. In the morning she was gone before he could belt her back. I'd gone yabbying for a couple of days to let him cool down and to have a place where I could laugh in peace at what she had done.

Yabbying with a community was fun. Once we had arrived at the chosen dam, dogs would be grabbed and tied to the utes and cars until after our big 'catch'. Hot and panting, they would all want a swim but since their disturbance would chase away the yabbies they just had to be patient and wait. They'd bark and whine and scratch until the catch was finally over and, like springs let loose, they would throw themselves into the water in a barking frenzy of delight. To punish us they would emerge dripping, come into the circle of humans and shake! The women would scream and the men and children curse.

'Git outa here, you bloody mongrel dogs!'

'Piss off, ya mangy bastards.'

'Ahhh shit, I'm all wet.'

'Clear off, ya bastards.'

'Stop swearing. You're teaching the kids bad manners!'

We learnt to curse along with 'mum', 'dad', 'thank you' and 'please'.

The dam rang with instructions.

'Put your hat back on.'

'Someone pull that baby away from the edge.'

'Shut up, you bloody dogs.'

'Put the blanket over there in the shade and watch out for them bull ants.'

'Careful putting those bottles in the water. Make sure they don't float away.'

'What do you think you are bloody well doing!'

'Honestly, kid, if you don't stop whingeing I'm gunna slap you.'

'Someone take this kid, will y'.'

The noise was like an army in full battle. The yabbies knew we had arrived!

Small yabbies were thrown back. 'Let them grow a bit. You want more than a mouthful. We'll get them next time,' my father would say.

Yabbying with a big mob turned into entertainment that a

circus would envy! It always began peacefully enough. We kids would quietly yabby away, doze, talk or go for a walk. The women would sit in the shade of trees and talk and drink tea from their thermoses. Or some mother would boil a billy, gentle laughter coming from their circle, their frocks hitched up to show shocking white thighs. Across the dam under other trees the blue-singleted men would sit and drink. We could smell the tobacco that tinged the air grey-blue around them. Their voices were deep, always carrying that man tone of authority.

After a lunch of roast-lamb-and-sauce sandwiches, or curried egg, or fritz and sauce, all washed down by tea, beer or cordial, the day would shimmer into lethargy. Snores would ripple the heat and compete against the drone of the blowfly. I'd doze and tune in to the day. The sound heat makes when it shimmers between the baked earth and old gum trees. The smell of eucalyptus from those cooking trees. The red moving earth, blistering and stretching. The snoring men and wuffling women, sighing dogs and sleepy conversations. I'd watch the earth spirits come and explore the sleepers, who would move and scratch, feeling the exploration as a soft touch of heat upon their cheek or hand. Heat spirits like tongues of controlled fire that reached out in skin exploration. 'It's bloody hot,' would yell some man as spirit fingers explored his red face. He'd sit up and swat at the presence, fall back into snoring, mouth open, small flies searching around the edges, seeking moisture. Another would howl, 'An ant just bit me. Bugger!' Men would roll and turn, blaming the day, not the spirits of heat that eagerly explored them. I'd watch and grin.

My father could see the spirits of places too. Slowly he'd sit up, brush them off, make faces at them and grin at me. He'd sometimes come and sit with me, roll his smoke and just sit. We'd watch quietly together. Slowly the men would come awake, farting and groaning. The spirits would retreat to the trees.

The women would wet tea-towels and washers. They'd wipe the young kids' faces, change nappies, wipe their own faces, arms and legs. They'd tuck a wet hanky down between their breasts. My father would stoke up a fire, boil water and make tea. The smell of burning gum would mingle with the smell of wood. I'd laugh at the spirits that would place their long, thin fingers up their noses. My nose felt like that, hot from the inside. I'd turn my laughter into a cough, my grin into a sneeze. I learnt that cover-up trick really early when I realised that most people simply didn't believe what I told them I could see. My nana didn't disbelieve; she'd just shake her head at me.

Everyone would sit drinking sweet tea and waking up. My father would take the nets from some ute and lay them all out on the back of the buckboard — all untangled and ready to have the bait tied in. Sandwiches and cake would be devoured. Men would walk off for a piss, kids would hunker down behind a car wheel and the women would 'hang on'. If some woman desperately had to 'go' then comments would snigger among the men.

'Bloody carthorse having a piss,' they would comment and laugh at their wit.

'It's a bit early yet,' my father would comment, swatting flies and eyeing the cold bottles on the edge of the water. He'd sit himself in the water and open a bottle of beer. The other men would join him, hidden under their ex-army hats, swigging like babies on their bottles. The women would come from the shade to paddle, their frocks held above their knees. I never saw them swim. Then one or two little kids would fall in. Some father would lumber to his feet, swearing and cursing. Water would run from his body, turning him into a big, grey, dripping elephant or a skinny, ribbed, bow-legged bird of some sort, slightly tipsy and unbalanced.

The spirit people would wake up. The fun was about to begin. A drowning kid would be hauled from the water crying and screaming. 'Chuck the little bastard back in,' some father would holler.

'At least that would teach it to swim,' my father would comment. I'd glare at him. Some mother would come to the little kid's rescue, all arms and smelling of hot powder and breast sweat. The fathers would roar laughing and pass the bottle. One would get up to piss, slip in the mud and down he'd go, skidding under the water. The men would shout, the kids would laugh and the women grin. Dogs would bark and the father who slipped would stand uttering curses and staining the water yellow in a circle around his private parts.

'Ahhh, ya dirty bastard.'

'You jack arse.'

'Get your feet outa the water.'

Hilarity would follow. The yabby catch forgotten, the men would play. They'd splash and swim and duck each other, yelling for the kids to join them. Some kids would, never to repeat the experience! They'd be ducked and squashed and chucked from man to man like a ball! The kid's fun would last about two seconds or until some mother would flap over, shouting and telling the men to be careful.

'Let them grow up tough,' some male would yell, splashing the concerned mother. The dogs would bark and whine in hot frustration and it would be the cue I was waiting for. I'd release their ropes and end their torment. Dogs and kids would head for the other end of the dam away from the clutches of the men.

Finally we'd all crawl from the dam. The men would go back to serious drinking from their tree shade and the women would towel us dry and fill the insides of us with cordial. The dogs would flop in the shade, aware that the dam was off-limits now as the shadows lengthened towards the serious business of catching yabbies. The dogs also had their antennae up, watching the men. Like the women and kids, they knew when a happy drunk could flick the switch and turn nasty. Always a fine balance between peace and violence.

Twilight would colour the edge of the sky and reflect from the dam. The women draped cardigans across their shoulders. My father would add the meat to the nets and slowly throw them into the water. Each kid or pair would be given a line. We would sit wriggling with excitement, impatient to begin hauling the nets in.

'Wait. Wait,' my father would call. 'Give the buggers time to bite.'

Patience. Yabbying takes patience.

I'd look across the brown water at the women, their floral

dresses hiding their tired faces and bodies in a blaze of colour like a flower garden at dusk. A roar of delight would bounce from the water as the first kids drew in their nets and pulled in a mass of snapping blue bodies. Net after net would be pulled and thrown. Kids would count the yabbies in their buckets and scream their tally. It would become all too much for one or two of the fathers who would decide that they were missing out on all the fun. One last guzzle of beer, and male expertise would lumber into a half-upright posture and attempt to walk a straight line towards the nearest yabby net. Kids' warning bells would send messages bouncing between them as they made way for the fathers. 'Oh-oh, here we go.'

The men were here to help. Kids scattered, women sat up to watch. Fathers would roar and curse as yabbies bit them or they staggered into the dam. Finally, some father would fall into the dam! Women would scream. Dogs sat up, barking. Kids yelled. No one laughed. No one ever laughed at the men — at least not until one of the men laughed first. I'd wet myself in unvoiced laughter, not daring to look at another kid. Like volcanoes we were ready to erupt. 'Arse up,' my father would roar into laughter, and we'd all explode. The men would bang each other on the back and drag the wet hero from the water. Someone would find the bottles they had stashed 'for later', and the dam would become the domain of the kids once again.

Water would chill to grey as a galah sunset filled the sky. Jumpers would be pulled over kids' protesting heads while other mothers gathered wood for a fire. Bags of bread would be buttered, vinegar and salt put out on a cloth and the billy placed ready to sing the song of the tea. A clean square tin, complete with wire handle, would be filled with water and placed on the fire. The last of the yabby lines would be drawn in.

The dogs knew it was over. Silently they would appear, sitting by the nets. I'd cut up the meat that had been used as bait and share it among them, trying to give equal portions and not start a dog fight. The trick was to feed all the dogs without causing so much as a growl. Dogs are like all of us. Some sniff their food first, some just swallow it as quickly as possible, while others chew slowly. One sniffs around the meat, trying to bury it, while another may guard their bit and growl at any movement in their general direction. There is always one who gulps the meat down and then tries to pinch the meat from another dog. One or two dogs also see an opportunity for a good fight. A dog fight or serious growling stand-off, with hackles raised and stiffened legs and tails brought the men like warriors to do battle. I'd make all the dogs sit and I'd try to keep it all smooth while sharing out the bits. 'Sit, sit. Stay, stay,' I'd hiss.

By the time I'd fed the dogs and placed all the nets in the back of some ute the women would have drained the yabbies and dumped them into the tin of boiling water where they'd be turning pink in death. If any child spilt their bucket of yabbies on the way to the fire pandemonium would break out. The men would jump to their feet, yelling and cursing as they grabbed yabbies and threw them back into the bucket. The dogs would break into a bout of barking in the hope of a possible fight. Some father would take a swipe at the kid who'd tripped, and the mothers would arrive for battle. One would take the screaming kid, others push the fathers up the bank towards the camp while those of us left would gather up the remaining escaping yabbies. The fathers would be yelling about 'useless' kids and tension would snap the air tight. The spirits of the bush would hide.

My father would give a bottle a quick shake and open it. Beer would explode and he'd aim it at glasses, never missing a drop. 'I learnt that trick in Egypt,' he told me. 'It always breaks the tension.' A kid would clap or a man laugh. The rubber band would relax.

When the blue-black crow cawed his song across the sky the feast would be ready. We would all sit in a circle, cracking, sucking and sighing. The warm blanket of night would enfold us, but two steps away from the fire and the dam was a cold presence. Cockatoos would split the air with their screeching, kangaroos would patiently wait for the circus at the dam to go home so they could drink.

Full-bellied, with the billy brewing the tea, we'd lean back on elbows and listen to the men tell war stories. The women and the kids drank tea. The men cracked open a flagon of red wine. The bush spirits sat just beyond the firelight, listening.

Slowly the conversation would begin — a quiet buzz. Usually one of the women covered any sleeping children. I'd lie back and watch the stars. Sometimes I'd wonder where my mother was. She only ever came yabbying with us once. That was a family picnic too, and she sat drinking with the men. From then on we only went on family picnics when she wasn't with us.

The only stars my mother liked were those in the horoscopes she read out from magazines. I remember how amazed I was when I first learnt that the stars don't 'come out at night', but are always there! I'd ask my father about the stars and he'd point out the Little Dipper, the Milky Way, the Dragon's Tail and the Southern Cross.

'What do the Aboriginal people see at night?' I once asked an adult who thought he was clever.

'The stars!' He roared with laughter. He told that as a joke for years!

I still ask people about what they see. The stars have so many stories! As a child I knew the gentle, dark-eyed people of this land had stories about the stars. I was curious to hear those stories. An old uncle, sitting around our camp fire, once told me, 'You see that up there. Those stars. White eyes, white thought. That they call the Southern Cross. Now, that's an old fella with his arms around his people. That over there, that's the Seven Sisters. The Pleiades. They watch over us, and one day we have to answer to them on our way.'

I watched the stars. 'What happens after you die?' I asked.

'The spirit does not die.'

'Will I have to answer to the Seven Sisters?'

'Probably, probably,' replied the old man.

'When I was in Egypt,' my father said, 'I heard that the Egyptians believed that before you could enter paradise, you had to name the Seven Sisters. I think they judged each soul.'

The old man laughed. 'We end up facing seven women for our deeds here on earth, eh? Oh, won't those holy fathers be upset!' And he laughed until the tears streamed down his face.

My father looked at me. 'Well, we'll all be buggered then.' I often thought back on that night as I watched the stars and made my own stories.

The men's talk would become slurred and the songs begin. When the war songs began the women would start to load all the picnic gear and gather the sleeping kids, wrapping them cocoon-like in blankets side by side in the back of the utes. Then the fathers would begin on some lusty verse or another and one would suddenly roar, 'Keep it down, keep it down, mate. Women and kids, women and kids.'

The women and the kids had heard all the songs. All the verses.

It was time to help the men onto the back of the buckboard. They travelled there by themselves. No kids, no dogs, no blankets. We would all be warm in the back of the other cars. Those of us who were still awake would tell ghost stories all the way home.

Mrs Young would drive the buckboard. She would deliver the fathers to their homes, then collect the dogs and me and leave us in our yard. She'd walk across the paddock to her home, whistling to keep the spirits from scaring her. I'd tuck a couple of blankets around my father and leave him snoring on the back of the buckboard. I'd be up and gone the next day before he surfaced. I didn't like his hangovers. I'd head off to another dam for a quiet time yabbying, and we'd eat my catch for tea that night. The dogs and I. My father would take a couple of days to recover from his sour stomach. If he decided 'a hair of the dog' would help, then he might go on and binge for a few days until he passed out or the alcohol ran out and there was no money or means to get more.

One summer my father and I were living at a place called Olary in the hot mid-north of South Australia. We had followed my mother there and it was the height of summer — shimmering air, baked earth and the endless drone of blowflies.

The stone hotel where we lived was shaded by one exhausted

pepper tree. The inside of the hotel was dark and hot. The darkness gave the illusion of coolness. The only excitement was the rumbling of the giant ore trucks as they passed the hotel, shaking mortar from between the stones as they thundered into the desert.

Occasionally one would stop and a heavy-booted, heavy-voiced truck driver would enter the bar to guzzle down beer, washing the red dust into his huge belly. I'd stare up at the monster vehicle sitting and sinking into the bubbling tar of the car park. I couldn't reach up to the step to satisfy my curiosity by climbing inside. In the evenings men in shorts and blue singlets would fill the bar.

My father would hose down the verandah, the front wall and the men's toilet. The smell of piss and diesel dominated the air; even the fried onions smelt of stale pub and men's sweat. I'd sit for a time on the verandah listening to men's talk that floated on the heat of the night. Always the same. The nights never breathed. The dark held her hot breath until morning. The cockies stopped screeching. It was time to go and get the manager's wife.

Every night at dusk my father and I would walk to the dam to bring home the manager's wife. The dam provided the town's water supply. A dismal place of no trees, no yabbies and no shade. Just the red cracked earth. The manager's wife would sit on the rim of the dam, drinking red wine from a flagon. We helped her home and my father would take her shoes off, lay her on the bed and cover her with a blanket. I'd put the empty flagon on the pile of bottles out the back of the pub.

'Let's go,' called my father one boiling hot evening. He banged the screen door behind him. I galloped ahead like a dog suddenly set free from a chain. Over the lip of the dam, unable to stop, I skidded to a halt next to the manager's wife.

The dam was red. Red earth, red water. Blood-red soaked the ground. I stood looking down at the silent woman. I could hear my father's voice shouting, his boots skidding.

'Don't look,' he yelled. It was too late. My mind registered the slit wrists, the fly-encrusted razor blade, the near-empty flagon, the cloud of flies buzzing angrily at being disturbed. I picked up the flagon and poured the last of the wine over the woman's hands.

'What the hell do you think you're doing?' yelled my father, coming back into himself.

'Saying goodbye,' I replied and threw the flagon into the dam. We both watched it sink.

'People drink that water,' he said.

'Then they can drink to her death,' I said and walked away.

The dogs, my father and I left Olary that week.

I rarely yabby now — only when children visit and want to 'have fun'. But I still sit by a dam, watching the dogs, talking to the water spirits and remembering the manager's wife whose face I have forgotten, but not the ending of her story.

Tea-leaves

I was instilled with the notion that tea was 'the very essence of life'. The nectar of the gods. Even more important than alcohol and definitely preferable to coffee, cordial or water. Tea. Black and aromatic. Never tea bags. Tea made with leaves. The pot warmed with boiling water, a teaspoon of tea for each drinker and a teaspoon for the pot, then fill to the required level with boiling water. Turn the pot three times one way then three times the other way. Let it brew for a couple of minutes. After that it was a matter of taste or custom. Black or white; medium or strong.

As soon as a child could walk it was given a cup of tea. White, two sugars. I have been involved in, and listened to, many arguments about tea and milk. Should the milk be placed in the cup before or after the tea? As one old witch told me, 'If you put the milk in first the tea mixes instantly. If you put the milk in after the tea you have to stir it. So give 'em a spoon but watch where they puts it. If two spoons are put in a saucer there'll be news of twins. And if the spoon is put upside down then someone close is gunna get ill. Also, you watch out if two people pour from the same pot, 'cause one's gunna have a baby by the end of the year.'

People I knew used to share their cuppa with a dog or cat; they always gave their companion its share in the saucer. Long before mugs became fashionable people drank tea from a cup and saucer. Most drank their tea from a cup but one old aunt always poured the tea into the saucer and sipped it slowly and delicately, while my father's friend Tom drank from the saucer in big slurpy gulps. He strained the tea through his bushy, nicotine-stained moustache, leaving tea-leaves to hang on the hair and be an endless source of fascination for me. I would wait until he rolled a smoke, hung it from his lip and started to talk. The black tea-leaves would dry and drop to his chin. Sometimes I'd giggle and giggle, mesmerised by the slowly drying tea-leaves.

'Bloody funny kid you've got there,' he'd remark to my father.

'She's easily amused,' my father would reply while giving me one of those 'Behave!' looks.

My nana was once horrified when she caught me sharing a cup of tea with my dog.

'You'll catch disease,' she screamed. 'Worms, worms. You'll catch worms. It's bad enough that you kiss that dog — how many times have I told you not to! You'll die of a dog disease. You don't know where that dog has had its mouth.'

'But I do,' I would reply.

'Well, do you now,' my nana sarcastically retorted. 'I'll tell you where its mouth has been — licking its bum, that's where!'

'My mother says the same.'

'Then stop it and stop sharing your tea and your plate of food with the dog or I'll send you back where you came from.'

She would too. But not to my father. She always threatened to send me back, under protest, to my mother. In fact we both protested. My mother and I cramped each other's style! Besides, how can a woman look and be so young and ultra-glamorous with a snotty-nosed, big-mouthed, never-miss-anything child tagging along!

So I became careful not to let any adult catch me sharing with my dog.

My nana's cat loved her morning cup of tea but she had it from her own bowl. A cousin who often stayed with my nana would take the bowl outside for puss, then drink the contents herself. There was a big hoo-ha when my nana caught her. She gave her the old disease story — as if that would really impress a four-year-old! I told my cousin she was drinking the tea that was meant for the cat and now the cat had none. She stopped drinking the cat's tea.

We played tea parties together. Dressing up her dolls, my teddy and the dog, we would sit under the lemon tree and play ladies. My cousin had a real dolls' teaset. China. Small teapot, tiny cups and milk jug. We would play for hours and it was an improvement on the tin cans that I used in my own tea games.

My nana taught me always to give any cold leftover tea to special garden plants. Her favourite tea plant was a huge, waving, broad-leaf fern that was attached to a board and then wired to the fence. I once told my nana that the plant had a belly like old Mrs Brook, and my nana slapped my ear and said I was very rude. 'Mrs Brook has fifteen children,' said my father when I told him. 'My God, girl, she *deserves* to have a belly like that!' He went off laughing and I heard him telling the other drovers that 'Old Madge has a fat belly like mum's old tree staghorn.'

My nana loved her staghorn. She didn't like Mrs Brook too much. She said, 'She doesn't take care of herself.'

I hadn't a clue what she was referring to. Later I realised it had to do with contraception and not with Mrs Brook's looks which were fairly ragged at best. Mrs Brook had no teeth, great big bosom, belly, thighs, and wore no shoes. Shoes hurt her bunions but when her eldest daughter married and insisted that her mother wore shoes to the wedding Mrs Brook did. She cut holes in the shoes so her bunions stuck through and her feet were comfortable.

She could never remember who was who in her big family and always mixed up the kids' names.

'Teddy, Rose, Nola and … no, Teddy, Rose … well, what's your bloody name then? Are you one of mine?' she would ask me.

Mr Brook worked on the railways. He had false teeth and when he wasn't at work the teeth sat in a jar on the kitchen mantel. I'd sit at the table watching that pink grin and be fascinated by those choppers for hours.

'They're bloody uncomfortable,' he'd moan before he put them in, and when he removed them he'd let out a long sigh and say, 'Ahhhh, that's better.'

Mrs Brook sprinkled damp tea-leaves around the house before she swept. 'It keeps the dust down,' she would roar as she wielded her big broom or sucked up all the debris with her vacuum. Mrs Brook called all vacuums 'Hoovers'. 'I'll just hoover this rug,' she'd say.

When I was little she would chase us all with the vacuum and we'd run screaming into the backyard and make ourselves hysterical by running around like a vacuum, sucking up all the kids.

My Aunty Hilda once chased me with my nana's vacuum down the long passageway and into the kitchen. The game went too far and I climbed onto the kitchen table, knocking sauce bottle, jam and butter to the floor. My nana had to comfort me because I thought that my aunt really did mean to suck me up! I can still remember the fear and the maniacal laugh of my aunt in control of that big sucking machine.

That same aunt must have been very disappointed on her wedding night, for in the early morning hours she removed her engagement and wedding rings and placed them around her new husband's flaccid penis. She awoke to find him hysterical and in deep pain. The rings were sunk into his erection and he had to be hospitalised!

My Aunty Hilda hid her blackened eyes behind dark glasses. Her husband took away her spirit and when she rediscovered it he beat her. Finally she left, taking all she could hold on her bike. Her death a few weeks later from a brain haemorrhage collapsed a bridge inside my nana and she began to slowly fall apart. She put herself back together in a world that only she inhabited, or perhaps she danced with her daughter and the ghosts of friends.

My Aunty Hilda loved tea. She drank huge pots of it laced with sugar and milk. My other aunty would sneak six sugars into her tea when she thought no one was watching. If anyone was watching she took only three teaspoons of sugar. She had a metal teapot covered with a knitted tea-cosy. It still burnt my fingers.

Some tea-cosies became collectors' items. The plainest

tea-cosies were knitted or crocheted. Some extended to several colours while others were creative designer pieces. There were teapot covers with fluffy pom-poms on top, or baubles sewn to the sides. There were doll tea-cosies, the cosy a skirt while above smiled a knitted black-mammy face or a Barbie look-alike. There were smiling cats and long-eared dogs and my nana's friend Mabel had a fairy doll tea-cosy that had her constantly slapping the small hands that tried to touch it.

Women won prizes for their tea-cosies at local fêtes or shows.

'Oh yes, yes. I won the tea-cosy prize at the 1957 Wanga-Wanga show,' they would proudly exclaim and out would come that prize piece, kept all those years in moth balls, never to grace a teapot.

I grew up in the era when little girls sat in 'domestic science' classes making tea-cosies and aprons! These were for our 'glory boxes'. A 'glory box' was a part of a woman's dowry. The bride came with linen galore — sheets, pillowcases, tablecloths and 'His' and 'Hers' towels. Mothers, aunts and friends all contributed while the men looked on with amusement as their daughters were encouraged to 'nest' and to come to a marriage 'well provided'. The men didn't have glory boxes, they had tool sets.

We cross-stitched and hemmed and made 'tray-covers,' for no tray was ever to be presented naked. And doilies! These were the teacher's speciality. Cover every surface with an embroidered doily.

'Keep the home beautiful, girls,' Miss Knight would say, every five minutes. 'It's a woman's job to make a happy home and keep idle hands busy!' Most of us sat and stared at this woman who spouted doctrines that did not fit within the reality of our lives. Miss Knight drank her tea with one little finger politely pointed out!

Wood stoves were ideal for keeping the teapot warm. 'Make a fresh pot of tea for God's sake, Mary,' my father would say to my nana. 'Don't reheat it over gas or electric — it tastes like weak piss!'

My nana swore that tea could cure most ailments. Drink it down or rub it in, preferably both! Add to that her philosophy that 'a cup of tea, a Bex and a good lie down' would cure almost anything, and you see in microcosm a nation of women addicted to those little white powders. The poor woman's laudanum. A generation of women became addicted and then exchanged those powders for a small pill called Valium.

My mother used to have her leaves read. So did my nana and her friends, and so did many other women and a few men. My nana also read the leaves and people would come, their cup wrapped in a clean teatowel, or they would have a cup of tea with her. I never saw her charge money for her readings.

My mother too could read the leaves, but often she would search out other readers to validate her prophecies. She also believed in divination by cards. When she had her cards read she would take me but leave me outside the door, safe and snug in my pram and later pusher. The last time I went with her I was walking and exploring the world. She tied me to a verandah post and went inside for her reading. I sat happily and watched the dance of the street. My mother kept popping in and out of the doorway, 'like a ferret looking for a mate,' as my father would say. As she untied me she hissed, 'You ruined that reading. I couldn't concentrate at all. I thought someone would steal you!'

Years later, when I told my mother I had had my cards read, she was horrified and urged me not to mess with those 'gypsy women'. She said it was all nonsense. I reminded her that she used to have her cards read and that she'd leave me in my pusher outside the door. 'That was the problem then,' she replied. 'I must have parked you too close to the door and now you're hooked!'

I wanted to know what the gypsy women were like but she refused to talk any more about 'those old times'.

Those gypsy women were probably women like my nana — women still in touch with the 'knowing' part of themselves and having a perception of others. Able to read energy, to divine messages, to see auras; clairvoyant — looking into the lives of the women who came for reassurance.

My nana was the gypsy woman of her neighbourhood but she would have been horrified to be called that. She read the tea-leaves, palms and eyes, but dressed in conventional clothes, making sure that she attended to her Catholic faith. Those faithful women knew the stories of their ancestors. They were reminded of those stories by their church. They knew about the burning times; they understood persecution. They were wary and conventional, almost socialised. They had 'the fear of God' and the Catechism pummelled into them. But the old knowledge remained within them and, like embers of a blackened fire when blown upon, it could glow red hot, ready to burst into flame.

They knew 'women's business'. They knew that the men who were their lovers, brothers, husbands, father, sons and strangers could turn against them for their beliefs. So they made light of it, called it women's nonsense, old wives' tales. They hid it under layers of what was required of them. They survived. It was a powerful, defiant woman who could dress with difference, who would wear colour proudly and accept the stigma of being called a gypsy woman.

My nana dressed like all nanas; my mother was a fashion plate with two painted eyebrows like arches across her forehead. My Aunt Julie curled her hair tight, and our friend Olga wore spotted head scarves and bright red lipstick. They were wild women, you could hear it in their voices, see it in their walk, hidden under the layers of propriety, ready to be peeled back, recognised by those who sought such women.

Women came to my nana and my mother to have their tea-leaves read. They came from far and wide, by foot, bus, car, taxi and train, trailing toddlers or with a baby on their hip. They came in head scarves, curlers, or with their hair newly permed, leaving the smell of chemicals in the room when they left. They came seeking a dream or a solution.

I would sit in silence at the kitchen table, or under the table or against the fridge door, listening. Not moving, scarcely able to breathe in case they asked me to leave.

This wisdom of women and spirit was a part of the everyday. It was passed from generation to generation of women over kitchen tables, washing lines and the heads of children. Without formal recognition or the repercussions of the moralists it was handed

on. I loved to hear the leaves being read and the gasps of recognition and acknowledgement from the listeners as stories and
predictions revealed the truth.

'I see a letter ... I see a man ... I see travel ... a new baby, a
debt to be paid, a broken heart ...'

'This bird means ... this animal means ... these dots mean ...
and, look here, do you see this ...?'

How did they know about my nana and my mother? How did
they know about the gypsy women who read the cards, the hands
and the crystal ball? How did they know about the women who
talked to spirits around a table or those strange churches where
people spoke in tongues? Certainly there was no advertising, there
were no 'New Age' papers. I never once heard my nana, my
mother or any other woman tell any of the men in their lives about
divination. It was known through woman-talk.

'Now there's a woman who ...'

'I met a character the other day...'

'Mrs So-and-So's husband passed over and she's been seeing
him in the garden ...'

'Elsie heard something about Jack. You know who from?
That woman in Brighton. If you want to find her take the bus to
so-and-so, go left, third street on the right, second place on the
left. Bird bath out front, two yellow roses beside the gate.'

'Ring this number and ask for Ruby.'

Woman-talk!

I never saw my mother or my nana take any money for a
reading.

Now I dabble with my cup of leaves and hear the voice of my
nana in the reading.

It was my father who taught me the art of making billy tea.

Boil a billy of water over a wood fire, add a good handful of
tea and gently swing the billy back and forth. Those with a sense
of daring would swing the billy round and round in a full arm-
length circle, the billy arching above their face and not a drop of
tea spilt. This settling of the tea-leaves is a definite art and should

be left to those who don't mind the occasional accident. Hot tea on the skin is simply not acceptable and yet the show-off in me loved to swing that billy high! I practised the trick with cold water for years before trying it at first with lukewarm water and building up to hot. Mumbling a magic spell gives the trick added dimension!

'All tea-leaves should settle to the bottom,' my father would say. 'That is the art of a good tea maker. That and a good strong brew. If you get bored add a eucalyptus leaf.'

But for our everyday brew, we used a pot. The biggest pot I ever saw was at a country dance. It was a copper. Used more often for boiling clothes. Like a witch's cauldron it stood over the fire, full to the brim with bubbling tea.

'Yeah, I remember a time when I was a young blood,' said my father. 'It was someone's wedding and the bride's people were real wowsers. All holy-rollers and fire and brimstone. No grog. Not even a whiff of it in the air. Well, we were all the "best men" of that poor mug who got himself tied and we wanted to have a party. The place was as dry as a witch's tit after she's a hundred. So we thought we'd give those holy-rollers something to really moan and shit about. It was so bloody funny. We laced that big copper that held the tea with Epsom Salts. There they all were, holding on to themselves and racin' for the creek. Best laugh I've ever had at a wedding.'

Men's marches and ladies' lounges

I learnt to dance standing on my inebriated father's feet while being waltzed across some RSL hall floor. He taught me every Anzac Day. Anzac Day. How I loathed that celebration of war.

My father would be up 'at sparrow's fart'. Just before dawn. Whistling, he'd shower and shave, yelling at me to 'Get up now; we're in a bloody hurry.'

I'd try to stay asleep, complain of a stomach ache, cold, anything that could possibly reprieve me. Any excuse not to go. For my father it was a sin not to attend Anzac Day.

'It's to remember all of me mates. Those dead and those alive. It's about respect.'

'I hate it!' I'd yell back. 'It's all about war.' And getting pissed, I'd think to myself. But never say that aloud! That was the forbidden, not-talked-about-except-with-humour area of discussion. The only times I tried to raise the matter with anyone I thought would listen they seemed to give me the same answer: 'But of course they drink, dear, they went to war!' Anzac Day was always a day of celebration. With sighs of patience my father would explain it again, and I'd yell back at him how much I hated it. Especially the RSL halls. But no matter how much I hated it I'd be dragged along.

There were several ways we celebrated Anzac Day but usually my father would head to the city of Adelaide — plenty of mates there to commiserate and celebrate with. Sometimes we would hit a local RSL hall in the country. Usually there were no women at those country celebrations; the drinking wasn't so heavy either. But the Anzac Days I preferred were when we were out bush and my father would just visit a mate or two.

In one town we went to visit three brothers. Joe, Jack and my father were in the same battalion. Joe and Jack had fought for their country while their mother cared for Harry who was 'short of a quid or two'. When the brothers returned from war they moved back home to care for their ageing mother and brother. Now there were just Joe, Jack and Harry.

'Some people are intelligent,' my father would tell me, 'like Joe there, who reads books and is a thinking man. Now Jack, he is not a thinking man, he sees everything in black and white and is just plain ignorant. But Harry, he's not intelligent or ignorant, just short of a quid or two and he lives in a different world. It doesn't mean he's dumb like Jack — he's just different.'

I liked going to visit them because Harry cooked cakes, but I didn't like Jack who smelled and could only talk about race-horses and racing dogs. He hated both animals unless they were on a racetrack. I'd ask my father why they all lived together and he'd reply, ''Cos they are used to it.'

Harry smiled a lot and would tell me about his aching feet. He didn't drink alcohol and so, while my father and the other two brothers would share a flagon of wine and listen to the Anzac march on the radio, Harry and I would sit and drink lemonade and eat hot cake.

One year we were way out bush for Anzac Day. My father had met up with some of his mates and we were all sitting around a camp fire while they shared a flagon of wine. Irish was an old friend of my father's. They had been 'boys' together once, taking local girls to dances on their bikes. Irish had a million stories and about as many wives and children. 'The women love 'im,' my father often said. 'They run to him like bees to a honey pot. Must be that bloody big donger hangin' in his pants.' Now a bloody big donger was something every man seemed to be very proud of, especially if one of his mates had such equipment. I used to look at the bloody big donger hanging out of the bull and I imagined that such a width and size must hang in the trousers of some men, and that women must be fascinated by it somehow. The dongers I'd seen weren't that big at all! Tiny shrivelled bits of meat that even erect didn't come anywhere near the bull's magnificent appendage. I figured that a few men had freak dongers and the rest wanted them. At least that's how it seemed to me. Men were forever discussing someone else's 'trouser snake' and I knew reams of stories about them, but no teacher in the many schools I attended ever asked for such stories.

Irish seemed old to me. Very old with his pouchy face, stained, droopy moustache and wild, bloodshot eyes. He was a master story-teller. My father also called him 'one of the old people'. I certainly knew of 'the old people'. They were the ones given the greatest respect and it had nothing to do with their age. When old Irish began to tell stories the spirit people would crowd around him ready to listen. I had often seen spirit people come to listen to stories or attach themselves to some human, but old Irish seemed to pack the spirits in. He was aware of them — he'd stamp his feet and wave his hands every now and again, yelling, 'Give a man room to breathe.' He'd stretch his back and hands, take a drink and begin.

'Once upon a time there were two giants. Two big, big, fellows. One was as gentle and as kind as a man can be while the other was born nasty and mean. Always boasting of just how good he was. Those giants had never met but they knew about each other. The first giant was hoping that they would never meet but the second giant was always itching for a fight. He wanted to show the world that he was the biggest, toughest, best. So he crossed the sea to find the first giant to do battle with him. The first giant's wife heard that the second giant was coming and she was worried because her husband didn't really like fighting.

'"I have to fight him!" yelled the giant. "It's my honour that's at stake."

"It's your head that will be broken," said his wife.

'They both worried as the giant came closer and closer. Then the wife had an idea and dressed her husband up as a baby. She placed him in the pram, dressed in a sheet for a nappy, with a bottle and a dummy. Just in time, because the second giant arrived spoiling for a fight and yelling for her husband to come out and see who was the strongest of the two giants. "Who's that?" yelled the giant, pointing at the pram. "That's our baby," said the wife. "Baby!" yelled the second giant. "Then how big is your husband?" "Oh, he's big," said the wife. The second giant looked at the baby, thought for a while and said, "If that's the baby then the husband must be …" "Yes," said the wife. Away ran the second giant.'

All this was told as a story-teller does, expressed with gestures of the hands, head, eyebrows that danced and bloodshot eyes that for a short time became blue — brilliant blue like the sky on a hot, hot day.

'He was a bloody coward letting his wife dress him up as a baby,' said one of the men sitting around the fire.

'No,' said Irish. 'He wasn't a coward. War and fighting just prove nothing. They just lead to more war and fighting.'

'But you went to war and you fought,' said my father.

'Yes,' said Irish, 'and what a bloody big, bloody adventure that was. And we're still bloody well fighting.'

'Yeh, well,' said another man, 'we need a few wars every now and again. It keeps the economy ticking.'

'Ah,' said Irish, 'we need no bloody wars at all. War just shows how bloody stupid we all are.'

Silence from the humans, except for the sound of the red wine being poured into their pannikins. The tobacco went from hand to hand, the fire was stoked and I watched Irish closely, observing his thick white hair and the rough hands of a hard-working man. One had to be a bit careful about all this war business because, after all, it was Anzac Day. So I changed the subject to safe ground.

'Do you believe in fairies?' I asked him. All the spirit people looked up and turned to old Irish.

'I've got a thing or two to speak to them about,' he answered.

Another man at the fire yelled, 'A thing or two! I've got more than a thing or two to talk to them about. They are always mucking around in places that they shouldn't be and upsetting things.'

'You are always whingeing and blaming the little people for anything that goes wrong,' my father said. 'You blame every bloody woe on them and they're probably bloody sick of it.'

Old Irish interjected, 'If you show them a bit of respect and you do them a bit of honour you won't have any trouble.'

'I'll show them bloody respect,' the old man yelled, standing up. 'Where's me bloody shears, you bastards?' The spirit people were dancing around and pulling faces at the old man. Irish looked at me and grinned.

'Well, he's certainly not going to get anything back the way he's demanding it,' said old Irish, and began to laugh until the tears ran down his face and he used the biggest handkerchief to wipe them away. My father, observing me watching old Irish, said, 'He uses that handkerchief to cover his face when he does robberies.'

'When he does what?' I asked.

'Hold-ups,' replied my father.

'He robs people?' I asked, wide-eyed.

'No,' replied old Irish. 'I just helps meself to a little bit of their wealth. After all, they can't take it with them and I need a little bit of it here. It makes it all go around a bit, like.' He winked at me. The men laughed and drained the flagon. I never really knew whether old Irish did really rob people or not, but my father embellished the story by telling me that old Irish had a good teacher. It seemed he was related to Ned Kelly.

I told my father about the spirits. 'Yeah, mate, they're always around the old fellow. He says they came with him from the old country but I reckon they're breeding here — he has so many more each time we meet. They tell him things and help him out. You just give respect to them and be polite.' I could always tell my father about the spirits. Sometimes my nana too, but carefully. I learnt early who could be told and who couldn't. When I listened to most adults I heard them talking about spirit life in terms of their childhood fantasies or their religion. My father always listened and for the gift of believing me I have thanked him a million times.

Another year we were out bush on Anzac Day, sitting around a fire with two men who were having a competition between them about whose poetry was the finest, Banjo Paterson or Henry Lawson. Both men were elegant speakers of verse and knew all of his respective idol's work.

Into our camp came an old man leading two camels. Mohammed had arrived. He was one of the last wandering traders who went from outback station to outback station, isolated community to isolated community, selling cloth and sewing needs like needles and threads, scissors and beads. My father and he greeted each other in Arabic and introductions were made. I had met the old man before and gave him the respect due to an 'uncle'. My father had told me that Mohammed was a very learned man who not only spoke several languages but knew how the stars made patterns of stories across the sky. Mohammed sat at the fire, brewing his coffee and refusing alcohol.

The two drovers continued their debate on which poet was the finest. Stopping for a refill, one of the men asked Mohammed which poet he preferred, and Mohammed replied:

> *'The Moving Finger writes, and, having writ*
> *Moves on: nor all thy Piety nor Wit*
> *Shall lure it back to cancel half a Line,*
> *Nor all thy Tears wash out a Word of it.*

'Omar Khayyam,' he grinned at me. My father smiled. The two drovers sat with their mouths open. 'What the hell was that?' said one.

'Poetry,' said my father. He took a long swig from his pannikin and said:

> *'Here with a Loaf of Bread beneath the Bough,*
> *A Flask of Wine, a Book of Verse — and Thou*
> *Beside me singing in the Wilderness —*
> *And Wilderness is Paradise enow.'*

'Jeeesus,' said one of the drovers. They returned to their debate and my father and Mohammed visited another world.

But in the city we watched that long grey march, men like seabirds in formation — marching oh so solemnly, usually in the rain. A funeral march, a remembrance march, fuelled with musical interludes that charged the emotion to tears of mourning for all of one's personal miseries.

My nana would watch the march on television. My mother would attend the march. She loved watching all those men in uniform. My Aunt Julie waved my uncle off to the marches, his medals banging proudly on his chest. My friend David's father went in a wheelchair and was pushed the length of the march by another 'digger'. David's father's big body was grotesquely heaped into a lump resembling what had been a formidably sized man. His amputated stumps stuck out in front of him and his one good arm held a waving flag. 'My dad says women like to touch his stumps for luck,' David told me in great secrecy. 'Oh, that's horrid,' I replied, looking at the ends of those scarred and puck-ered limbs which poked out of his shorts like fat pink slugs. His wrinkled grey penis and hairy balls used to dangle out of the shorts too. No one had the courage to tuck that ugly mass away. I didn't want to look but, like most curious people, just had to.

Many of the war heroes my father knew were injured — an arm, an eye, a leg, hand or foot. So many of them used walking sticks. They were all hung with medals that they were proud of and they would endlessly tell me what each medal represented as they sucked their cigarettes right down to the stump. Yellow-tar-fingered men whose war experience bound them all together for this once-a-year celebration.

Stories were told.

'Do you remember that sergeant? Jeez, he was a right bastard.'

'Made me peel spuds till me fingers bled.'

'Didn't his missus run off with that Yankee GI?'

'Bloody good thing too.'

'Yeh, but what about Bob, poor bastard? He came home

from that Singapore fiasco, after being in the water for four days, to find his missus in bed with a GI.'

'Yeh, poor bastard. He took his kid, who was still in nappies, to me sister. She showed him how to change a nappy and make a bottle. That boy now drives the train from Port Augusta to the Alice. He turned out all right.'

'Those bloody GI Joes with all their money and silk stockings. Like rats up a drainpipe. We are off fighting a bloody war and those bastards are up our bloody women.'

'Not like the Brits — they didn't get into our women.'

'No,' yelled Jezza, 'we got into theirs!'

'Remember the time Jerry went to the same brothel as us?'

'Jesus, what a bloody scare that was. Here we was, face to face, heading into the same place and we were supposed to be killing each other.'

'Jimbo threw a penny to see who'd go in first. He was a bloody good Two-Up champion, he was, and he sure as hell wasn't going in after Jerry.'

Loud men's laughter, men's business, would bounce off the walls. Stories were washed down by copious amounts of golden beer that had a topping of thick white foam.

'Never, never wash a beer glass in soapy water,' my father instructed me. 'It makes the beer go flat, no matter how often you rinse the glass out.' He taught me how to pour a beer. 'Tilt the glass, then slowly raise it until you get a white topping of froth.' The men on Anzac Day would make a tower of the empty glasses. They played Two-Up on the floor while shouting and singing out and exchanging money. Then someone would start a sing-song.

> 'Hitler had only one brass ball,
> Goering had two but they were small,
> Himmler had something similar, and
> Poor old Goebbels had no balls at all.'

Men would slap each other's backs and laugh with tears running down their faces.

Away they would go again.

> *'There was a young sailor named Gates*
> *Who useta rumba on skates*
> *But he slipped on his cutlass*
> *And now he is nutless*
> *And practically useless on dates.'*

They'd roar with laughter, slap each other on the arm, back or head and someone would climb on a table and begin to yell,

> *'The boy stood on the burning deck*
> *His pocket full of crackers.*
> *One went off, two went off*
> *And blew away his knackers.'*

The room would roar with male approval and comradeship. Then someone would say, 'Sh, sh, enough now. Women and kids.'

'No more dirty talk.'

Serious drinking would begin. No more dancing as the shoes became splattered with vomit. Men fell down on the floor, slept with their head on the table, and cried into their beer.

'Piss talk,' the women would say. 'He can cry now he's full, but I have nights of him yelling and screaming that the bombers are overhead.'

'Ted still gets bouts of malaria. He sweats, mutters and turns yellow. He's a mess for days.'

'Bill wakes up screaming.'

'Fred punches the wall and once he kicked a hole in the toilet door.'

'Joe has bloody nightmares and I'm a mass of bruises.'

'Bluey walks in his sleep. I followed him once and he turned around and tried to kill me. My screaming woke him up. He said he thought I was one of those bloody Nips sneaking up in the grass behind him.'

'Walter keeps too many guns. It scares me.'

My father would be one of the last to leave the RSL halls. If we were just two we'd arrive home and he'd open a flagon of port. Some time during the night I'd get up and help him to bed, drag off his shoes and cover him with a blanket.

One Anzac Day we were living with my mother. The streets ran like rivers and still the rain teemed down. We arrived home in a taxi. I squeezed past my drunken father as he tried to pay the cab driver and I ran for the house. My mother opened the front door, let me in, then firmly shut and bolted the door. My father cursed and pounded on the door to no avail. All went quiet. Next morning I found him asleep on the back verandah, curled up with the dogs on their mattress. His hat, coat, pants and shoes were floating around the pool we once called our backyard.

My mother loved 'ladies' lounges'. This was the secret place, away from men.

A room with tables and chairs, and a hatch in the wall, opening into the bar so the ladies could order their sherry or port. Or brandy. Or stout. The women would sit at the tables drinking and smoking Turf or Craven A, while opening their compacts to check their lipstick line. When no men were present the women made up their faces openly, but when men were present they headed for the toilets.

I once watched a woman powder her face and replace her lipstick line while using a silver salt shaker as a mirror. A mirror over a fireplace in the ladies' lounge was usually essential so the women could keep check on their image. The ladies' lounge smelled of the perfume of women. Helena Rubinstein, Revlon, Coty, and Ponds battled across the tables. Bottles of Oil of Ulan went from hand to hand and nail polish and lipstick colours were eagerly inspected. I'd sniff the women in and I liked the smell of the old woman who wafted lavender strong enough to 'kill a brown dog'. As my father would say, 'They smell like a brothel in the busy season.' The ladies' lounge might have smelled like a brothel to my father but for me it was a sanctuary away from the rest of the pub that smelled like men — beer, vomit and piss.

The ladies' lounge didn't have the football, the races or the cricket bouncing off the walls. It came through the hatch muffled and left the room to the stories of the women. Woman-talk.

I'd sit as inconspicuous as possible and slowly sip a raspberry-and-lemonade, pretending to read a comic, while my eyes watched and my ears soaked up the conversations. I learned the art of listening to several conversations at once, my ears bouncing from table to table, life to life. The women talked as if I wasn't there. I'd keep my head bent and peer up under my lashes at the beaded soft jumpers, shoulder-padded coats and cashmere twinsets. Powdered, wrinkled throats, whiskered chins, china-smooth make-up, clip-on earrings, necklaces of pearls or glass — all were noted as I smelled each woman and my brain connected each story.

My mother was a fashion plate who had no money and so she shaved her legs smooth and used her eyebrow pencil to make a line down the back of her legs to simulate silk stockings. With legs like Marlene Dietrich she showed off her line to perfection. She spent hours beading her jumpers. Beautiful patterns crossed her shoulders and breasts. She loved earrings and necklaces. Every Coles store held an Aladdin's Cave of delight for her. Each lipstick end was saved, dug out with a match, all the pieces heated and melted together into another lipstick. When she couldn't get eyebrow pencils, she used charcoal. She dyed her red-gold hair jet black and went to bed every night in spiky rollers.

She painted her fingernails but never her toes because she said it was cheap to paint one's toenails. My mother also, like many of the women, would put perfume on her hankie and tuck it between her breasts. With great glee I would watch a woman pull a hankie from between her breasts, spit on it, wipe a child's face and pop the hankie back in its resting place. The child's face would smell of spit, perfume and the breasts of the mother.

Sometimes a man would enter the ladies' lounge and all conversation would stop. He'd stand at the door and gaze around; he knew he had entered sacred territory and he would take off his hat. Awkwardly he'd approach his wife, mother or sister, and quietly speak. Sometimes he'd buy a round of drinks for the table where his relative was sitting. He'd serve the women, receive their thanks and leave. Seldom did a man ever join the women.

Mixed business was done out in the beer garden. Men and women would sit drinking while the kids and dogs ran riot. Drunken men would curse and be yelled at as they tripped over dogs and kids on the way to the toilet. The women's toilet would always be packed, especially the space in front of the mirror. I'd squeeze against some woman's stomach as I tried to wash my hands and she'd be shoving my face into the sink with her body while vying for space at the mirror and spraying hair spray all over both of us.

Before I even began school, I'd seen fights, vomiting, pill-popping and face painting in women's toilets that would have left a film effects person gasping. I'd watch women add hair pieces to their own hair or spray their hair into an immobile mass, and once I watched in fascination as a woman removed her wig, scratched her bald head and replaced it, with fresh tape to hold it in place. She turned to me, saying, 'My Joe now, he doesn't know I'm bald. He has never seen me without me hair.'

'And mine's never seen me without me teeth!' screeched one.

'Or me false leg,' yelled another.

'And mine,' said one woman, 'has never seen me with the lights on.'

I watched women attach false eyelashes, draw on eyebrows, add paint, powder, glitter, lipstick or rouge, and pluck out hairs while keeping up a never-ending chatter of gossip. In those toilets I helped paint toenails, fingernails and tease hair. I'd watch women pull up their roll-ons, lace up corsets and stuff their brassieres with tissues. I'd watch women flush pads of blood down toilets while others wrapped theirs up in yards of toilet tissue and, finding no bin, would put the offending package in their purse. I'd watch women wipe their hands on grey towelling, paper, panties, petticoats and hankies. Stockings would be straightened, and black stiletto shoes cleaned with spit and a hankie. I'd watch women compare stretch marks and operation scars, and I was fascinated by a diabetic woman who gave herself an injection; it made me determined that I'd never be a diabetic because of my fear of injections. The women's toilet was a theatre like no other.

Burn marks from cigarettes were on every surface. Butts were stubbed out underfoot or lay hissing in bowls or sinks. The sound of pissing. 'Like a bloody carthorse, you are, Mavis.'

'Oh god, I needed that. I've been holding on fit to burst.'

'Pass me some toilet paper, will you?' Wads of paper would go under the door.

Someone would sing:

> *Red sails in the sunset*
> *Far over the sea,*
> *To carry my loved one*
> *Home safely to me.*

Once I was waiting to enter a toilet when the door flew open. A woman was bleeding into the toilet from her 'private places' while standing straddled over the bowl. She looked into my wide eyes. Her voice cracked at me, 'Close the door.' I did, and waited and waited.

Another door opened, a woman hurried out. I entered and peed.

I came out, washed my hands and re-entered the ladies' lounge. The light green walls swam in nauseous turbulence. I held onto the table and looked into the faces of the women drinking and smoking at the table.

'A lady is bleeding in the toilet,' I said to the table.

Chairs scraped and in seconds I was the only one left in the room.

Slowly the women filed back in. My mother and another woman did not come back. Someone bought me a lemonade-and-raspberry. Slowly the lounge emptied until only one woman and I were left. She took me to the police station and they telephoned my nana. My nana spent her 'bill money' on a taxi.

The next day my tall, unamused Aunt Julie visited, frowning when she saw me. She bent her face for a kiss. I hugged my favourite aunt while her reaction spelt anger and disapproval. I sat on the front steps hearing her berating my nana for my mother's misdemeanours. I tried to explain to my aunt that my mother was helping a 'bleeding lady', but my aunt only heard her own anger with the favoured daughter, my mother, and she replied, 'They are always falling down drunk and bleeding.'

My nana stood behind my severe aunt, shaking her head, as she did many times to warn me to shut up and not answer back.

This time I kept quiet; my aunt needed very little fuel to rage against my mother.

My nana told me that my aunt was angry with my mother because my mother always pinched her boyfriends.

My mother always said, 'Julie has no idea how to have fun.'

My aunt would always say, 'Margaret would be in the bar all made up, swinging her hips and putting on a show for the men while I would be running around doing all the work.'

My father told me he had asked my aunt out until my mother walked through the room and, according to him, he fell instantly in love. My aunt was forgotten.

My mother loved men — all sizes, shapes and types, so long as they were male. There was never any placating my aunt as far as my mother was concerned for my mother lived on the wild side that my aunt possibly could only dream about. My aunt's home was spotless and she would follow me around with a brush and a broom whenever I visited. Everyone said that she was the perfect wife and mother, and she was the example that was pointed out to me as a pillar of respectability. Much as I loved her, she lacked a passion that my mother manifested fully.

Three weeks later my mother reappeared. We left together to live in a big house in the city of Adelaide. A home for young girls, all pregnant. The home was run by women in grey uniforms, with titles like 'Captain' and 'Brigadier'.

They were kind, quiet, religious women who must have known about the nocturnal visits of the boyfriends.

I'd lie in bed and hear the boyfriends try to climb quietly up a ladder beside my ground-floor bedroom window. If the window was open I could smell them. Nervousness, fear and cigarette smoke would waft into the room. The men would walk in what they thought were quiet steps, sneaking across the corrugated iron roof to the first floor of the two-storey building which housed all the girls and the army that cared for them.

My mother told me it was possums. I'd always reply to her, 'Possums in hobnailed boots!' and she'd tell me to go to sleep. I'd strain to hear their voices — men trying to whisper, not knowing how, and the sounds were like frogs with sore throats. I'd lie, trying to put the words into coherent meaning, when another set of feet would begin the squeaky tin waltz. I'd go to sleep counting the visitors.

I never stayed awake long enough to hear the feet retreating in the morning.

One day I climbed the ladder and walked across the flat roof. The window entrance was closed, the outside area thick with cigarette butts.

Some evenings my mother and I would walk to the local shops to buy a cheese she particularly loved. On the way she'd deposit brown-wrapped bottles in street bins.

My mother bought a drink called Sedna. She got it from the chemist on Sundays when hotels were closed. A one-pint-six-ounce dark brown bottle that gave the illusion it was a bottle of medicine, not wine. It was a 'tonic', a 'pick-me-up', 'good for the blood'. It was for 'the pressure of business, for a weak stomach and all manner of other complaints'. The label read, 'This mixture contains 33 per cent proof spirit to which is added macerated kola nut powder, to each fluid ounce of wine 15 grains of kola nut powder' and 'Sedna, refreshing, exhilarating, stimulating, nourishing wine'. The label — in orange, green blue and yellow — showed a rural scene of three cows surrounded by a frame of grapes and leaves.

The Sunday I finally told my mother, 'No. Go get your own bloody Sedna', was a day when all the street seemed to be out visiting but for one pregnant young mum across the road. I was thirteen and moody. My mother, in her early thirties, was angry at my refusal. She stamped off down the street. I sat on the front fence watching the bitumen blister and listening to the heat of the day.

I heard the young mother crying out. I looked up and down the street. Empty. Houses shut tight against summer heat but no feel of people.

I crossed the road and stopped at the front gate. I could clearly hear crying and 'Help, help!' I walked up the side of the house and in the back door. The toilet led from the back porch. I looked in. The young mother was sitting on the toilet, rocking, her eyes streaming tears, her body energy all pain. She looked at me; she didn't see me — just the pain. She fell forward, crashing to the floor.

I pulled her straight and looked her over. Blood was pouring from between her legs. I looked into the toilet bowl and there was a tiny being. I reached in and lifted it out. Dead. I put the seat down and placed the once-alive on top. Then slowly I pulled the mother into the kitchen, bit by bit. I put newspaper under her hips and bath towels between her legs. I put a pillow under her head and a bed cover over her. I took a tea towel and wrapped the once-alive in it, placing it beside the mother. I washed my hands and ran out of the house, down the driveway, down the street, around the corner and into the phonebox. I dialled emergency. I could dial it in the dark. The phonebox never had any light. I ran back to the house and stood outside. The ambulance came in an energy of urgency. No one in the street came out. Not even a curtain moved. A stretcher came out, carrying the young mother. An ambulance man said, 'She'll be fine. Home in a few days. Get your mum to tell her husband when he comes home that his wife is in hospital. Okay?'

I nodded. I returned to my fence-sitting. My mother didn't like the husband.

I'd tell my father to tell him, I thought.

My mother came down the street, happy, with a man friend on each arm. They came level with me. 'The lady across the street had her baby,' I said. 'She's gone to hospital.'

'Good,' replied my mother. 'We'll celebrate our way. Wet the baby's head and all that. Weston's got a flagon. Hide this for later.' She handed me the Sedna bottle. Laughing, the adults went past into the house and shut the door.

My father arrived home and took the Sedna bottle from me. I told him what had happened. He threw the bottle at a Stobie pole, exploding it into the smell of the day and staining the concrete-and-steel pole with a wet, dark stain that made a picture and told a story.

No place for a child

My father found work in Whyalla, a city of men who built ships. He couldn't take me because he'd be living in the single men's quarters.

'You can't come. It's all men.'

'So what?'

'Well, it's no place for a child.'

'Why not?'

'Because it's all men! Because … It's way out of town and no kids are allowed.'

'Why not?'

'Because it's for men. Now shut up. Like the front bar in a pub is for men. Men need places without women and without kids.'

So I was sent to my nana at Seacliff, and my father went to Whyalla to be with men. 'He's sick of women and kids,' I told my nana. Tex and Tiger had both died and I only had Tip now. I didn't like living in suburbia. I missed being on the road. I missed the people we met on the road. There were plenty of 'characters' around Seacliff, especially on the beach, but to most I was simply a child, while the people we met in camps treated me as if I were a small adult.

My mother and her new boyfriend turned up at my nana's. They had a great place to live. I went to stay with them in an old, run-down, disused pub in a country town called Roseworthy.

The small town consisted of an agricultural college and not much more. The small wheat community was dying and dwindling. A new pub stood on the highway and the old pub rotted into its watery cellars. It was a fascinating place to explore. So many rooms.

Clydesdale horses roamed paddocks and I spent my days watching and talking to them. Tip and I ran free and wild.

One week I realised that I had not seen my mother for three days. Not that unusual, with a new boyfriend and lots of drinking to do. I had fed Tip and myself each day, but now I became concerned. Going into the adults' bedroom I found it deserted. No clothes, no make-up, nothing.

'Gone again,' I muttered, and searched the place for money. I gathered up what I could, packed my things and walked to the highway. There, the dog and I caught a bus for Whyalla.

Whyalla. It was like a vision of hell — the sky alight with flames and the smell of hot metal in the air. Sparks like fireworks showered the air, challenging the stars with the brilliance of man-made galaxies. Big iron ships were being built and the place was billed as 'a city of men!' (I told my aunt later that Whyalla had eleven men to one woman and she replied, 'Wait until someone tells your mother; she'll be up there with her skates on!')

Now I was here, looking for my father. The driver stopped the bus and yelled, 'Single men's quarters.' The dog and I stood in the red dust watching the bus disappear.

I left my bag with Tip and entered the office. No one was there. A big green ledger was open on the desk. I turned it around and scanned the names. I found my father's name and room number. When he came off his shift he found us sitting at his door.

'Jesus fucking Christ.'

The next day he arranged for me to board with Ron and Bea Bennett. They were to be my 'guardians'.

Bea Bennett was a massive woman with a bitter tongue and a sour temper. Her husband Ron was a huge wreck of a man. A punch-drunk alcoholic. I could not have my beloved Tip with me. My father gave him to someone on a station. I cried and sulked and raged. 'It's no good, mate, he has to go.'

'But he's my friend and you told me that a dog is for life.'

'I know and I'm sorry, mate, but it's either that or I dunno what. They won't take him, your nana won't take you, and I'm buggered. So just give me a break. Look. He's a beaut dog and they want him to father puppies. He'll have a great time.' I cried and cried.

In me Bea Bennett had a servant. I washed and cleaned and mowed and polished while she kept up her threats of 'the Welfare', and her slaps were hard and vicious. I ran away.

My father found me down at the local racing stables. We moved into a commission house together. It wasn't long before my mother joined us. My father came home with a skinny black pup. 'Looks like a bit of a mix. He's called Bozo.'

'Bozo?'

'The boof.'

Bozo the boof grew into a huge black dog, half Great Dane. He liked me and came riding as he grew. I had great fun with him — he was such a willing, happy clown of a dog.

I attended the local primary school where, for the first time in my life, I wasn't teased by the other kids or the teacher. I stopped the other kids teasing me after two magnificent school-yard fights which I won against older bullies. Not one of the teachers at that school ever questioned my background or gave me the impression I was less than the other students. Mrs Gilmore was my teacher for one-and-a-bit years and she is the only primary school teacher I ever truly respected. She recognised my love of reading and taught me how to use a library. I remember a tall dark-haired woman with glasses. In my mind I can see her clearly — her smile, her hands and the true love of teaching; her humour, understanding and compassion. She understood my passion for books, reading, language, talking, dogs and horses. She understood my need to have my dog with me at school. The dog slept under my desk. Nothing was said. She understood my aversion to the compulsory dancing and sport days. I excelled at throwing and hitting a ball. She encouraged me to play softball. I couldn't run and so I had to hit hard so I could lope around the bases.

For that short time school became a place where I wanted to go.

Since Whyalla was a city of migrants, most of the students spoke broken English or no English when they first arrived in the school. We immediately taught them all the swear words. Mrs Gilmore understood and tolerated that quirk in children. She understood our shit, bum and tits obsession. She was kind and patient. She made learning come alive and she opened the doors of geography, history and science for me. When I turned up with nits in my hair she sent me off to the hairdresser with a note. It did minimise the embarrassment and, compared with my father's usual scrub with kero, it was a huge improvement in smell and treatment. Mrs Gilmore never told me my clothes were wrong or old or asked after the non-existent uniform. I asked her about sex and she gave me a thick book on anatomy. The year finished far too soon.

I harassed my father continually for a horse. I managed to acquire a bridle and a brush. 'No, no, no, we can't afford it.'

Someone down at the racing stables told me of an old broken-down trotting horse for sale for five quid. 'But be careful buying from them, kid. They're hillbillies and they'll take you down. They deal with the knackery and they'd sell their granny for a bob.' I went to see the horse. He was old, with four white socks and a white blaze. He was like a bear in build and covered with as much hair. His name was Ginger.

The owner was greasy and unkempt. 'Yep, he's yours for a fiver or he'll go to the knackers.'

Two teenage boys stood next to their father, leering at me and picking their teeth. They looked like ugly characters. 'Your folks know you want a horse?' asked one.

'You're kinda young, kid,' the old man laughed and his breath was like a cesspit. I decided I couldn't leave Ginger with them.

'You got a place to keep him?'

'At home,' I lied. I arranged for them to drop Ginger at a local stable I was hoping to rent.

On the way home I asked the owner if I could rent the stable and small paddock. He agreed.

My father used to give me one pound a week for bus fares to and from school, my school lunches and something towards a new pair of shoes.

I walked to and from school carrying my shoes to stop them wearing out, and I didn't have any lunch. My aunt then sent me her old bike so I was mobile and free — and I had a horse. And I figured I could afford to keep him!

The five pounds needed to pay for Ginger I easily acquired that week. I went through drunken men's pockets and wallets.

I never stole from my mother or father, or my nana. No friend or relative. My mother's drunken men-friends were another matter, and many a pocketful of change fed me fish and chips.

I was now eleven, going on twelve.

I adored Ginger. Every morning and night I'd cut fresh grass to add to his hay and chaff. I took an old, grey, army blanket from the house and made him a rug to keep him warm. With the mat of hair on his body I could have made myself a rug! I brushed him and talked to him, sang to him and told him stories. Ginger and I rode the saltbush and bluebush scrub around Whyalla and we lived many stories. The bush spirits were different out in that rugged country. The horse saw far more than I. He'd stop, his eyes wide open, ears on alert. Sometimes he'd snort or want to sniff something that caught his curiosity. The area is heavy with iron energy. I loved my days riding, each ride an adventure. Always something new to see, always the expectation of seeing eagles in flight or coming across one sitting motionless on a post, the eyes constantly alert.

I stole money to buy Ginger oats, but not for a saddle. I rode bareback. Sometimes I saw the 'two ugly sons', as I had nicknamed them, driving around with their mates in a hotted-up car. A couple of times they chased Ginger and me, and I was frightened of their bullying.

Then a car hit me. Two thugs, having robbed a local milk bar, came roaring down a laneway in a stolen car. I was emerging from that lane on my bicycle. I felt myself fly through the air, then skid along the gravel on my face and hands. The thugs kept going, leaving me unconscious, face down in my own blood.

I awoke in hospital. My face and hands were bandaged. A kind nurse looked down at me. 'Oh good. You're awake. We had to clean a great deal of gravel out of you, young lady. What a mess. Your hands will heal in a few days and we've put a few stitches in your face. You won't even notice the scar. In time. Now you'll have to eat sloppy foods for a few days. Ice-cream and jelly. Won't that be nice?'

She kept going on and on while all I could think about was Ginger. I thought of my best friend Marissa. I knew she'd be in school and wondering where I was. I usually told her if I was going to wag school. She loved horses though she wasn't as passionate about them as I was. I visualised her sitting in the sewing class making a cross-stitch pattern on a tablecloth. I went into her head and told her that I'd been hit by a car, I was in hospital, and could she please feed Ginger until I came home — hopefully tomorrow. I then saw her scream and stand up. The class was silent, all mouths open. She said something to the teacher and ran from the room. I knew she had gone to feed Ginger.

Marissa came to see me that night and to give me a report on my beloved horse. When I returned to school we were placed in different classes. 'You have far too much influence over each other.'

My father came to the hospital after work. I told him what had happened and about Ginger.

'Jesus Christ! And I thought you were just mucking around in someone's stables. Oh, shit. Well, you've been managing, so it's a pound you've been getting and a pound you'll go on getting. Your mother's gunna be hysterical when she finds out.'

'What — that I'm in hospital?'

'No. That you've gone and got yourself a bloody horse!' In fact, when my mother heard she said, 'Don't think you're so smart, young lady. You'll get sick of it all. Just keep out of my hair.' Phew!

She was busy with a couple of new loves. My six-foot-tall, magnificent-looking mother always chose the pits in men. Except for my father. My mother turned heads with her model's figure but her blokes were nearly always shorter than her — thickset and violent. All were drinking men. Con men and boxers, race-horse trainers and pub managers. Thugs, men who carried guns and fat wallets. Shifty-eyed businessmen and ship builders. She swooned over a man in a uniform, but not cops! At that uniform she drew the line!

My father came home with a battered saddle that he had acquired from one of his mates in the pub. I cleaned and polished it until my bum squeaked every time I rode in it.

The promise of high school filled me with excitement — a different teacher for each subject and the thrill of nearly being adult. It was not the expected dream. More the repeated nightmare of enforced regimentation.

The school was Whyalla High. It was built like an asylum and it smelt. There was no other high school I could attend, and the Catholic school was out of the question because of the fees. My father once again seriously threatened me. I tried to explain how I felt about the place but he was busy trying to sort out his relationship with my mother, the grog and all the other men who came and went from our house. Also he was in war injury pain and trying to hold down a job with the 'Big Australian', BHP. So school it was for me, come hell or high water.

The school was ranked — prefects, well-bred, and 'others'. The prefects and well-bred controlled the school. They wore the best uniforms, had smart tennis racquets and knew we were the children of the 'workers'.

English was boring. No life in it. The teacher often went to sleep! I loved science but there was never enough equipment to go around and the workers' kids were always 'watching on' while the 'real' students did all the experiments.

In maths the big, young, dark-haired teacher threw a student across a room, threw another out the door, told us all we were bloody idiots and threatened us every day. One day he belted up a young student and that student's brother belted up the teacher.

The young man went to jail, the teacher kept belting into boys and we all became afraid to report him.

Miss Brice wore no undies and had the boys hysterical. She would walk along the first-floor metal walkways and down the metal ramps, the boys looking up from underneath. Those she sufficiently excited into yelling or whistling she had caned. She would sit in class with her legs open and all the boys would continually fight over the front-row seats and drop objects on the floor so they had to bend down to retrieve them.

The toilet doors were removed in the girls' toilet block because the school had the highest unwanted pregnancy rate in the country.

I hated the teacher who picked his nose and ate the pickings; the one who smelt and roared at us; the one who was always telling us to 'be good girls' while peering down our developing fronts.

The school was sport mad. Academia came a very poor second and reading was considered sissy. The head sportsmaster looked like 'The Hulk' — all rippling muscles. He wore short shorts, as tight as possible, and oiled his body until it glistened. The older girls were hysterical over him. I thought he looked crude and not at all 'drool material'. The students had physical education one afternoon a week — Monday; sport, running around the oval etc. every Wednesday; and sport every Friday. It was sport, sport, sport, two afternoons a week and all day Friday. I hated it.

Whyalla is a hot city. There we'd be in 100-degree heat being told to run around an oval. I'd sit down. The sport teacher would stand over me screaming. I would not run, hurdle or crawl. He would drag me up to the office and yell for the head to beat me. He was very civilised!

I couldn't afford a tennis racquet so I was allocated to pick up balls. I threw them from court to court while tennis was being played. Back up to head's office!

I refused to play hockey and the only time they persuaded me to play netball I was embroiled in a punch-up and smacked another girl's nose after she punched me in the stomach! Out she went like a light. 'She hit me first' was no excuse. My father was brought to the school; the police were brought; and the respectable parents were in the room, tight-arsed and bitter. No one listened to my side of the story. I was threatened, my father was threatened, and a great deal was yelled about my being 'uncontrollable'.

I attended all my classes except sport. During sports period I went riding. The truant officer caught me. Back to the headmaster's office. My parents were called. My father came. I tried to explain that I was 'doing' a sport — I was going riding.

The head suggested that if I stay at school and attend all my lessons then they, he, would allow me to go home at lunchtimes on Friday so I could ride. This was considered a very special privilege. I agreed. I didn't stick to my side of the agreement. Every sport class I went riding.

The truant officer had to work hard to catch me this time because I went bush. But he found out where I kept the horse and he was waiting. He drove me home expecting to speak to my father. My mother answered the door and it wasn't long before they were sharing a bottle or two.

The headmaster, the truant officer, my mother and I were at the meeting. On the way to the meeting she was threatening to kill me and do all manner of other unpleasant things. When we entered the office she was as sweet as pie and she left with the truant officer.

I could still have a half-day on Friday to go riding but, on the other sports days because I couldn't be trusted, I'd be locked in the library.

About this time the two ugly sons of Ginger's previous owner turned up at the stables demanding a ride. I refused.

'You never paid our dad for that horse. He lent it to you and it's really ours. So we're gunna come back for our horse.'

Several times those boys returned and a couple of times I found the gate open and Ginger wandering around the yard. I decided to shift him. The threats became intimidation. They'd run up and down the lane banging sticks along the corrugated iron fence. They stole horse feed and Ginger's rug. They'd roar their hotted-up car down the lane.

I found another place to stable Ginger but the morning I arrived to shift him he was gone. I raced out to the road and searched for him. I found him in someone's front yard, scared and shivering, his front legs bleeding from a fall to the knees. He was also bleeding from gravel rash on the nose.

'Four boys in a hotted-up car were chasing him,' one man said.

'Yeah, the horse came down and they shot off.'

I led him home, crying. I bathed his nose and knees. It took me hours to pick all the metal from his flesh. I cleaned and put salve on the cuts and fed Ginger oats and a warm mash. Into the yard suddenly stormed Ginger's previous owner with his two boys. 'What have you done to me horse?' he yelled.

I stood up stunned.

'Look at him, all injured. I can take you to court for this.' The sons stood grinning.

'He's my horse. I paid for him.'

'Yeah? Then get the receipt. I leased you this horse and I've come for the next five quid, and what do I find? My bloody horse is injured.'

Receipt! I didn't have a receipt. I'd handed over the five pounds and hadn't thought any more about it.

'He's mine and I paid for him.'

'You leased him, girlie! Now either give me the five quid for the next six months or I'll take me horse back.'

'Just give me time to go home and get the money.'

'Nope. I want it now. Will you look at the state of that horse!'

The man grabbed Ginger's bridle and pulled him out of the yard. Yelling, I went for him. A big meaty hand slammed into my head, then into my face, then another whacked into my chest, sending me sprawling into the dirt.

'Guttersnipe!' roared the voice. 'Try to do me outa me horse. I should kill you.' Hands roughly picked me up and threw me into the stable. A truck rumbled away.

I lay in the straw and manure and cried. After a time I sat up, aching all over; I was covered in dirt, horse poo and blood. Slowly I pedalled my bike home. Bozo greeted me.

'I should have taken you, boy. Maybe your size would have scared them.' Bozo just grinned. He couldn't growl at anything. He had a pup's joy in the world and nothing could change that, not even a robber! I tried to sneak into the laundry. I was running the water quietly into the trough when my mother entered the room. I felt her behind me and slowly turned. I don't know what she saw or presumed but the next moment she had me by the hair and was dragging me around the yard screaming and belting into me with her other hand. I was screaming blue bloody murder.

The back gate crashed in and my mother's friend Olga came roaring into the yard.

'Margaret, leave her alone! Jeeesus, leave her alone. You'll kill her.' Olga dragged me from my mother and wrapped her large self around me. 'Stop it, Margaret, stop it.' My mother continued to scream.

Olga sat me down; took my mother by the arm and led her inside. I sat dazed and sick in the dirt. Olga came back, lifted me in her arms and took me to her home. Between sobs I told her what had happened. Gently she bathed me, cleaned me up, fed me and put me to sleep on her couch. I stayed with her for a week.

My father came for me. He said, 'She didn't mean it.'

'She did, she did.'

He sat there slumped, looking old.

'I'm not coming back into that house.'

'She's left.'

I sighed. Him, Bozo and me. 'Who is it this time?'

Does it matter?'

'No. All that matters is that she's gunna turn up again.'

'She's sorry.'

'I'll bet.'

I moved back home. I was watched at school. I still spent sports time in the library and I left on Fridays at lunchtime.

I never saw the two uglies again and although I knew where they lived I was far too scared to venture anywhere near their home.

For a time we seemed to have the Welfare or police forever at our door. Then a run of wives looking for their husbands. I missed my nana but I knew she was about to marry again and I couldn't go to her. I worried about her, as I didn't like this Mr Loose who was her boarder and was now about to marry her. He was smarmy! A do-gooder with a bitter twist to his words while his veneer of niceness was very thin indeed. He'd say, 'Now, Mary, you've had such a rough life, just put your feet up and I'll deal with it —', 'it' being her money, assets, life and getting rid of the other boarders and all of my nana's independence.

As time went by, he made her dependent and he sucked her vitality dry, leaving her a husk of a woman. One morning she awoke to find him dead of a heart attack beside her. She had no idea how to cope with the world as he had changed it all for her and at the same time the currency had changed from pounds and shillings to dollars and cents. She couldn't find herself and when she looked into the mirror a small, old, worn-out woman stared back; she gave up.

'Why do women end up with bastards?' I asked my father.

'Because all men are bastards.'

Tex

I started riding my bike home from school by a different route so I wouldn't have to pass Ginger's stable. Passing there made me cry. The way was industrial with men working on car bodies, welding, sanding furniture and a great deal of swearing. I liked passing the woodyard because of the smell — earth, fungus and wood.

Standing on a pile of wood, throwing large pieces onto a truck, was a cowboy. Or someone who looked like an American cowboy in chaps and chequered shirt. The hat was definitely cowboy, not an Akubra. I leant against the fence and stared in at the scene. The figure was slight but fit and muscular, a boyish face with a 'rollie' drifting smoke around the person like a halo of silver light. I stared.

'That's a good person,' I thought.

'Gidday,' said a voice. I re-focused on the cowboy. 'Watcha doin'?'

'Going home,' I replied. 'You look like a cowboy out of films.'

Laughter came in a loud roar. A leap from the woodpile, a few big strides and a hand shot out and came between a gap in the wire. 'Tex. I'm called Tex.'

I looked into a pair of brilliant blue eyes, like the sky when the blue hurts my eyes with its brilliance. 'I'm Catherine.'

We shook hands. Tex leaned against the fence and smoked. I told Tex the story of Ginger.

'I've got a couple of horses. Cattle cutters. I use them for rodeo. I like to keep them fit and so I go riding on the weekends if you wanna come. I get sick of leading one all the time and could do with another rider. But I like to go for a few hours. Take lunch. None of this prissy English riding for me. I like the range.'

I jumped at the offer to ride again. We arranged to meet on the following Saturday at the paddock where my new friend's horses were kept. I pedalled home full of excitement.

It was when I was sitting with Bozo while he ate his dinner that a thought suddenly hit me and I smiled, knowing it to be true. I knew what it was about Tex that I couldn't quite put a finger on. It wasn't being a cowboy that had puzzled me. Tex was a she being a he! Two people in one.

I talked to my father about my new friend. 'Yeah, everyone knows Tex. He's a she. Wants to be a he. So she is a he. Got sort of trapped in the wrong body. You know, like God was real busy, overworked and real stressed. Sent a couple of souls into the wrong body and Tex ended up in a woman's body. He reckons he's always known he was a he. I dunno. Anyways, what's his colours like?'

'Fine. The spirit is disrupted.'

'Yours would be too if you woke up in the wrong body.'

'I like her. Him. Tex.'

'That's all that matters then. You can have any friends you choose so long as you like them. Bugger what other people think.'

'I'm going to ride with Tex.' I told him about her horses.

'Enjoy yourself.'

My father was not looking well these days. He seemed grey, his colours had faded. The shrapnel in his body caused him a great deal of pain and his hernia was bothering him. Alcohol was taking its toll and he preferred drinking to eating. He was missing work and he no longer whistled.

Every weekend for the next few months I went riding with Tex. Her horses were quick and alert. They could 'turn on a six-

'pence'. A bay and a chestnut — both loved to work. Even coming home they were eager, and although I learnt a great deal from both horses, for me they were never a relaxing ride as both were forever 'up on their toes'. Riding in a Western saddle was also new for me.

We'd ride through the scrub out to some dam, rocky hill or mine. Occasionally we'd visit one of the out-stations where Tex had friends and share a billy of tea and hot scones.

Tex talked horses, rodeos, America and ranches non-stop. She sang corny cowboy songs and introduced me to the music of Patsy Cline. We'd sing into the wind, 'I fall to pieces each time someone speaks your name,' and 'South of the border, down Mexico way'.

We always stopped for lunch, boiled the billy and shared our sandwiches. We didn't talk about ourselves in a personal way. It was all about horses. And cowboys. And America.

One of Tex's horses liked Coke so I photographed the horse drinking from a bottle. We dreamed of millions, advertisements and fame. Coke sent us a crate of Coke. That was enough and the fame went out the window as we shared bottle after bottle with the horse.

School was school and the weekends were my life. One Saturday Tex and I were brushing the horses when three other riders arrived. We talked for a while and I was offered a ride on one of the horses. I said yes. As I mounted, someone hit the horse hard on the bum, thinking it would be fun. The horse plunged, I fell backwards and my foot went through the stirrup. The horse bolted, taking me with it.

I awoke in hospital with a thumping headache and thinking, 'Oh no, not here again!'

I can't remember the incident, only what I've been told. I can't remember any of that week. My mother was sitting beside the bed.

'Good, you're awake.'

'What are you doing here?'

'I went to visit your nana. She's just re-married. I went to the wedding.' I groaned.

'Now that's enough out of you!' She leant down and spoke quietly and vehemently. 'What are you doing with that — ? How could you be friends with that thing? It brought you in here. What have you been doing?' She was spitting out the words.

'Riding. We go riding.'

'Riding! I'll give you bloody riding. You've been mixing with that thing. That not-normal thing. Half man, half woman, and it's going to stop. Do you hear me?'

'We're friends.'

'People will think you're queer next.'

'I don't give a damn what people think.'

'Friends! Can't you get decent friends? No one is friends with that. It's not normal. And I'll tell you another thing, my girl; you are not going to see that thing again. I'm going to tell it to keep away. You find other friends. You are too young and it could lead you into all sorts of trouble. Tex. Tex. What sort of name is that? We had a dog called Tex.'

I heard my mother's voice bounce through the wall as she thanked Tex for bringing me in and said that my father had now forbidden me to ride so I wouldn't be seeing Tex again.

When my father brought me home my mother was still not satisfied. She made sure my friendship with Tex was dead. 'If I ever see you even talking to that half-and-half I'll call the police. Do you hear me?'

I nodded.

'Good. Because I'll get it into serious trouble. You're under age, girl. Do you understand me?'

'Under age? We went out riding. What the hell are you suggesting?'

'You know quite well what I mean, and I mean you keep away from that thing or I'll get it into trouble.' I was horrified and fled to my room. My father said nothing.

I lay on the bed. I couldn't believe what I had heard. 'The vindictive shrew,' I thought. I knew my mother could be bigoted, but this was beyond me! I knew if I remained friends with Tex my mother would get her into trouble. Woe betide anyone my mother didn't like.

I knew it was the end of our friendship but my mother, never one to allow any incident concerning me to rest, prolonged the drama. I'd walk into a room and, if there were people present or not, she'd start. She'd raise her glass and say, 'Have you got any decent friends yet?' I'd walk past.

'Riding! Little bitch said she was going riding. I bet she was!' The men with her would laugh. My father would sit in pain and drink. If I answered back my mother would get into the full swing of her abuse until I had to run from the room or engage in a screaming match which only ended when she shrilled that she would have me locked away.

One time we were alone and she started. I tried to leave the room but she grabbed me by the arm and leant down, screaming abuse at me.

I yelled, 'Shut up, shut up!' I threw my arms wide and my right hand smacked her in the mouth, side on. We both stopped dead and looked at each other, horrified for different reasons. She pulled out her top dental plate. It was broken in half.

'Look what you've done, look what you've done. You've broken my teeth. Your father will kill you!'

I grabbed the teeth from her hand and headed for the kitchen.

'Where are you going?' screamed my mother. 'Come back here; those are my teeth.'

I pulled the tube of Tarzan's Grip from the shelf, dodged my mother and raced back into the other room, putting the table between us.

'I'm mending your teeth,' I yelled.

'You're what! Give me my teeth. Your father will bloody well kill you. Hit your mother, will you. Tramp! You hit your mother, you little trollop. Whore, slut, garbage. You hit your mother. He'll kill you.' Meanwhile, we're circling the table and she's also looking for something to throw at me.

My father kill me? Ha! I could remember both the occasions when my father had belted me, and both times it was after I had sworn at him angrily.

It was difficult to run the liquid glue up the sides of the teeth, join the pieces together and hold them tight so the glue would set, while dancing the table get-away waltz.

'Stand still, bugger you! Stand still and let me hit you,' said my frustrated mother.

'Bugger off or sit down. I'm mending your teeth.'

Finally I put the teeth down and leapt for the front door. As I crashed into freedom my mother charged out after me; then, as in a cartoon, came screeching to a halt, did a very fast turn around and was back inside before I could blink. A man friend of hers was coming up the path carrying a flagon of wine.

'Hello,' I said, happy to have escaped my mother.

'Gidday.' The man strode past and banged on the door. 'You there, Margaret?'

My mother opened the door with a full set of smiling teeth.

If she told my father then he never told me he knew. The teeth were not mentioned again for thirty years when my mother rang to tell me she had just bought a new set of teeth. The teeth had worn out but the Tarzan's Grip was still holding. I suggested she send the old ones to the manufacturer of Tarzan's Grip.

I was back to having no horses. I frequented the racetrack where trotters, pacers and gallopers were stabled. I started by just hanging around, then grooming horses, then riding track work. Sometimes I'd drive horses on the track in a work-out. I began to know the men and all their connections. They loved their horses but they loved to win too!

School was not going well. I was still spending time in the library. On my half-day I rode track work. I loved the feeling of flying with the horse as part of my very being, the pounding of the hooves, the pumping of the heart, the flare of the nostrils. Living, breathing and racing.

My father was not recovering easily from a hernia operation and he was ill, all his fight fading. He stopped arguing with my mother. When I challenged him he'd reply, 'It's easier to go along with her, Skeeter.'

'You're crook, Dad.'

'I am.'

We'd sit together with the dog around a fire in the backyard, the billy singing.

My mother was pregnant and wanting to keep the child even though she had, at my nana's wedding, offered the child to my Auntie Julie who refused it. My father had told me that the child to be born was not his; that he had not 'been with' my mother in months. In fact he was so ill that sex seemed of very little interest to him. This situation came at a great cost to him for sex had bound him to my mother in a way I was yet to understand.

I believed what he said about the child, and I told him that she said it was his. His reply: 'Your mother couldn't lie straight in bed. Let her write what she wants on the birth certificate — I don't really care any more.'

We both cried.

Jillaroo

I turned fourteen years of age.

My mother took me with her to the employment centre. There she met with the truant officer and they entered the stone building together, leaving me to sit and wait on the hot, concrete steps outside while they decided my fate. Working men kept coming and going, in and out of the building. They looked dusty and poor, their spirits low. Many had hands that shook.

Finally my mother, looking like a hothouse flower, came out, followed by the truant officer. She waved a piece of paper under my nose.

'There, girl! This piece of paper says you can leave school and go to work and that's exactly what you are going to do. It's all sorted out. I've cooked your smart little goose for you.'

My mother told me that she'd organised a job for me as a jillaroo, a companion on an outback sheepstation. I was to be paid three pounds a week and my keep. She expected that I would send some, if not all, of that money back to her so she could look after my father. (I thought, 'She must be bloody kidding. Three pounds a week! That money is for books, not booze!')

My mother went with the truant officer to the pub to celebrate.

I walked the five miles home.

My father woke me before dawn the next morning. With Bozo, we walked into the city centre where a big blue and silver bus stood waiting. It was to offload me in Port Augusta where I'd catch the mail-run car, which would take me out to the station I was to work on. Just as my father was saying goodbye, a taxi pulled in and out hopped my mother and the truant officer.

'I've just come to make sure that you really get on that bus.'

I turned away from her smirking smile, hugged my father and climbed on board. My mother and the truant officer climbed back into the cab and drove away, leaving my sick father to walk home with the dog. My eyes filled with tears. His spirit people seemed insubstantial; I knew he was dying. I didn't know that would be the last time I saw him alive.

Daylight exploded into blue heat as the bus left Whyalla. I cried all the way to Port Augusta. It was breakfast time when the bus stopped at the post office. Mail and parcels were exchanged and I stood with my belongings on the warming pavement. A battered white ute was the only other vehicle in the yard.

A short white man, as tall as he was wide, introduced himself and told me he was the mailman and would be taking me out to Yudnapinna Station.

'You must be the new girl for the Willmotts,' he said. 'Ya had breakfast? No. Well get in and I'll stop at the roadhouse so you can grab something. A couple of the roadhouses around here are open all night for the truckies. Best food. Always stop where you see trucks and you'll get a decent meal. Big steak, lots of eggs, big burgers. Good tucker.' While he talked he threw boxes and bags into the back of the ute. I threw my bag in. It contained all I owned except Bozo. A change of clothes, a jumper, pyjamas belonging to my father and my rifle. Two blankets were my bag.

The mail-run delivered mail, groceries and any other requirements to the stations and out-stations. The mail-run was vital to people living in the bush and the mailman was a gossip. He knew everyone and they knew him.

We stopped at the roadhouse for a can of Coke and a burger for my breakfast. I bought some sandwiches for lunch as I had noted a large plastic container of food and two thermos flasks on the front seat.

We went from station homestead to station homestead,

delivering. In each place I was introduced as 'the Willmotts' new girl'. I stayed in the ute and hardly spoke.

The mailman stopped for morning and afternoon tea. We demolished cakes and tea, sitting under a shady tree. The day was alive with heat. Lunch was eaten as we drove.

The mailman still had the plastic covers on his car seats and my skin crinkled and stuck to that plastic like chewing gum. He noticed my discomfort.

'Well, I told the missus I'd keep the inside clean.' He grinned. 'She said the last ute I had wasn't even fit for the dogs, so this time at least I've got a clean seat.' I laughed. My legs were ankle-deep in papers, tins and rubbish.

I told the mailman, 'I had a guardian called Bea Bennett who kept the plastic over her car seats and lounge. She said that I was such a dirty little guttersnipe I'd probably spread disease if she didn't have all her stuff covered.'

The mailman looked at me. 'A real nice, kind sort of woman, eh!' We both laughed.

But I was bewildered. Work! Yesterday I was at school, arguing with my mother and trying to care for my father. I didn't mind working. My play, such as yabbying, was also work, and I had worked on farms with my father. Working was part of existing. But now work had become my way of life. There was no home, no father, no school.

The land we drove through was dry and scrubby. Lots of salt-bush and bluebush. There were sheep everywhere, their wool the colour of the land. Bred for meat, they looked skinny and dry. There were rocky outcrops where wallabies scaled walls and bounced from rock to rock. I watched kangaroos bounce away into the bush, camouflaged in seconds, and the emus ran the fence lines like athletes in a marathon.

I saw brumbies galloping along ridges and up dry waterways. A proud stallion stood silhouetted by the sun. He was a horse from a picture book. The mailman said, 'Isn't he a beauty? All stallion. The owner of this place bought him for a fantastic sum and set him free. He'll improve the blood lines of the brumby. Give them some blood and bone. The owner next-door put an

Arabian stallion into his stock. Bejesus, those offspring are all beautiful — like fire to ride. But he says the buggers will work all day.'

Late that afternoon we bounced the ute over a rough gate-grid with such force that my teeth rattled. The sign on the gate read, 'Yudnapinna Station'. For miles we drove along a dusty track, then a huge red dam came into view, towering next to it the largest windmill I had ever seen. Beyond that were smaller towers with two wide blades rattling in the wind. Wind power that drove generators so the houses had thirty-two-volt electricity.

The main-station was ringed with holding yards, and a large homestead had a green garden surrounding it. I could see bunkhouses and a cookhouse. There were sheds and several smaller houses — none had gardens. Big open sheds held equipment and utes. Everything was built in galvanised iron. I smiled when passing the owner's homestead. It was stone.

The mailman saw me looking. 'The owner's in Adelaide. A manager runs this place. He lives there. The owner comes up once a year. You'll find the manager fair, but I guess you won't have much to do with him, being on an out-station.'

We pulled up beside a tin shed with a sign 'Store' painted in white on the corrugated iron. The mailman said that the store opened when anyone needed anything — tinned food, tobacco, wide-brimmed hats, boots, pocketknives, toothpaste or bullets.

The stores, mail and I were left on the small verandah. I sat and looked around. Dogs were tied up on chains everywhere. A drum for a kennel, a hessian bag for a bed and a large tin of water. Working dogs. Mostly kelpie, a few cross-breeds. They lay panting in the dirt. Flies droned their presence in the hot air around my face. 'Persistent little buggers,' my father would have said. I wondered how he was. Probably drowning his sorrows in a flagon of red.

I sighed and stood up. Stretching, I wandered around the open sheds, looking in, talking to dogs but not patting them. My father taught me not to pat working dogs unless the owner gave permission. 'Men don't like their working dogs fondled. They reckon it spoils the dog. Bloody nonsense but there you go — some mean-spirited bastard gets a queer idea and like sheep the other bastards follow. Always talk to the dog; they recognise kindness in your voice.'

I returned to my swag and sat down. I felt like crying.

A battered old Land Rover came roaring into the yard and pulled up in a cloud of dust.

'You for the Willmotts?' asked the old man at the wheel. 'Throw your swag and all that Willmott stuff into the back and we'll be on our way.' I climbed in. There were no doors. The seats were uneven, the windscreen patterned with cracks, and talking was impossible over the roar of the engine.

The ride to the Wilmotts' out-station was bone-jarring and it was a relief to climb out to open and shut gates. I was bounced from seat to dashboard to open door, and it was only by hanging on to the thick safety handle under the windscreen that I avoided being thrown out.

I kept taking side looks at the old man. He was old. Very old. His hair was white and white stubble covered most of his face. His hands were those of a working man — knotted, scarred and heavy. He was built like my father, 'nuggety'. He wore faded, well-washed clothes. I looked down. His old boots were dusty but polished. My father valued men who cleaned their shoes. He used to say, 'Take pride in yourself. Just because we're poor doesn't mean we're dirty. All you need is one bucket of water to give you and your clothes a wash. Do your hair and clean your boots. Keep your dignity and self-respect. You can tell a fella by his boots.'

The old fella at the wheel suddenly turned to me and roared, 'We're nearly there.' The old man's eyes were opaque. He was blind! I sat there stunned.

'He couldn't be completely blind,' my mind told me. 'He's driving.' If you could call it driving. We travelled slowly and erratically from one side of the road to the other. The wheels would hit the bank on one side of the road and the old man would pull the car over until it bumped the other verge. Branches caught the sides of the vehicle and a couple of times I had to duck. I thought this was because the old Land Rover was so old and heavy. I became terrified.

'Last gate,' yelled the old man.

'He must be able to see,' I thought. 'A little at least, because he called every gate.'

'Home paddock,' yelled the old man into my ear as we side-swiped another branch.

'Just keep your eyes on the road,' I yelled, and the old man burst out laughing.

The home, or house paddock was five miles by five miles in size — considered small. A corrugated iron house, surrounded on three sides by a sagging verandah, came into view. A fence surrounded the dusty house garden which consisted of two rain-water tanks and a huge green pepper tree. There was a small tin shed used as a washhouse, a large open tin shed for farm equipment, a chook shed surrounded by a high wire fence and, standing proudly on the small hill sheltering it all, the 'dunny' with its door facing the house.

There were several dogs, tied to metal drums, all barking furiously as we shuddered to a halt.

A tall, dark-haired man in overalls came out of the shadow of the house, calling, 'Gidday. Are you the new girl for us?' He was followed by a small, skinny woman in a faded print dress and bare feet. Her blonde hair hung down to her shoulders in a straggly mane. She carried a small boy on her hip and a cigarette drooped from her mouth. 'I'm Sandra and this here's Wayne. And (nodding towards the man) he's Brian.'

To me they both looked old. They were probably in their twenties.

'Mrs Willmott,' I managed to squeak.

'Nope, Sandra and Brian. Now come on in. Kettle's on.'

I liked them all immediately. Open and friendly.

'What you see is what you get,' Sandra would say. It was her expression for everything. Brian had a long, slow smile and he was naturally a slow, quiet man with a wonderful sense of humour. He always looked as if he were concentrating. 'What ya can't fix with string or wire, forget it,' was his motto. 'Use a nail in an emergency.' Sandra was the talker. She loved company and was starved for the company of women; even though I was only a girl she treated me as an equal. Never once did I feel less than part of that family. Never once did either of them make me feel as if I were employed to do a job. Sandra had a natural gusto which made her enjoy her life. Wayne, their son, was a happy two-year-old who babbled away and explored his world with delight.

The iron house was relatively cool even though a wood stove was the source of heat for cooking. As we drank tea and Sandra riffled through the mail, Brian talked of making an emu-feather fan for the ceiling

'I saw a picture of one in a book. It looked bonza. A huge fan made of feathers. You pulled a rope and it waved across the room.'

'Yeah,' interrupted Sandra, 'and you'd have Wayne here pullin' that bloody rope all day — unless that employment service could send us a rope-puller too.' She burst out laughing.

The kitchen held the black wood stove, sink, cupboards with wire mesh at each end and a big laminex-covered table that stood in tins of water to keep the ants from climbing up. It was surrounded by old wooden school chairs with hard seats and chrome chairs with the stuffing leaking out of their padded seats and backs. A bottle of sauce and a kerosene light stood on the table.

The place, called, 'Five Mile' because it was five miles to the nearest dam and its home paddock stretched five miles in all directions, had a wind generator for power but this usually didn't work. Brian was not too clever in maintaining it and it was far too temperamental for Sandra or me to understand. When it was working we had soft yellow light of an evening for two hours! So kero lamps of all descriptions were needed — or candles. During my stay Brian decided to modernise the power and he bought an old diesel motor which powered a generator and gave us a longer soft yellow glow at night. It was housed in the metal shed and when running sounded like World War III. After a week of diesel power Brian turned it off. The noise gave him a headache. Sandra and I had been threatening to throw a spanner at it and worse. It made such a din that it shattered the peace and made

Sandra scream, 'If I wanted to live next-door to a bloody railway line I would be living in the city.'

Brian tried to quieten it with bags but it overheated and stopped. We moved it out under a tree and the dogs howled in accompaniment. We stayed with the wind power and kero.

The fridge also ran on kero and it sat in the small entrance-way belching black smoke and 'odour de kero'. 'Shut the bloody door and don't let the fridge in,' Sandra would yell to anyone entering the kitchen. Caring for that fridge was also a delicate operation. To get it to run cool, you had to keep it alight without smoking and make sure the door was firmly shut. It never ran cold — never cold enough for ice-cream. A hessian water bag swinging on the verandah kept the drinking water cooler. The telephone on the wall was in the same area as the fridge which nearly asphyxiated anyone talking on the phone.

The telephone we used can only be found in antique shops now and, unless converted with a dial on the front, these beautiful pieces are no longer practical in today's de-personalised technology. This was the time of people-operated telephone exchanges, when the operator was a true gossip. Like the bread man in the city she knitted a community together.

We would crank the telephone to alert the exchange that we needed help, usually to be connected to local towns or cities. If we wanted other homes on our line, then we knew how many rings would bring them to answer our call. Our signal was two short, two long, two short. We knew the exchange operator listened to the calls going through her area — we could hear her breathing and the occasional cough. Other people along the line would listen in as well. But the kero fridge stopped any of the 'Five Mile' lot from eavesdropping!

When the phone bell rang all conversation would stop and everyone counted the rings.

If we weren't wanted we would continue our conversation. If the call was for one of us, the silence continued as we all listened in to hear what the call was about. If we were outside and didn't hear the telephone, then the operator was like an answering machine — she took a message. Sometimes one would be talking on the phone with several people listening in and giving advice!

The telephone ringing late at night or early in the morning was like receiving a telegram — you always feared it brought bad tidings.

We had a large lounge room with board floors polished a honey colour and a large unused fireplace. There was a lounge and big comfortable chairs — the house dogs slept on these. Wayne's cot was also in this room, and the ironing board someone had given as a wedding present held nappies, pins, powder and all sorts of baby needs. Any ironing was done on the kitchen table. Our irons were black metal, heavy and hot-handled when heated. Sandra did invest in a new iron while I lived with them but it scared the hell out of me and I refused to use it. It had to be pumped up to achieve pressure and heat. I hated it and, as with pressure cookers, I always imagined it exploding. It never did but the pressure cooker did and we had long strings of lamb dripping grease from the ceiling. The lounge room also had kangaroo skins scattered across the floor and flower-print cotton curtains at the windows.

Sandra and Brian's room held a big, double wooden bed, huge looming wardrobe and a wooden dressing-table. My room was the sleepout, holding a skinny wardrobe, table and single bed adorned with a blue candlewick bedspread. The windows had wooden shutters that opened out. One night I had a dreadful fright in the early hours of the morning. I awoke to feel a hot breath travelling up and down my body. I froze. Rigid. I couldn't scream or move. I was terrified and it was so dark that I couldn't see. In my head I was calling for help but my voice would not work. Up and down, up and down, went the hot breath. Then the breath snorted and I nearly passed out. Reality banished all the gruesome scenarios in my mind and I laughed with the explosion of relief. The horse that had come into the house yard and put his head through my window was startled and threw himself back, banging his head on the wooden window frame and snorting with surprise.

'Bugger,' I thought. 'The house gate must be open.' It was far too dark to go hunting for horses and in the stampede that would surely follow I'd only wake the household, including the dogs; the whole performance would turn into farce. While I was thinking this and relieving myself outside, I became aware of being watched. I looked up, straight into the eyes of a big red kangaroo who was gazing down at me and scratching his belly. I shrieked and bolted inside. At breakfast the next morning Brian handed me my pyjama bottoms. In my fright I had leapt out of them and left them on the ground.

The bathroom was one of my favourite places because of the size of the old enamel bath. It was huge, like a small swimming pool on legs. Long, wide and very deep. Water was boiled by an incredibly efficient chip heater. I'd fill up that bath and lie up to my chin in steaming bubbles of perfume. Sandra adored bubble bath and we had bottles of the stuff stacked in every corner of the room. Every time she hit a town or city she'd head for the chemist or Coles. The bottles came in all shapes and sizes, colours and perfumes. It would have been worth the drive to our place for any Avon lady with her fancy bottles.

My job was station work, housework and company. On weekdays I rose at dawn when the sky took on the colours of the galah. I'd light the kitchen fire and put on the kettle. Then my job was to lay the table for breakfast and prepare the porridge. Also bring out any bread ready for toast and make up the day's milk from powder. While all was cooking I'd race outside, feed and water the chooks and dogs, have a quick face-and-hands wash, clean my teeth and be back inside just as the kettle started to boil for tea. I'd also make sandwiches if Brian or myself were to be away at lunchtime. At the weekends we had fried eggs for breakfast and could take a little more time around the table. Sugar was heaped into everything. If a food couldn't be sugared then it was heavily salted. We had tea with every meal. As a special treat after Sandra and I had struggled with the washing, or Brian and I had finished some repair job, we would have coffee made from bottled coffee essence. I'd lace mine with sugar and it was like sweet tar.

My other housework jobs were sweeping and washing the floors and helping with the laundry. Sandra and I both hated that chore. Boil up the copper, cook the clothes, scrub them, rinse them, hang them out. It was hot, heavy work, and farming clothes are built tough and rough. I also collected wood chips, cut wood, fed the dogs and chickens, made sure all animals had water and went for long walks with Sandra pushing Wayne in his pram. Out of doors I'd help Brian dress a killed sheep or kangaroo and I was expected to bring home my quota of rabbits. Which wasn't hard as our hill was a minefield of warrens. I'd sit up there at dusk and each bullet meant one dead rabbit. It was as though the bunnies had decided some should die because I'd be shooting away and after a time they would just keep grazing. I began to feel very guilty and started to hunt the bush for rabbits with a wilder streak of survival in them.

It was part of my job to help during crutching and shearing, to help with any station maintenance that was needed and to be able to drive anything! I could drive a car and a tractor.

'Can you ride a motor bike?' asked Brian.

'No.'

'I'll teach you and then all you'll have to do is practise.'

So he taught me how to fill the bike with petrol and oil, how to start it, what the gears and throttle did and how the brakes worked. Then he left me to it.

'You'll be righto. It's like a pushbike to balance but you don't have to pedal.'

My pushbike had never gone so fast. I roared around the house paddock in straight lines. Then I travelled the dirt tracks with over-confidence. I skidded around corners and into banks. For a while I was off the bike more than on. I took bends too fast and found my body flying in a different direction from the bike. Battered, bruised and with a sore ego I hobbled around.

'I prefer horse,' I groaned.

'Not some of the bastards I've had to ride,' grinned Brian.

The first time Brian took me with him into the main-station there was a mustering of sheep and we went to help.

'Can you ride?' asked the overseer.

'Yes,' I replied. 'I've been riding for years.'

'Good. Jump up on that grey there and let's go.'

A beautiful dapple grey stood saddled and waiting. I placed my foot in the stirrup and as my bum hit the saddle I knew something was up. All the men had stopped working and were watching me. The horse went rigid under me. My mind yelled, 'Get off!' The back arched, the head went down between her legs and she bucked hard. I flew from the saddle into the dirt. Laughter followed me, the men returned to their work. I was initiated!

'What if I'd said I could only ride a little?' I asked Brian.

'Then they would have given you the bay. She bucks slower and the fall isn't as hard.'

Baptising new workers was traditional. I was a new worker and there were all sorts of different christenings, as I found out. I'd had the horse-baptism but not the blood one. The most important. To be blooded.

I was helping to bring in a mob of young steers to be branded and castrated. We were moving the stock through the chutes to the accompaniment of yelling men and cattle, screams of pain, barking dogs and flying dust. As I leant against a rail, taking my hat from my head to wipe away some of the grime, four big hands grabbed me, dragged me into the circle of men and cattle and wiped my face with a bloodied pair of bull's testicles. I swore and spluttered. The men all laughed.

Brian said, 'You're lucky, the last jackaroo was branded!'

'What else do I have to expect?'

'I reckon that's about it.' He laughed. 'But ya never know.'

I kept practising on the bike until I felt I was a fairly reasonable rider so long as I didn't try to be a hoon and speed! It was certainly quicker to check the fence lines, tanks and troughs by bike. With a horse I would have been out for days.

The day before I was to begin my fence run I rode down to our dam. It was of rich red dirt and I would often go down there at dusk to watch all the animals and birds that came to drink. The bird life in that place was amazing — so varied and colourful. But this day when I arrived like a volley of exploding fireworks, there were no birds to be seen, just Sandra and Wayne having a quiet moment on the side of the dam. I rode up to them like a bronco rider, too big for his boots, and sat there revving up the engine while holding the bike still with the brake. I thought I was very smart and cool. Rev, rev, rev.

'For Christsake turn that bloody bike off,' screamed Sandra above the din. I gave the bike a huge last rev and let out the clutch, presuming it was in neutral. It wasn't. It was in gear. I roared straight down the slope and into the dam! Sandra stood laughing until the tears ran down her face.

I could only laugh at my own stupidity. We dragged the water-sodden bike from the dam and I pushed it home. Brian wasn't too amused. I had to clean out all the mud and water under his instructions until it was as good as new. And it was. It was sparkling clean for the first time since it was new. But afterwards, whenever that bike played up, Brian would comment, 'Never been the same since you tried to wash it in the dam!'

My driving improved and I enjoyed the time I spent travelling the fence line and checking dams, tanks, windmills and troughs. I checked the sheep too, though I dreaded the fly-blown bums I had to clean and clip around. I also dreaded climbing windmills. I have a fear of being high up on a structure that sways. If I heard a faulty windmill I'd report it to Brian.

'Take a spanner and have a look what's wrong with it.'

'I can't. It scares me.'

'Best way to overcome it then.'

'I can live with some of my fears.'

He'd just laugh and go up the windmill himself.

Fire and flood

One day Brian came running down from the hill at the back of the house, yelling, 'Fire, fire!'

The phone was ringing and we could see black clouds on the horizon. The message on the phone was that the fire would probably pass us by, but we should be ready to get out. The car was brought to the front of the house and loaded. Brian roared away on the motor bike and returned, herding the workhorses before him. Sheep followed through the opened gates. We locked the horses in the yards, locked the chooks up and tied all the dogs around the car in preparation. Brian brought out the old ute and we filled a tank on the back with water. Water drums were placed on a trailer behind and heavy metal knapsacks filled. We could smell the fire.

'Come on,' yelled Brian. 'Let's make sure it misses us.'

Wayne was shut in the house with a couple of dogs for company and away we drove to meet the fire. We heard it, smelt it, and saw it. A wall of flame.

'Shit, I'm going to die,' I thought. 'Brian had to be kidding. Fight that!'

He strapped a water container on my back, showed me how to pump it and gave me a push towards the fence. Sheep were streaming through the gates. We fought the fire along the fence line and although we were on the very edge it felt as if we were in an inferno.

We kept filling our packs all afternoon, Sandra returned to fill the tanks with water, check on Wayne and returned to continue fighting.

The wind kept the fire from our home paddock but it licked along the fenceline and we sprayed it frantically.

'Don't be a hero,' yelled Brian. 'If it looks like turning — if that wind changes even slightly — we're outa here. Got that?'

The sheep kept coming through and many were smoking. We now used the water on them. A few staggered in, badly burnt, and dropped. Brian shot them. Then no more sheep came through. We fought on.

By evening the fire was moving slowly away from us. We jumped in the ute and travelled the fenceline down to where it threatened to swing around. It roared along like a huge red train. I was terrified. The three of us fought on, to keep it back.

It was dawn when I next became aware of myself. We were black and beyond tiredness. The fire was heading away from us. We dropped where we were and slept. I awoke to find Sandra and Wayne prodding me. They had breakfast ready. Fried eggs and onions between huge slabs of bread.

We put out small spot fires all day and tried to rescue burning trees. We could still hear the fire roaring. At dusk we returned home. The verandah was alive with lizards, sheep and exhausted birds. I noticed snakes lying on the steps. All creatures seemed exhausted and I was well and truly buggered. My hair was singed and my boots smelt of charcoal. Brian went on the phone to report. He managed to get through to our neighbours but not the main station. I fell into bed. My face and hands were clean.

The next morning we ate porridge before dawn and at first light we were out fighting the fire once again. This time we were following it and once again putting out trees that were alight and small spot fires. We lived on fried egg sandwiches and sweet tea.

The fire roared into the distance until we could no longer hear it. All around us was burning or black. The smell was over-powering but the danger had gone. It had come close. It was five miles from our house to the gate where we had started fighting on the edge of that raging inferno.

That evening Brian fed the sheep while I released the horses. If we had been forced to flee, we would have had to set them free to take their chance. After a meal we sat on the front verandah. The reptiles had vacated it but exhausted birds still leaned into the tins of water we had given them, and weary sheep lay panting around us. 'That was bloody close,' said Brian. 'A whisker away.'

'Too bloody close,' said Sandra. 'Never again, Brian. Never again will I let us be that close. It was too dangerous.'

'Well, we survived.'

I just stared at him, too weary to react. I slept where I sat.

The next day I took the bike, Brian the ute and Sandra the tractor. We loaded up with water and bullets. Brian allocated us paddocks. We shot burnt and injured birds and animals. I cried and spewed, cried and spewed.

Never again could I stand the smell of a barbecue. We cleaned out tanks and water troughs and noted down all that needed replacing. We pulled dead, bloated animals out of dams. We wrapped hessian around our boots to help save them but I still burnt holes in the soles of my boots.

'We'll get you a good pair of boots in return,' said Sandra.

I was saving for a coveted pair of R.M. Williams boots. This was not the way I expected to get them. But I thanked her and we selected a pair for each of us from the mail-order catalogue.

Dying and burnt animals, smouldering logs and trees, hot twisted metal and blistering days greeted us. Day after day we cleaned up. We collected hay from the main station and fed those sheep which survived. Brian rang a head count through to the boss and he promised more sheep would be sent to replace those which had died. We had heavy losses. The fences would have to be repaired first, then troughs and windmills replaced or repaired. Brian whistled when he added up the cost. 'Jeeeesus,' was what he said. He could not describe the level of destruction the fire had caused. Talk went on for months about how it could possibly have come about.

'It was human error,' said Sandra. 'Probably a camp fire.'

Brian snorted. 'Yeah. A bloody big one.'

'I think it was deliberate,' said Peter, a jackaroo who had come to visit.

We looked at him blankly. We couldn't at that stage understand why anyone would want to light a fire that caused so much destruction. That sort of realisation came later.

I now had time to lie in the bath at last. Sandra complained that I was using all the bubble bath so we selected a big range of fragrances and fancy bottles from the mail-order catalogue and sent the order off. When the goods arrived they were different colours but they all smelt the same!

Dark clouds rolled across the sky.

'Shit. That's all we need — a downpour.' Brian scanned the sky.

'I thought you'd be pleased,' I said.

'Yeah, but you just mark my bloody words. It will now bloody flood. We'll end up like what's-his-bloody-name in the ark — stranded.' As he spoke the thunder rumbled and the sky went black.

Brian ran for the motor bike and took off towards the main station. He arrived back well after dark, soaked to the skin. We had waited up for him.

'The creeks are up. She's pouring up north. We're in for a flood.'

He had returned with stores to help us through — tins of meat and baked beans, flour, sugar and tea.

It poured all night, a ceaseless drumming on the roof.

It rained and rained. For days we sat on the verandah, watching the rain. Sandra and I had placed plenty of wood in the shed so we could cook food and boil water. The phone went dead. Still it rained. The land couldn't hold the water. It flooded. The water ran black from soot, then red with mud, then brown with rock and clay. Finally it eased into a fine rain and we could slosh our way around.

We had caught the horses and they were tethered in the big shed; they would have been up to their knees in water in their yards. When the level dropped to shoe depth we started work. We rode out to see the damage.

It was another world. A world of water. The earth was water-logged and running. We pulled corpses from waterways and dams. We could not get out and no one could get in.

The fine rain continued. 'It's like that bloody forty days and forty nights,' complained Brian.

'I didn't realise you knew the Bible so well,' commented Sandra.

'I remember my old gran's stories, and we had to do that stuff at school and go to church on Sundays,' Brian answered. 'We have to do something about him too,' he added, nodding towards Wayne.

'Wadda ya mean?' asked Sandra.

'So he doesn't go to hell and all that. You know. Dip him in water.'

Sandra was laughing. 'Christening.'

'Yeah.'

'How're you going to get him done out here? We don't even have a visiting priest.'

'We'll have to get him fixed up in town.'

'It sounds like a sheep you're castrating,' laughed Sandra. 'What do you want him done as?'

'What do you mean?'

'What religion?'

'I dunno. Catholic? No, no, Church of England. No, no, you're not that. What are you again?'

I left them discussing Wayne's possible christening and went to make tea. We were getting low on wood and drying it in the oven now. I thought, 'Wayne will have to wait unless they just dunk him in the water outside,' and I started to laugh. I then suggested to Brian that we dip him in the creek, and Sandra fell around laughing, but Brian said we were both 'sacrilegious' and that he was going to bed! He huffed away with all his feathers ruffled. We kept laughing.

It kept raining. Then the rain suddenly stopped and the sky

turned blue. Water turned to mud — thick mud. Still we were stranded.

It was extremely hard to ride. Brian ranted and raved at some invisible God.

'Oh well,' said Sandra, 'it will stop him thinking about getting little Wayne christened. He's too upset with God now. We might as well wait until we've got a few kids and have them all done at once. It would be cheaper.'

Sandra was pregnant.

'Nothing bloody well fazes her when she's like that — in that condition. The bloody sky could fall in and it wouldn't worry her,' raved Brian. He was out of tobacco.

Our stores were running low. We ran out of tea and sugar. We could still shoot rabbits. We had rabbit fried, baked, boiled, stewed.

'I'm beginning to look like a bloody rabbit,' complained Brian.

With the sun came mushrooms. We ate damper, mushrooms and rabbit. Wayne had powdered milk.

We had some custard powder so we mixed it up with powdered milk. From then on I gagged at the very thought of either.

Our diet left us with cravings. I wanted chocolate and a Coke. Sandra wanted tobacco, tea, Coke and a thickly sugared cream cake. Brian craved tea, chocolate and tobacco; Wayne, milk and a jam sandwich.

Brian's mood was really foul. 'I'm gunna walk to town,' he yelled at the sky. But town came to us in the form of a helicopter. I heard it before I saw it and called to the others. We raced up the side of the hill and waved and shouted. Then something was falling from the sky.

'Bejesus, they're bombing us,' yelled Brian and, grabbing Wayne, he ran towards the house. On the way he passed the toilet and ran in, banging the door.

'Bastards!' he yelled. 'What are they doing?'

I was scared, more by Brian's behaviour than the long silver cylinder that crashed into the soft earth. Sandra was sitting on the nearest rock, laughing so hard she was crying.

'Oh, my god, you should see your bloody faces!' she hic-cupped. 'It's food, you silly bastards.'

'Food!' Brian came out of the toilet. 'I knew that. I was just scared that the nipper here would be hit.'

Wayne was bawling by now. Sandra took him and laughed. 'It's all right, sweetheart. Your father panicked.'

'I never panic,' replied Brian, his dignity quickly returning.

The chopper did a big circle and we watched it retreat.

'Bombing!' giggled Sandra.

'I hope some bastard up there smokes,' said Brian as we made our way to the shiny cylinder. He broke the seal and undid the lid. We sat around that shiny cylinder in the mud and ate a loaf of fresh bread. We pulled that bread apart, grinning and stuffing it into our mouths.

Brian did a dance when he discovered tobacco. 'Hooray and beauty! Thanks to the bloody smoker!' Sandra joined him and they cavorted in the mud like happy children.

I went back to the house to get the wheelbarrow while they sat in the mud like two happy tortoises and had a smoke.

We had tea, sugar, flour, jam, tinned meat, onions, potatoes and a pumpkin. There were tins of vegetables, a jar of Vegemite and a big tin of powdered milk. Brian threw the tin of mush-rooms down the dunny.

It was the packets of jelly that made us excited. We made up three packets and waited anxiously for them to set. It was our big treat.

As soon as the earth could be safely ridden on Brian went out, following the telephone line. He returned, covered in mud. 'It was down all right, in bloody feet of slime, near that wide creek.' We had gone from soot to mud. Our clothes stood up by themselves, caked and baked in brown soil.

Then the paddocks exploded into colour. Green came, new shoots threw themselves into the wind and the air was full of song. Even with my fear of heights I climbed to the first ramp of a large windmill to see the view, and it was spectacular; I could see for miles. A paddock of yellow, another of blue, another of purple, another, red. I looked out on a giant patchwork of colour. Climbing down, I sat in acres of desert pea — a sea of red and black. After the devastating fires and the flooding rains the earth had come to new life in a colour show of stunning beauty.

A fencing team arrived; we cleaned out troughs and counted the sheep loss. We repaired gates and caught up on news via the telephone — who had lost what; what had happened to people and stock. The mail came through once again and it was funny to read in the national papers about war and politics but nothing about our fire or flood. This suggested to me that really most of what's happening in the world is irrelevant unless we are personally involved.

Brian and I would make sure we were in the vicinity of the fencing team for morning tea. Their cook made huge sultana cakes and, washing this down with mugs of sweet black tea, I felt I was living in paradise.

We took eggs to the cook and Sandra and I also did a couple of big loads of washing for the men. The day before they departed they gave us a huge sultana cake as a present.

'See, it all evens out between the seesaw and the swing,' said Sandra. My nana used to say the same.

A day in town

The Willmotts' family car was a huge, green Ford Customline, an American gangster car with running boards and suicide doors. It may have looked great in movies but this old girl had seen far better days. The front wheels leaned in because the wishbones were 'shot'. The two back doors were wired together across the back seat, the tension kept in the wire by a broken axe-handle strategically placed in the centre of the car. This stopped the back doors from flying open. The driver's door was welded on. It didn't quite meet in all places. A tree had originally removed it when Brian was chasing horses one day. Trying to round up a mob of brumbies in a huge gangster car may have been a good rustling story but it was not practical, and when Brian skidded into the tree and lost his door he just threw it into the boot until several weeks had passed and Sandra needed to go into town. The door was attached 'temporarily', never to come off or open again! The window didn't shut either. In fact, none of the windows would stay closed. They crashed down at the slightest movement. Only the front passenger door opened. The boot lid banged and its interior smelt of petrol and oil. We had to carry petrol, oil and water at all times. Every five miles or so we had to top up the water and oil. The old girl constantly boiled, and she guzzled oil. Under the bonnet a mechanic's nightmare was revealed. Everything was held together with wire and baling twine. The battery floated around on a construction of wire that made it look like something from science fiction. But the radio worked! We could get the ABC or a country-and-western station. Sandra would flick constantly between stations so she could hear both. I loved the wide running boards on each side of the car. I could stand outside and hang on — easy for opening gates.

To go anywhere in that car took planning. It took all day to go into town, some eighty miles (128 kilometres) away. Often we would stay the night in Port Augusta and come home next day rather than travel by dark. The lights were 'two piss-holes in the snow', according to Brian. Sandra preferred the phrase 'two candles in the snow', but Brian would say, 'My piss would give more light than that thing. We should get rid of it.' But we all liked it and its gangster image.

I loved to stay overnight in the town because Sandra would chose a local motel and that was an adventure to me. Until then I had never stayed in a motel but I had always wanted to. Travelling with my father in my childhood, we would pass motels and I'd want to go inside, shower and lie down on a clean bed. Now I had the chance and it was bliss! The motels Sandra chose were cheap but antiseptic clean with starched, stiff sheets, laminex-topped furniture and a toilet covered with paper that said it was now 'hygienic'. It had polished linoleum on the floors, cigarette stains on the furniture, venetian blinds that one could look out of yet not be seen, and an air-conditioner that rattled and groaned cool air into the room. Each bed would be covered in a soft chenille bedspread and we'd carefully fold the cover back to the end of the bed to keep it clean.

Breakfast would be brought to the door on a tray. Glutinous fried eggs and hard bacon, or tinned spaghetti on toast. Extra toast would be wrapped in a paper napkin, and little pats of butter would glisten in a small dish. We were excited when we received small individual containers of jam or Vegemite, and fruit juice — orange or pineapple — was a big treat for us. We could make tea or coffee in the room but the silver pots that came with breakfast had a brew inside that stood our hair on end!

I'd stand under the hot shower until I wrinkled.

It was all luxury for us!

One afternoon as we headed home to the station we decided to stop at the last milk bar and treat ourselves to a big cold milkshake. After our treat we piled Wayne and the dogs back into the car, I slid behind the wheel. The car wouldn't start, even after much pumping of petrol and whirring of the starter motor. 'Ahh shit!' exclaimed Sandra. 'Buggered battery. I've been telling Brian that the old girl's got a battery problem. We musta left the radio on.' We had.

The car was loaded! Kid, dogs and groceries were packed into the back seat; the boot was crammed with horse feed, groceries, oil and sundries. The middle of the front seat and any available floor space was loaded as well. The weight made the wishbones groan even harder and the tyres spread out like an elephant trying to gain balance.

Out we climbed and lifted the bonnet.

'We'll have to push it,' said Sandra.

Push! It would be like pushing the *Titanic*! I peered into the mess of engine. Suddenly a voice said, 'Can I help you, ladies?'

Ladies! We knew only one sort of person would call us ladies! Ladies we did not resemble. I was dressed in well-worn jeans, boots, shirt and hat and looked all of twelve! Sandra was very pregnant, dressed in a faded flowered dress that hung low down at the back, and over her belly like a mini-skirt in the front; she wore thongs. Her blonde hair hung down to her shoulders and she had a 'rollie' hanging from her bottom lip.

We turned. Sure enough, the police. There he stood, clean and scrubbed and pink. All pimples and slicked back hair. 'Could you give us a push?' said Sandra, pulling out the axe-handle that held the hood up. The hood came crashing down, making us all jump. The copper's eyes had boggled at what he had seen of the engine. 'Flat battery,' she yelled at him as she opened the only door and shoved me behind the steering wheel. She was far too pregnant to fit behind the wheel.

'Get in, get in,' she hissed. I slid behind the wheel.

Wayne and the dogs were leaning out of the windows, the dogs barking at the copper and anyone who passed.

'Shut up!' yelled Sandra, adding, 'Excuse me' to the nice young policeman. She began to push the car. The copper woke suddenly, leapt to the back of the car and began to push. As we rolled, Sandra shouted, 'Gun 'er up, gun 'er up. Get the bloody old thing going, for Christsake!'

I bounced the old girl along in first gear and suddenly she exploded into life. Sandra leapt in, leaned out the window and yelled, 'We'll be right now, mate, thank you,' and we roared off. I looked back through the outside rear vision mirror. There stood that nice policeman in the middle of the road, shaking his head. The old girl had left her calling card, like a dog leaving piss on a tree; he was covered in black from our exhaust.

Sandra lit a smoke and leaned back. 'Jesus, that was a near miss, eh. We need a new bloody battery.'

We didn't go into town too often as the mailman brought us most of our requirements, ordered by catalogue or over the phone. On mail day our treat was always the fresh bread.

A day in town was a celebration. We always ate fish and chips, washed down with a Coke, and finished the outing with a cold milkshake. Sandra would buy cartons of tailor-made cigarettes and huge bags of lollies. Soft drink was loaded up and sugary cream cakes packed in for later.

We'd be chugging along when on would come the oil light, and the radiator would begin a familiar dance. We'd pull over under a tree, lift the bonnet and wait until the car cooled down. On the way out it was tea and sandwiches as we waited. On the way back it was cream cakes, soft drink and tobacco.

Emu

While the contractors were mending the fences after the flood, a team of surveyors arrived. They were joined by a young bushman who had an emu as a pet. He had raised the emu from a chick and it would follow humans around. When bored, which was frequently, it would entertain itself by getting into mischief. It explored packs and bed rolls, bags and food bundles. It also followed the surveyors around and pulled their precise pegs from the ground. They did not think this was funny. Their work was serious and this emu was making it a mockery. The emu had to go, but none of them was willing to kill it so the young bushman asked us if we'd take it. We did.

The emu was about half grown, cute and friendly with a huge sense of humour. He'd follow us, peering in through windows and doors. He lifted tools from the shed and we found them scattered across the yard. Brian was not too amused at this and tried to remember to put things away after he had used them. Things went missing — spanners, shoes, car keys — and Wayne found them in the emu's nest; that made us think that maybe he was a she. The thieving began to be a nuisance. Then our pet emu began to chase the dogs and the poultry, and tried to lord it over the horses who were not too keen on having a whirling dervish come at them in a whirlwind of feathers. After Brian had

been thrown a couple of times he ordered the emu to be confined in the stockyards but Wayne said it cried and he let it out.

The crunch came after a morning of laundry. Sheets, rugs,
mats, clothes. Anything that could be cleaned by water and soap.
We had slaved in the tin shed, washing and wringing until the
lines groaned.

'There, it's done,' said Sandra proudly. We took a tea break.

Suddenly all the washing hit the ground. In slow motion, line
after line fell. Into the dirt. The emu came into view. Those big
feet trampled our work into the earth as he or she wove a dance
pattern that made Wayne clap his hands with joy. We sat trans-
fixed.

Sandra exploded, leaving the verandah in a volley of oaths
that would have turned a sailor's head. Like a banshee, she covered the ground in seconds. She grabbed that emu around the
neck and started shaking it. I pulled her off before she killed it.
She sat in the dirt and howled. I pushed and pulled the bird into
the hens' house and locked the door.

When Brian returned late that afternoon we were still re-
washing the washing. One look at Sandra's face and he left us to
our work. Wayne told him what happened.

The emu had to go.

It couldn't be put in the back of the ute or behind the
tractor, so it would have to travel inside the car. Getting a nearly
fully grown emu into a car is not easy. We had to organise a rope
around the car to hold the back doors on once Brian released the
tension which held them in place. The emu was reluctant to get
in the car despite his or her previous curiosity. We pushed and
shoved, trying to fold up the emu's legs, hold its neck, and not
let it get irate and bite us — all while the dogs were barking and
Brian was swearing.

'Bend the bloody legs, bend the bloody legs,' he yelled at
Sandra.

'I'll bloody well break the bastards,' yelled Sandra. We
heaved and pulled.

'I'll bloody well eat you,' yelled Brian to the emu and it
popped into the back of the car.

'We got it,' he yelled, and the emu jumped out the other side. Brian tied the door shut and we started again. He tied the emu's legs together and we'd lift it into the back seat. By now the emu was very cross and started to retaliate. We undid its legs.

'Bastard, bastard, bastard,' yelled Brian.

'Bastard,' yelled Wayne.

I went to the house and returned with a loaf of bread which I waved inside the car window at the emu. It took one look at its favourite food and leapt into the back of the car. Brian slammed the door into place while Sandra tied it on. We all climbed into the front seat, me feeding the emu small pieces of bread to keep it amused. We found a large gathering of emus two paddocks away and stopped. By then all the bread had been consumed and Brian was swearing as the emu tried to clean out his ears.

We released the emu. It came from the back of the car in an explosion of feathers. It stood rigid, looked at the emus, turned and leapt back in. Brian swore. We pulled and pushed to get it out of the car. We were now surrounded by emus who had come out of curiosity to watch the performance. Brian turned. 'Oh, Jesus Christ, we'll have all the bastards in the back seat next.'

That did it. We sat on the ground and laughed and laughed. Brian rolled a smoke and sat on the bonnet.

The emus began to call. Our emu popped out of the car, like a cork from a bottle, and ran into the mob. Brian sprang from the car bonnet. 'She must be a girl. Quick, get in!' We threw the doors into the back seat, scrambled into the car and roared off.

We never saw 'our girl' again.

But I did find an abandoned nest of emu eggs while out riding one day. I checked the area. No emus. The eggs were very cold. I knew an old Aboriginal man who carved emu eggs and I thought it would be a great gift for him. So I tucked my shirt into my jeans and carefully loaded the eggs inside my shirt front, next to my chest. I climbed back on the horse and headed for home, walking. All went well until the last gate. I bent down, opened the gate and gave it a push. It swung open and we went through. As the gate swung back I leant down to fasten it. The horse stepped sideways slightly and my fingers missed the gate and it slapped into the horse. This horse was well trained, but a bang on the bum was never tolerated. He bucked and I sailed into the air and came crashing down on my chest. The eggs exploded. They were months old!

The horse galloped for home. He couldn't stand the smell either! I gagged and spewed and staggered the five miles home, green and sick.

Sandra would not let me anywhere near the bathroom. I washed in the laundry and, with a hessian bag around me, lit the copper for an outside bath.

I couldn't eat eggs for about a year, and I never touched another deserted nest again!

Visitors of various kinds

Visitors from all walks of life came and went. We'd had the fencing contractors, hardworking men in singlets who belonged to the seasons that had weathered their bodies into bronze or burn. We had kangaroo-and goat-shooters — men who came in utes studded with lights and guns. Taciturn men in wide-brimmed salt-encrusted hats, with blood and gunpowder beneath their nails who considered themselves hunters, getting rid of pests whose meat and skins brought in the money they needed to live. Their lifestyle was quite different from the weekend shooters who came to kill for sport. The last would shoot anything that moved — dogs, horses, sheep. They'd leave campfires smouldering and beer bottles in shards around the camp, having used them for target practice. We often found water tanks dry, riddled with bullet holes. In dry country every drop of water is precious and to have it deliberately wasted would send Brian into a frenzy.

The 'roo shooters were professionals who took their work very seriously. They shot to kill and, if they maimed, the dogs would be sent in to complete the job. Feral goats were a big problem and one shooter always arrived with a refrigerated truck to hold all the meat he would shoot within a few days. We also had feral cattle on the property, but these were rounded up and trucked to market.

We had many surveyors visit — clean, neat men in new four-wheel drives. They talked of their 'outback experience'. One man brought his wife. She was not enjoying her outback experience. It was too hot and dry; she hated the flies, the endless screech of the galahs and the lack of water. He was concerned that she wasn't having a good time.

Too many of our visitors were inexperienced bush drivers. The people who came on government service were usually from the city. They drove new four-wheel drive vehicles and lacked experience in handling them. It was usually impossible to give them any advice. When a fifteen-year-old jillaroo began telling them about road conditions and where they should be careful, their eyes would glaze over as they dismissed me.

The town surveyor and his wife were not experienced in the bush though he tried to convince us that all his camping holidays had made him extremely knowledgeable about bush lore.

Brian muttered, 'Not another bloody one.' He called them 'boy scouts'. Brian would get the tractor ready. This bloke received lessons in managing his four-wheel drive and he proudly showed us his 'beauty'.

Feeling sorry for the woman, we directed the couple to a beautiful camping spot. It was a rocky outcrop with deep watering holes, some of which could be used for swimming, and the abundance of wildlife in the area was breathtaking. It was an oasis and we often went out there to camp at night. We'd swim, and boil the billy, and sleep beneath a canopy of stars close enough to touch. It was a special place and we treated it with respect and rarely told anyone about it.

'It's a place where Aboriginal people come to sing,' said Brian, 'and they have given us permission to use it.'

Anxious to get there, the man drove too fast. He came to a sandy bend, skidded, braked, left the road and crashed down into a dry creek bed. His wife fell forward, crashing her head into the dashboard and splitting her forehead, her eyes, nose and mouth. She collapsed into unconsciousness, blood pouring. The husband panicked. He left her unconscious and bleeding while he ran back along the track, screaming for help. The dogs heard him before we did. Sandra had to slap his face to stop his screaming long enough for us to understand him. He collapsed, yelling, 'She's dead, she's dead.'

Brian raced for the motor bike and screamed off in the direction of the accident. We followed in the old car and left the man sitting in the dirt crying, little Wayne giving him cups of water and patting him on the back.

Brian had pulled the woman from the car and sat her up when we arrived. We used our first-aid kit as best we could but the woman was badly injured and her eyes were glassy. She kept wanting to sleep so we walked her around. Blood seeped from beneath the bandages. Brian went to ring the main station while Sandra and I loaded the woman into the back of the car. One arm was broken and she said her back ached.

We drove fast but carefully. The husband was still sobbing in shock. Brian came running from the house, scooped up Wayne and threw him into the front seat. He hauled the man on to his feet and pushed him in with his wife.

'Shut up, ya bloody grizzlin' moron, and hold her head.' He turned to us. 'Get her to the main station. The flying doctor is on his way.'

We arrived at the main station before the flying doctor and helped the station hands remove rocks and sheep from the runway. The runway was kept pretty clear at all times but it was in a sheep paddock.

We heard the plane coming. 'Hooray,' breathed Sandra. 'She's pretty knocked up.'

They air-lifted the couple to the hospital at Port Augusta.

We towed the four-wheel drive from the creek and washed the blood out. We used that vehicle for weeks before we got a telephone call to let us know someone would be arriving on the mail-run to collect it and could we have it in at the main station. We had even taken that four-wheel drive into town and we were there and back in record time, not having to stay the night or play 'spot the copper and hide the car' games. The vehicle was scrubbed clean, ashtrays emptied, rubbish removed and no trace left of our having used it. Wayne picked up every piece of sheep's poo from the back! (It had been excellent for shifting stock.) Brian drove it to the main station and we followed in 'the old girl'.

An ill-humoured, officious public servant awaited us. He shook hands with Brian and turned his back on Sandra and me. Brian explained that we had saved the woman's life. The official walked to the car. 'They would have saved a dog's life just as willingly. That's what women do,' he said. 'Have you used this vehicle? — because if you have you will be charged.'

'Bugger off,' replied Brian and walked back to us.

We watched the official roar down the track away from the station. Brian said, 'Nice fellow. He should have had a good look at the fuel gauge, that bloke. He's gunna have a long walk.' Sure enough, about twenty miles along the track the vehicle ran out of fuel. The officious officer had no choice but to walk back to the main station. There he had to wait until a station hand could take him back to the car with the fuel for which he had to pay cash, from his own pocket. Because his rudeness had been noted, he was well charged for that fuel. When he complained, the jackaroo said, 'Well, mate, walk it, 'cause I ain't takin' ya shit. It doesn't work out here.'

Another time, four men arrived from the Museum of South Australia. Brian had found a sheep with a golden fleece.

We were all excited (all those on the party line had heard the news too). Brian talked of fame and money. He had found the long fleeced sheep with the big horns and unusual head and had brought it home.

'Big money and fame! Don't kid yourself, honey,' said Sandra. 'It's just a bloody goat that's mated with a sheep. Bit of a freak — that's all. Why you had to go and ring the bloody museum and carry on, I dunno. We'd have been better selling it to a freak show.' In those days every local agricultural show had their version of 'freak alley'. We all loved freak alley. To go and see the dwarfs, the seal boy, the man with two heads, the fat lady, the lady with the beard — it was deeply fascinating stuff. I loved to try and meet these people, to talk with them. In our politically correct world it's hard to go up to someone who is obviously different and ask them about themselves. Freak alley made this possible for me and I'd hang around behind the tents and talk to the little people or the half-man-half-woman.

'Anyhow, if it's a cross between a goat and a sheep, those museum people won't want it,' said Sandra.

It did have a long fleece, like an angora goat, but the rest of it resembled a sheep. It was a nicotine colour until Brian scrubbed it with Sandra's precious packet of Lux soap flakes and it came up gold in colour. Brian was extremely excited; a pen was built for it in the shed and it was given the best feed. He brushed and pampered that sheep and every day he expected the museum people and the national media. He'd rung every radio station and newspaper he could think of.

Then it happened. He was on the news.

Sandra screamed us into the house to hear, 'Mr Brian Willmott of Yudnapinna station has discovered the lamb with the golden fleece. A sheep has been found on the outback station resembling the mythological sheep of the 'Jason and the Argonauts' story. The sheep is reported to have a yellow fleece. Mr Willmott, who found the sheep, described the fleece as gold. The South Australian Museum will investigate.'

Brian expected helicopters of reporters to arrive. Clean overalls were even ironed! For days he was neat and tidy, all scrubbed and brushed, as he scanned the sky and would not miss a news report. One day, while I was out on my trough run, four men arrived from the museum. No media and no fame came with them. No money either. They took the sheep, thanked Brian, shook his hand and told him they would let him know the results of the tests they would carry out on the sheep and its fleece.

When I arrived home Sandra met me with the news. 'Don't talk to him for a while. He's out on the front verandah.'

'No fame?'

'No fame.'

'No money?'

'No money. No talk of any money. Just "Thank you, we'll let you know." I told him we should have sold it to freak alley.'

We did not hear from the museum. There was nothing further reported on the news and nothing in the papers. Sandra eventually rang the museum and was told the sheep had been given to a farmer and no, Brian's sheep was just an ordinary sheep. Yes, it did have an unusual fleece but the fleece was wool and not gold! Brian felt as if he'd been robbed.

'It was gold. Gold. They stole it. Now it's in a bloody private collection. It *was* gold! You both saw it' (nod, nod) 'it was on the news for Christsake! Bastards! Someone is gunna get famous because of it and it was supposed to be me! I had things to buy.' For weeks he was like a broken record.

So when he arrived home with an unusual cocky, all excited about his find, our response was very subdued.

'Look at it, look at it! It's a cocky crossed with a galah. And those experts reckon that doesn't happen. Well it does! Look at it! Now this is a real find and I'm gunna take it down to Adelaide meself.'

Next morning the bird had flown — accidentally 'escaped', and Sandra had a big grin as she listened patiently to Brian's lament.

For weeks he went around trying to find another unusual animal or bird that would bring him glory. He bought a book on birds and a pair of binoculars but the novelty soon wore off and he went back to his normal 'bush talk' rather than raving about fame and money.

We also had a visit from a team of archaeologists. A lake nearby was packed with Aboriginal artefacts. These men had been digging out there for a few days before they visited us, wanting drinking water. They explained to Brian that they had permission from the owner of Yudnapinna (who lived in the city).

'But what about the owners of the stuff you are packing in those crates?' asked Brian. 'I don't think they'll be too happy that you're takin' their stuff.'

The archaeologists explained again that they did have permission and if he had any issues then he should raise them with his boss. Brian did. He was on the 'blower' to the local manager immediately but hung up red-faced and angry. 'He said if the boss in the city said it was okay then it *was* okay and I had to butt out. Bejesus, I'm not happy about this! What are those people gunna say and think when they come back and their stuff is gone. What do I tell them? That the boss gave permission? Jesus Christ!' He roared off on the bike as angry as I'd ever seen him.

The dry salt lake was a special area and it was surrounded by red sand dunes. 'You should see this place when it rains,' Brian told me. 'It's beautiful — all green and blue, with thousands of birds. The Aboriginal people come and stay and there is lots of singing and dancing.' There were spear heads, grinding stones, axes made of Mount Gambier lava, cutting tools, old, old structures used for shelter, and seeds for beading.

Brian was friendly with the people whose home this was and he'd take tea, sugar, flour and tobacco out to them when they arrived. Sometimes he'd stay out there for days with the earth people and come home with his eyes full of stories.

He found some of the 'walking people', as he described them, and told them what was happening. He brought the elders back to the lake to talk with the archaeologists. It transpired that a couple of the owner's sons and their friends had found the lake the year before while they were up on holiday. They had reported their 'find' to a university and it was considered valuable and significant.

The elders sat and talked with the archaeologists but to no avail. The owner of the land had given permission and, so far as the archaeologists were concerned, any dispute the Aboriginal people had was with the owner of the property and not with themselves. No compensation was ever offered or given.

The elders came back to our home and we shared tea and tobacco with them. They were very sad and they thanked Brian for his help. He was still very angry.

A few days later he took off on the bike, returning hours after dark. Tied to the back of the bike were three big boxes of Aboriginal artefacts. He knew the archaeologists were staying at the main station that night before they left for the city next day, and so he had gone and stolen as much as he could fit on the bike. The next day he returned those belongings to their rightful owners. They gave him a set of grinding stones, a small axe head and a set of spear heads in gratitude. He gave these to me. Years later I lent them to a friend's sister to show her classmates at school, as part of a talk about the Aboriginal people of this land. She returned without my precious gifts. Someone had stolen them.

Whenever Aboriginal people were on our land or came to the homestead, tobacco, flour, sugar and tea were always given. One old man often came to our door while the rest of his people and dogs stayed well away from the house. He was a shy man but he would always thank us. One time I said, 'You're welcome, Uncle.' He patted me on the head and smiled saying, 'It is good manners. It is good.'

Once, when I was out riding the boundary with Brian, he pulled his horse to a sudden stop and bent down to examine the earth. 'Look here,' he said. Some one walking with a sandshoe on one foot and a thong on the other.' I could see the tracks but could not interpret them. We followed those tracks and came across an Aboriginal woman grubbing out rabbits from their burrows. One foot wore a thong, the other a sandshoe. We dismounted and I held the horses while Brian approached the woman. She stood. I stared at her long, long, black legs. She had a freedom and grace in those long legs and she reminded me of the emu. Spirits danced around that woman with a joy I've seldom seen. She grinned at us and a light radiated from her that made us grin back. She took the offered tobacco and nodded her thanks.

As we rode away I said to Brian, 'She's beautiful.' He just nodded in understanding and I saw a great depth of compassion in him that even he was not aware of. He was a simple, good, kind man who operated from his heart and still had the simplicity of a child with a beautiful garden to live in and share.

It was to Brian I went when one dark night I was out the front of the house having a pee and I saw a light. It was a red light, like a tail-light, bobbing around in the bush. There was no noise to indicate it was a motorbike and, with its erratic behaviour, I knew it was not a vehicle. I watched it weave and flow through the scrub — it was a dance I witnessed. Suddenly it disappeared.

'You've seen the Min Min light.' said Brian. 'Jeesus! It's an Aboriginal spirit light, but few Aboriginal people have ever seen it. Mind you, not that they'd want to. Around here they say it brings death. Or it has something to do with death.'

We just looked at each other in the lamplight.

'Do you believe it brings death?'

'I dunno. I suppose so.'

I looked at Brian hard. 'Is it my death?'

'I dunno. You saw the light but you're a white person, so I dunno. Are you Aboriginal at all?'

'No.'

He shrugged. 'Then maybe you've just seen it, that's all. It may not be for you.'

We both just stared into the flame of the lamp. I didn't know what to think. Death surrounded us. The killing of animals for meat, the culling of kangaroos and goats so the sheep could survive. I had seen a great deal of death in animals and coming to terms with their death had been hard enough, let alone trying to conceive of a world without me! I had thought a great deal about death. And suicide. I think young people do. I had seen death and suicide but it was *my* death I thought about now. None of the religions had offered any answer to the puzzle of death. Believing the light to be a spirit of death, I was reluctant to raise the issue with the Aboriginal people. I pondered for weeks on the meaning of the Min Min light and then pushed it to the back of my mind for many years.

Shearing and shooting

At shearing time all the out-stations would drive their sheep into a central area where there was a giant shearing shed surrounded by stockyards. Brian told me it was the biggest shed in the southern hemisphere and I believed him.

Shearing was a time of excitement, dust and noise — the sound of machinery as fleeces fell; the bark and yap of dogs; the bleating of the sheep; the swearing and whistling of the men; and the neighing of horses as their hooves pounded the dirt. Everywhere were flies and dust. Endless hot days with blue skies. An endless trickle of sweat that left breasts stuck together in an itch of salt and dirt. The smell of sheep clung to everything. We were covered in prickles and lanolin.

When not on horse back, bringing in sheep or shifting sheep from paddock to paddock, Brian and I were on foot, pushing sheep into yards, through races and up ramps. Dogs worked hard, their tongues hanging out and their sides heaving for air in the heat.

We all stopped twice a day for smoko — morning and afternoon tea, and for lunch. The food was brought out in the back of a ute. Tea was boiled in billies over a campfire.

Smoko was tea with huge slabs of sultana cake; lunch, thick sandwiches of roasted lamb and pickles. The menu never varied. The sandwiches and cakes came in mountain-loads and was demolished as if a giant had appeared, opened his mouth and swallowed every last crumb. I was told that tea — evening dinner — was always the same: roast lamb, roast potatoes, roast pumpkin and tinned peas followed by pudding and custard. Plenty of bread. Breakfast also lacked variety: fried liver, kidneys, chops, eggs and tomatoes; lots of pickles, sauce and tea.

I swept the shearing-shed floor, threw fleeces onto slatted benches so the wool classers could sort them into the correct piles, and slapped tar on sheep that had been cut by the shears. I preferred to work outdoors because the smell in the shed and the terror of the sheep was overpowering. As well as all that, the smell of the diesel oil as it pumped into the big engines gave me a headache.

I thought my arms would fall off and I was so tired at night that I would go to sleep in the bath and wake when Sandra pounded on the door to check whether I'd drowned and whether she could please have the bath water! Then I'd fall into bed, too tired to dream. In the morning as I'd light the fire, every bone in my body would protest, but Sandra would drive us back to the shearing and we would begin again amid the dust, flies and terrified bleating.

Once our sheep were shorn, we drove them back to their paddocks or into holding pens, ready for the market. The dogs were able to shift big mobs of sheep by themselves or at the whistle of their boss. They never failed to amaze me with their understanding and skill while being called all sorts of names and threatened with all sorts of punishment. No human would have worked under such abuse. Yet these dogs were as valuable as gold to their owners. Curses would ring out, kicks were given, threats bellowed into the sweating heat and orders shouted over the top of others' commands to their dogs, but woe betide any person who gave orders to or touched another person's dog. No affection was shown to these dogs because it would make them 'soft'. 'A bloody woman's dog,' was the term, yet later I met men who gave affection and love to their working dogs and treated them well and those dogs were excellent workers and faithful friends. But the prevailing wisdom of the time was never to let one's dogs 'go soft'. I could not agree with such a philosophy and had many arguments with working men about dogs. On reflection I realised that the same men treated nothing with kindness; they were hard like knotted rope and had hidden any feelings in a locked chest they had sunk to the very bottom of their being. These men maintained a 'man's' role in the world which was one of their own making that ultimately left them empty and often alcoholic.

Brian did not subscribe to this cult yet he still believed in clearly-defined roles for men and women. Women's work was well beneath him and yet he was capable of cooking, washing, and caring for young Wayne as well as any woman. He never once treated his dogs indifferently or with cruelty. A good working dog was worth money and that spoke volumes. Bloodlines would be discussed and the value of dogs as workers weighed up.

By the end of shearing I was glad to return to the isolation of our place and even glad to spend a day washing clothes. It was a relief to get back on the motorbike, to travel the water lines and do things in my own time again. It was when out on the bike that I had the time to stop and observe. I loved to watch the kangaroos. The stature of the big red kangaroo. So magnificent when standing tall and so formidable to watch in a fight. I laughed at the agile wallabies who were able to bounce up rock faces. I'd sit quietly and watch kangaroos graze or watch pouches move with sudden force as the young would bounce in and out or hang out and graze while in bed!

Emus enthralled me. Like dancers who waltzed across the red landscape, they moved to their own magical rhythm. They would run beside the bike along a fenceline, Olympic athletes of stamina without drugs.

One evening Brian said to me, 'Get your gun. We need meat for the dogs. We're going to get a roo.'

Brian would not shoot a red kangaroo unless it was injured and preferably male. He would cull out an area if he thought there were too many males, but he preferred to shoot the grey kangaroo, male.

He had the bright idea that I should sit on the back of the bike and, while he was driving, shoot a kangaroo.

'You want me to shoot a kangaroo from the back of the bike — while we are moving?' I asked incredulously.

'You're crazy. I can't shoot a kangaroo, bouncing around on the back of a bike.'

'Yes you can.'

'I'll shoot your bloody ear off. Or your head.'

'Nope. You'll be right. You're a bonzer shot.'

'This is madness, Brian. I need to be still to shoot. This is not the Wild West.'

'Don't worry about it. Get on and just shoot when I tell you to.'

Away we went, the gun loaded, with me bouncing and crashing on the metal rack at the back of the bike, my legs dangling and only willpower keeping me on. I could hardly balance, let alone sight a gun!

We roared along the dusty track until Brian spotted some grey kangaroos and gave chase. He singled out a big male and turned the bike in his direction. The big boy bounced along in front of us, me bouncing up and down on the bike, fighting hard to stay on.

'Shoot him, shoot him,' yelled Brian.

I lifted the gun, knowing it would be a miracle if I could even pull the trigger, when I found myself airborne. I crashed to the ground, the rifle beside me. Thankfully it hadn't gone off!

Picking myself up, I coughed up dirt as I brushed myself down, feeling to see if I was still in one piece. I couldn't see Brian or the bike but I could hear his cursing. All his concentration had been focused on the kangaroo and not watching where he was going. He hadn't noticed the dry creek bed; the kangaroo had effortlessly bounded across. Now Brian lay on the bottom, the bike on top of him.

I dragged the bike from him. The exhaust pipe had burnt his leg, and his jeans smouldered.

'Did you get it?' he asked. I sat down and laughed. Brian just stared at me.

'I think that old 'roo is sitting up there laughing at us. He's got a great sense of humour.'

Brian looked at me. We both stood up and there was the big kangaroo, standing on the bank, scratching his belly. We both laughed and dragged the bike up after us. We walked it slowly home, Brian limping all the way.

Dunny tales

Angela came to visit. For an outback experience.

There were quite a few visitors on various parts of the station. They were all to be collected by mini-bus at the end of their stay.

She was a couple of years older than me and had never been 'out bush' before.

She was intrigued by everything. She was appalled by how 'primitively' we lived. The fridge, telephone and bath fascinated her. The telephone delighted her. 'It's marvellous,' she said in her London accent. 'Amazing. I've read about such things and here one is, actually working! Wow! But how do you manage a private conversation with all those people listening in?'

'Tell them to bugger off the line,' replied Brian, just as intrigued by Angela's London accent.

'Do they all hang up then?'

'Bejesus they do!' said Sandra. 'They just breathe quieter.'

Our toilet was the 'pièce de résistance' as far as Angela was concerned — the highlight of her visit.

'It's so unusual,' she commented. 'We haven't had toilets like this in England for over a hundred years. A genuine long-drop.'

Fascinating as our toilet may have been, Angela would not use it after dark. Walking up the long hill with a torch, lighting the candle in the toilet and sitting there with spider webs silver in the candlelight and all manner of insects angry at the human interruption — all this made her 'unable to go'! All the night sounds seemed amplified in the dark. Angela would wake me to go with her to the toilet and then ask me to keep talking while she was inside to keep her calm. 'Nothing here can harm you, Angela.'

'You don't know who could be out there.'

'Out here? You've got to be kidding. It's a long way for a prowler to come.'

'They go to all sorts of places following girls and women.'

'Angela, the dogs would tell us if there was anyone around.'

'They could be Abos.'

I burst out laughing. 'You've got to be kidding. They don't give a stuff what we are up to.'

'I don't know. I've heard stories.'

'That's all it is — stories. You've been living in Whyalla too long.'

Whyalla had its fair share of prowlers. Far too many. It took me years to recover from the nightly crunch of metal, faces at windows and heavy breathing beyond the flywire. Of all the places I've ever lived, Whyalla was the home of the nightly prowler. My father was coming in our back gate one night when he surprised a prowler. 'What are you doing here?' he asked.

'I live here,' was the reply.

'Oh yeah?' said my father as his fist crashed into the man's jaw. He came inside, washed his hands, and said casually, 'Got another bastard. Out cold. Ring the cops. Tell them I've left him in the lane.'

Angela was as prowler-shy as I had been. I tried explaining over and over that there was nothing out in the bush that would harm her. 'It's not a town or a city; we are in the middle of the bloody donga.'

I was sick of being woken up twice a night for the toilet marathon.

'I've got a weak bladder; I can't help it. If you were civilised people the toilet would be inside.'

'My father says it's civilised to have the toilet outside,' I replied.

'Well it's not convenient.'

I tried to talk her into squatting in the yard but all my arguments failed. I found an old potty in the shed and cleaned it up. Angela was thrilled. Peace at last.

The first night she used the potty she switched on her torch to light the procedure. Then, she used the potty by the light of the moon, familiar with the process. A couple of nights later she woke the house with blood-curdling screams. Brian had placed a layer of sal-vital on the bottom of the potty! It had fizzed up over the rim. We all laughed, even Angela.

On the day she was to leave, Angela got her own back on Brian.

Brian always went to the toilet mid-morning, if he was home. Straight after smoko he'd head up there with his cigarette. There he'd sit and do his business while reading a magazine.

The day before, Angela had placed a ladder up against the back of the dunny. The mini-bus was to collect her and take her back to Whyalla. She was the last pick-up on the route, so the bus would be full.

All packed and ready to go, Angela seemed anxious. We knew she had enjoyed her stay but 'the bush' was not for her.

As we refilled our mugs she watched Brian head for his morning contemplation. Sandra, Wayne and I followed Angela outside. We watched as she set off for the dunny. As Brian sat inside, smoking and reading, Angela climbed quietly up the ladder on the outside, carrying in her hand a very long, dead snake we had found in the toolshed. It was still fresh.

Our toilet had a pointed tin roof. Where the points met, there was a hole, which let in light, and rain. We watched with glee as Angela positioned herself and silently fed the snake towards the hole in the roof. Into the hole went the snake and dropped into Brian's lap. At that moment the minibus full of women arrived.

Brian exploded from the toilet, overalls down around his

knees, the snake tangled in cloth and skin. Brian was screaming and waving and trying to run towards us, his hands pulling at the snake as his legs tangled in it. The women in the bus stared, their mouths agape. Brian fought and yelled and stopped dead. He held the dead snake in one hand, trying to pull his pants up with the other. There he stood, his privates exposed, his face ashen.

Angela roared. The bus rocked with laughter. Sandra and I held onto each other, tears streaming down our faces. Brian recovered, covered himself and walked sheepishly over to us. Angela held out her hand and he took it, bursting into laughter. He appreciated 'being got'.

We had another toilet incident.

Brian announced one morning at breakfast that we were going to have to dig a new toilet hole. 'We need a new dunny hole. It stinks in there and I can't get me peace.'

Sandra and I had been complaining about the smell for days. No amount of phenol could disguise the rotting sheep skin Brian had thrown down the hole. He'd been coming home in the ute one evening when he'd hit and killed a neighbour's sheep. Even though the dead sheep was on Brian's land he felt really bad about its belonging to the neighbour. He brought the sheep home and dressed it, then threw the skin down the toilet in a sudden panic that he'd be accused of sheep stealing!

The skin brewed. We complained. The weather became hotter.

'Well, the old hole is years old. Time to dig another one anyhow,' said Brian. 'I've been planning it for days now. We will dig a new hole next to the old one, then wrap a rope around the dunny and pull it across with the tractor.'

Sandra and I argued that we should move the dunny first and put all the dug dirt from the new hole into the old hole.

'Yeah, that's a good idea,' said Brian, 'but we might not get the new hole dug in a day — that ground's bloody crowbar hard. So where would we go to the toilet in the meantime?'

We did it Brian's way and it took more than a few days of digging before we had a very deep hole.

'I need bloody dynamite,' Brian would yell from the depths.

Sandra and I hauled up buckets of dirt until our shoulders ached. Finally the hole was completed to Brian's satisfaction. We tied a rope around the toilet and hitched it to the tractor. Brian and I were to steady the toilet while Sandra, driving the tractor, slowly pulled it over to sit above the new hole.

'Okay,' yelled Brian. 'Take it slowly.'

The tractor had no first gear and it was a very temperamental piece of machinery. It kept cutting out rather than going slow. 'Give it a bit more choke,' yelled Brian.

Sandra pulled on the choke and the tractor leapt into the air, flooded the engine as it bucked, and stopped. The toilet followed the acrobatics of the tractor. Swinging sharply away from the old hole, it bucked, bent, groaned and lurched into space, throwing me back into the dirt and knocking Brian off his feet. He skidded and grabbed for the toppling structure. And missed. Down into the old hole he slid.

I pulled myself from the dirt as Sandra jumped from the tractor. Brian's howls would have woken the dead. Wayne reached the edge first and said, 'Daddy's down the hole.' Sandra and I burst out laughing.

'Shut up, shut up, you pair of bloody morons!' Brian yelled. 'Get me out of here.' We tried not to laugh as we looked at Brian, up to his shoulders in shit and flies. The rotting sheep skin surrounded him.

We had to push the toilet right away from the hole and get the rope off. We tried to hurry and not to look at each other. If we caught each other's eye we broke into hysterical giggles. Finally we threw the rope to Brian and he climbed out as we retreated.

We heated water in the washing copper as Brian pulled off his clothes and dropped them into the hole. He wrapped a bag around his waist.

'Hurry up, hurry up. Get that water hot. I'm diseased, for Christ's sake. I lost a full packet of fags too.' He cursed and yelled as we fed wood to the fire. Sandra gave him a bucket of warm water and a bottle of disinfectant. He washed and scrubbed, then climbed right into the copper as she scrubbed him again with soap.

The only disinfectant we had was phenol, the one used for cleaning the toilet. We couldn't go near Brian for days because of its lingering smell!

Starry nights

I made a friend of a jackaroo, a station hand called Peter, several years older than myself. We could talk station talk and horses and he was ever hopeful of something more; women were scarce in the bush. We'd go riding together and we often worked together.

'Peter likes you,' commented Sandra.

'Good. I like him too.'

'Nudge, nudge, wink, wink.'

'No, Sandra. Just friends.'

'He wants more than that and he's willing to wait.'

'Friendship.'

'He's a man.'

'Can't men be friends?'

'Some can, but I think their dick nearly always gets in the way.'

'Well, he's too old for me. I'm not interested either.'

'He thinks if he waits long enough you'll give in. Men are persistent.'

'No.'

I was determined to keep Peter as my friend and I made it clear to him that was all I could offer. He seemed fine about that and so our friendship grew and we had a great deal of laughter and fun. I forgot to heed Sandra's words. Peter had just decided to 'wait until I grew up'.

Once, Brian, Peter and I were asked to help with a large muster of cattle. Someone had once owned a few house cows. During World War I, the cattle were turned loose. Over the years they bred and wandered, making their home in a dense bush area on the far side of a wide saltpan. It was not easy country to get them out of.

'Be better just to go in and shoot them,' said Peter.

'The boss wants them off, but he wants to send them to market and get a bit of moolah,' Brian explained.

Away we went on the muster. For the next few days we rode in chaos — horses, dogs and cattle in a frenzy of dust and cursing. Those cows looked more like the cows of a Spanish bull-fighting ring than the domestic cow. They were untamed and angry at being pushed around. They had generations of freedom in their veins and horns to protect that freedom. I could hardly move each night, I was so stiff and tired.

On the day the trucks were to arrive, we were herding the last of what cattle we could find when one big bull turned and charged a horse, horns down meaning business. The rider spun the horse around but was not quick enough. Down they went, the big bull trampling them.

Whips and curses cracked the air. The horse came back on its feet, blood streaming from a horn wound in its side. The jackaroo staggered to his feet and fainted.

I helped tend the horse as others took care of the rider and the bull. We could put our fingers into the gaping hole in the horse's side.

'Someone get some rags. A towel or tea towel. We have to pack this. To stop it bleeding. Quick!' yelled Peter.

Towels were brought and held against the horse's side, but they were soon soaked. I went to my swag. I had started menstruating and had a supply of tampons and a few pads. Out of my swag I pulled two pads. Going back to the injured horse, I pulled them apart, stuffed the hole with the cotton wool, placed a towel over it all and held it all in place with a leather strap around the horse's belly. The men all watched. No one said a thing about the pads but I overheard: 'Bloody ingenious'; 'Who would have thought to use them?'; 'Not you, mate.' A great deal of laughter and friendly teasing followed.

I heard Brian tell Sandra that night: 'She fixed that hole with one of those women's things.'

Peter and I attended the Marrabel rodeo. Dust, heat, noise and flies. Horses squealing and neighing, men cursing, the audience roaring, beer bottles smashing and the smell of burning meat and spilt beer. Cowboys and cowgirls in fringed satin shirts and jeans or moleskins. Tooled leather boots and big hats. Bushmen in plaid shirts, riding boots, worn jeans and Akubra hats. 'Raw' riders dressed in all manner of clothing, and the grotesque clowns with thick white make-up, big red nose and lips, black eyes and a curly orange mop of synthetic hair. Their make-up ran into rivers of coloured mud and sweat.

We sat on the railings to watch the riders trying to go the rounds on big bucking bulls and wild-eyed horses. Most riders came off seconds after leaving the chute. It was the first time I had seen Brahman bulls up close. They had names like 'Chainsaw' and 'Bulldozer'. They were magnificent with their big horns and hump on the back, a white-faced clown rode one of these bulls around the ring.

Horses bucked, fell, foamed at the mouth and reared into the sky to remove the rider on their back while the rope crushing their penis or testicles pulled tighter and tighter. Some horses were unbroken and wild but most were taken from rodeo to rodeo until they became too injured or worn out to continue. They went to the knackers.

'Why do they do this?' I asked aloud, not really wanting a reply.

Peter turned and said, 'Because it's a sport and it takes skill to ride those bucking broncos. Look at that bloke. He can't ride. City boy.'

The boy hit the dust and blood poured from his nose as he stood up.

'Broken. That'll teach him to stay on,' Peter laughed.

'It's all about pain and terror. I don't know if the animals are enjoying this,' I said.

'Of course they are. They like the excitement and the chance to get back on us buggers that ride them.'

'The men are frightened too. It's a bloody tough sport. Sorts out the men from the boys.'

I felt really upset and knew that rodeos would never be 'my thing'. I said, 'I think I'll go for a walk to stretch my legs a bit.'

'But you'll miss a good turn coming up.'

I jumped from the rails and wandered away.

'Don't be too long.'

'About a hundred years,' I thought!

I wandered around to where all the trailers and trucks were parked. Women sat around a fire sharing tea. I joined them and introduced myself. A mug of brew was handed to me. I remained there until twilight. Women came and went, sharing stories and singing love songs. Two women yodelled a few songs, bringing a small crowd to listen. They talked rodeo talk, kids, dogs, men and the bush. Peter found me listening to a woman who was prac- tising her calling for the dance that night:

> *'Sashay round your boy and girl,*
> *Nip and dive and away you go,*
> *With a dosey do and a do, do, do.'*

'You could hear her over a bloody footy match with that voice,' exclaimed Peter.

'She'll need to be heard with all those drunken cowboys at the dance tonight,' I replied.

'You wanna go to the dance?' asked Peter.

'No.'

We drove back to the station. Rather than stay the night in the bunkhouse I rode a bone-shaking motorbike back to the Willmotts'. It had no lights and the journey home by moonlight gave me a new picture of the land. I often went out for a motor- bike ride with no lights, when the moon was full. It's never really dark, just a different light at the time we call night. Different

shades of colour and a softness that takes the sharp edges of daylight away. I also tried riding horses on full-moon nights but they
shied away from the spirits of the night.

'Never be afraid of the night,' my father would say. 'Only be
afraid of humans, and at night you can hear them coming
anyway. These people who came to this land think they can move
around quietly in the dark but they sound like a bloody herd of
elephants on a rampage.'

He taught me how to walk without making a noise. Taking
time. Being aware. He taught me how to crawl along like a snake,
how to hide, how to be invisible and how to move from place to
place without being heard. It came in really handy when I was a
child — I'd eavesdrop on adult conversations without their being
aware of my presence. I fancied myself as an 'Indian' and I'd crawl
all over the place, sneaking up on people. My father and I often
played a game where I sneaked around in the dark while he'd listen
and try to hear where I was.

'Learn to melt away,' he'd say. He taught me to cover tracks,
to lay false tracks, and to watch the road and bushes for signs of
animals or humans. How to tell if someone had been to your
home, land or camp when you weren't there. So many small
tricks of awareness he taught me. I have never been afraid of the
night. I always remember it's not the night that's scary — just
people with odd intentions.

I liked to sit on the small hill behind the house at night; to
watch the moon and stars and feel that I was this tiny living speck
in a vast universe; to contemplate the mystery of my being here.
Alive. I'd watch the night birds and rabbits, sitting quietly in
their world — they were great teachers.

My fifteenth birthday came and went. I bought myself several
volumes of bush poetry via the catalogue and I'd sit and read by
candlelight. Town life seemed planets away.

One day I was out mustering when Sandra came to get me.

'I had a phone message about your dad. He's in Whyalla hospital with a stroke. You'd better go.'

I jumped in the ute and Sandra took my horse. I drove like a mad woman. My father in hospital. My father in hospital... I pulled the ute into a carpark and ran towards the hospital entrance. I could think of nothing but my father. I hadn't realised what I looked like — wild, covered in dust and grime. I had come straight from working, no time even to wash my face. Dusty tear tracks were the only clean surface.

I ran through the doors to the reception desk. A tall woman in white stood there. The matron.

The receptionist looked up, aghast.

'What do you want?' the mighty white power boomed at me.

'To see Mr Johns,' I replied.

'He's dead. Who do you think you are?'

'I'm his daughter.'

'Well, see him at the funeral.'

The receptionist was suddenly very busy at her desk.

I drove to my friend Olga's place. My mother was in the kitchen. She looked me up and down as I entered. 'Mum,' I said and held out my hands. 'Dad's dead.'

She turned and walked from the room saying, 'It should have been you.' Olga held me while I cried. She put me on the lounge, removed my boots and covered me with a blanket. In the morning I met my baby brother.

I stayed for the funeral. It was horrible. My mother and her men friends, my tiny nervous brother, Olga and her husband Pat. They played the Last Post on the bugle as the coffin went into the ground. How I hate that piece of music!

Everyone retired to the pub for a wake. I stayed with Bozo at the grave and watched the men fill it with dirt. That night the dog and I slept on the grave beneath the stars.

My mother and I were arguing. She gave away to her men friends all my father owned. I fought over his beautiful boxes of cared-for tools.

'You are not having them. You are not having anything,' she yelled at me. I escaped with his photo album. Pictures of his life in the war and afterwards on the island. Pictures of Egypt, the land he loved; pictures of myself as a baby and little girl. An old leather-bound album, the photos held in place with brown corners.

I returned to Yudnapinna. The land, the animals, the spirits and my own dreaming helped to heal the pain of the loss of my father. I would hear his whistle, see his smile and at times smell him. My heart ached and the bush blurred with my tears. I retreated into myself to heal and my lack of response must have hurt Sandra and Brian but they left me alone to grieve. I walked with the dogs for hours, in mourning.

Another phone call came from Olga. My mother was busy 'drowning her sorrows', and my brother was neglected.

As I waited for the mailman to take me to the bus in Port Augusta I sat patting the dogs and watching the open space in front of me meet the sky. I wanted to stay but I shook myself into the now, hugged Sandra, Brian and Wayne. I climbed into the ute, waved goodbye and sat saying a silent goodbye to this land. Now I had two bags of possessions.

I heard my father's voice, 'She'll be right!'

As I entered the street where my mother lived in Whyalla, there was my small brother Ronald walking down the road — snotty faced, dressed only in a singlet, his bum and legs shitty. He had just learned to walk.

For the next few months I lived at home and cared for my brother. We seldom saw my mother as she was on a grieving binge, to drown her sorrows.

Then one Wednesday came a knock at the door. Police.

They informed me that complaints had been made against my mother and that on Saturday they would return to take my brother and me into custody. We were to be placed in welfare until we were eighteen. I stood stunned!

When they left I went to see Olga. Olga and Pat fostered

children and they were willing to take Ronald so long as we could get my mother to sign the papers. That part was easy, and so Ronald was settled, loved and cared for by that generous pair.

On the Thursday I had a job serving in a shop. On Friday night I still had nowhere to live. An old woman came into the park where I was sitting. She had a beautiful German shepherd dog called Flossie, and we soon made friends. The old woman sat down with a groan. Grievances spat from her, thick with venom. But the owner of the dog, her daughter Doris, had a room to rent at her home. So I had a job and somewhere to board.

Saturday morning I was waiting for the police. They came in a divvy van! I explained that Pat and Olga Walsh were legally fostering my brother and that I had a job and a place to board.

'Smart little bastard, aren't you,' said the man in blue. No longer a giant!

'Too smart for your own good.'

'You need a few lessons, kid.

They took me by the arms, marched me down the path and threw me in the van. I was taken to Whyalla police station and locked in a cell until the next morning.

'That'll teach you a lesson,' said the man in blue as he unlocked the door on Sunday. I walked the five miles home.

Pride and joy

The colour and heat of Whyalla constantly slapped me in the face. Day after day of heat, flies and red dust, blue sky and knife-edged shadows. I had settled in with Doris and Bill Griffiths and their son David. Bozo was with me and he adored David. Bozo had decided that David was to be his person and the feeling was mutual.

Doris was a tiny feisty woman. Bill, a hardworking stocky man, dreamed of living on a farm but worked gruelling hot hours in a steel foundry, those dreams being fed into the steel for ships to carry away. Immigrants from Yorkshire, England, they retained their broad accents and were proud of their heritage.

I worked in a drapery store owned by a kindly bear of a man, Mr Walker. Mrs Smoker ran the store and managed the staff. Straight-backed and straitlaced, always groomed, she belonged in a genteel emporium somewhere in London — not a store set in the centre of a volcano! She was stern but fair. Old school. Manners were extremely important to her.

I measured out fabric and ribbons, sold bras and corsets and pined for a horse. I bought a single-seat BSA motor bike. It was old!

Each weekend I'd chug down to the racetrack where the racing and trotting horses were stabled. I'd hang around, patting the horses and drinking in their smells, like a glass of water that

brings one back to life. After a couple of weeks an old man introduced himself. He looked like a crumpled, brown paper bag.

'I see you like horses. I'm old man Reynolds. My stables are
across the road — I don't like fraternising with this mob. Too
many eyes here for me. You worked horses?' I nodded. 'Good.
You want to come and strap for me?' I nodded. I followed him
on my bike. We drove about half a click to his stables — all made
of iron and tin, painted steelworks red. The yards were fenced
with thick piping.

'I can't pay you,' he said.

I looked at him. Oh well. Money wasn't the issue. Horses
were.

'You'll get something. I'll place a bet for you each race day and
if the horse comes in a winner the money's yours. Fair enough?'

'Fair enough,' I said and we shook hands.

So I started working for old man Reynolds each weekend. I'd
be up at dawn, splitting the air open with the sound of the BSA
rattling down the streets and across the paddocks to the stable. I
still wasn't quite old enough to hold a licence.

I was taught how to harness and drive the horses; how to
drive one and lead two; how to balance their food, and what they
needed for their health. I brushed them until they shone. There
were six horses in work and several more being spelled in the dry
saltbush paddocks.

Then I began to go to the stables before work. I would rise
before dawn, grab a piece of bread and head out the door. I'd be
back in time to shower, change, grab another piece of bread and
run to catch the bus for work. I'd often arrive at work late, having
missed the bus. I was forever apologising. 'I'm so sorry I'm late.'

'I suppose it's horses,' glared Mrs Smoker. 'Do you want this
job or not, girl? This is your future, not horses, so you just better
buckle down. There are plenty of young women who would give
their right arm for a job like this.'

I was young, enthusiastic and friendly. I could 'sell ice to
Eskimos', because I liked the job, loved the talking and enjoyed
the customers. I hated the endless dusting, cleaning, washing the
glass and mirrors and being told to, 'Get on with it. Talk only to

the customers. Be productive.' Talking was never seen as productive unless it was to sell. Signs like 'Time is money' and 'Don't waste time' hung on the walls. I was forever being told off because I would cut ribbon or cloth with a generous few inches extra. Measurements and maths have never been a strong point in my education. My idea of measurement is 'so long ... so wide ... so many cups or handfuls ...'

In summer, with the longer hours of daylight, I could race home from work, grab a sandwich and head off to my beloved horses, returning at dark. Doris would leave my food in the oven if I failed to show for tea, which, tradition dictated, was at 6 p.m.

Because I worked on Saturday mornings I couldn't attend race meetings unless they were in Whyalla. After each race day old Mr Reynolds would give me an envelope with money inside. 'Your winnings.' I saved that money for my dream horse and all I would need for her.

Old Mr Reynolds was a man who talked horses to me — horses, form, meetings, feeding and training. I never met his family and only met his wife a couple of times. I knew nothing about him personally and we never talked of personal things. He knew where I worked and lived. Beyond that, for him, I had no life story apart from horses. I enjoyed training the horses on the dirt roads and racetrack. Being a girl, I was barred from racing; I could do everything but actually race.

The horses enjoyed the dirt-road training. We'd trot along, the dust swirling in clouds so fine that it covered everything like a second skin. Sweat would leave track lines down my face, and my nose was always burnt from the sun and wind — scorching hot north winds, alive with wild spirits.

I never raced the horses, except on the track. I kept them working at a continuous pace, steady. If I was working only one horse on the dirt then I'd often let the horse set the pace and if she or he wanted to race I'd let them go, reining them back gently when I figured they'd had enough.

One morning a new horse was out in the paddock. A big raw-boned heavy-gaited pacing horse. He would race, but not out front — he liked to race within a pack, never as leader.

'Oh, he'll go all right,' I was told. 'Go all day but he won't race, and once the bugger gets going he's got a mouth of steel and is impossible to pull up. He stops when he wants to.'

'Pride' was gentle and stubborn. He enjoyed being ridden and loved to pace along the beach and play in the water. He'd dance in the sea, making waves with his hooves and throwing water into the air with his nose. He loved to swim and we had some wonderful mornings in the still waters of the bay.

I trained him in harness along the dirt roads and he'd set a pace and stay with it. He didn't change the pace when being raced, always staying in the pack, comfortable with the other horses. He'd always stop when the last horse pulled to a halt.

'He has to go,' said old Mr Reynolds.

'Go where?' I asked.

'The knackers.'

'I'll buy him.'

'Okay. Ten quid and he's yours without papers. He's not to go on the track. You pay for his feed and you can keep him here.'

Pride was mine. I rode him everywhere, same pace. His gait rattled my teeth and backbone; I had to turn him sharply to stop him, but he was such a loving horse that I loved him in return.

Pride couldn't or wouldn't canter. Occasionally he'd battle me about halting. We'd be trotting down the road, his head held tightly to one side; we would be eyeball to eyeball and still he'd keep going. I'd be yelling at him, 'Whoa, whoa! Stop, stop!' Hanging on to Pride and his pacing gait I wore the hair off the inside of my legs and it never grew back! I often felt like a yo-yo on his back.

But I was back in the saddle and loving it. The weather was mild, before the blazing heat of summer. I began to take 'sickies' from work, inventing all sorts of aches and pains. Mrs Smoker tried the quiet approach, the direct approach, then reported me to Mr Walker. We had a boss talk in his office. I explained that I felt 'shut in', and he talked to me about being responsible. He talked about jobs and the future, about security and savings. About settling down! I had to understand that I was young and, like most girls, I was going through a 'horse phase'. I would 'come out' of that and if I wasted my life now on horses I would always look back and regret it. I had a job, security and a future. He was willing to 'give me another chance' if only I would 'wake up'.

I heard him and sat there nodding but his words made very little sense to me. I'd often been told that horses were 'only a phase', that I would grow out of once I 'met boys'. Nothing had any value except boys. I'd grow up and be quite 'normal'. Once I began the 'sex, romance, boys' period of my life, all would change!

I tried to explain to the boss that horses were part of my soul.

I had heard all the 'Just wait till you get a boyfriend' rhetoric and it didn't make sense to me. Have security, a bank balance. Have a 'glory box'. All the young women I worked with all had those dream boxes full of sheets and towels and 'things' for their future home. My idea of glory was to use the things now! Why keep the best for tomorrow when the best is here and now! I'd often ask why men didn't have glory boxes. Didn't they want sheets and towels and 'stuff' for a home too? Or did they bring in the car and mower and help to start the all-essential baby? I would rather a new horse rug than waste my money on things for tomorrow's marriage.

One pay held a week's notice. Sacked!

I spent every day at the stables. I was free! I travelled to local race meetings and survived very well on my winnings. Doris was upset and puzzled that after a short 'holiday' I didn't seem to be looking for work. I paid my board, had money for petrol and needed few clothes. But in her view I was not being 'normal'. She was also annoyed that I spent all my waking hours at the stables.

'You should be working.'

'I am.'

'He doesn't pay you and you work like a dog for him. What do you get? Nothing!'

'I make enough to live and have my horse.'

'You live on your winnings. Betting,' said Doris.

'It's money.'

'And who will pay for your board and keep if you don't win? I'm not keeping you.'

'I've got money in the bank. I can afford to pay my way. You won't ever have to keep me.'

'Don't you be bloody cheeky, my lady. This is for your own good. You live here, and I'm not having any of your back talk.'

I told my friend Nancy about what was happening at home and she suggested that I give Doris a copy of *The Nun's Story* to read. Presumably it contained some message about compassion, but I was unaware of this at the time, and repeated the advice to Doris who immediately exploded.

'I don't need her telling me how to run my life.'

It ended with me in tears and Doris telling me that I could 'get bloody well out if I didn't like it because she was boss'. I promised to get a job, pay more board and 'behave' myself.

I looked for work and spent my time at the stables. I'd ride every morning while the other horses ate. Then I'd clean, brush and train until dark. I loved the life. It suited my dreaming.

Old Mr Reynolds was like most trainers. He may have had the occasional favourite horse, but overall horses were sport and money and they had to perform. Win. They were fed, raced, assessed and moved on. I'd be getting to know a horse and enjoying its personality when it would be moved on. There was very little opportunity to develop real friendships with the horses.

I poured all my love into Pride, hoping he'd respond and stop being a big wall that would happily trot for hours! He'd come to me and call out, he was well-mannered, but he didn't put himself out for humans. We were just there! He was in his element and seemed really alert and happy if I gave him a free rein to trot. Off he'd power, me bouncing like a ping-pong ball.

Pride was to have his day. Race day brought horses, trainers and 'special' people coming up from the capital city. Mayor this and high flyer that! Mr Race Meeting and Miss Australia! The racing people were in a big 'tizz'. The big day was complete with brass band and champagne. Guests all 'dressed up to the nines' arrived from the airport in long black limos. Flashbulbs popped, celebrities yelled, 'Darrr-ling', to each other and the crowd strained their eyes and necks to watch the wealthy and beautiful take their places in special boxes.

The Clerk of the Course was resplendent in his red coat, bleached white pants, shiny black, high boots and black velvet hat. Mounted on a reliable white horse he looked impressive. For each race he led the racers to their starting point, the hooter screamed, 'Go', and the race would begin. The Clerk's horse would dance a few steps, then wait until the race finished. Horse and rider would then lead the winning three horses on a walk past the stands so the crowd could clap and cheer. (Or cry if they had lost!) The second race was run, then the third and fourth. Kegs were tapped and the foaming ale ran freely. Champagne was replaced by cold lager.

The Clerk's horse suddenly went lame. Another horse was needed quickly. The Clerk had tried to keep cool with a few ales and he needed to ride — it was the only way he could hold steady!

Panic raced around the stables. Only Pride was available. Quickly he was saddled and bridled.

'You'll get paid for this,' slurred the Clerk. 'Sank you, sank you.'

The next race was announced. I went to watch. Pride led the racers to their starting points. The crowd fell silent. Expectant. The Clerk was beetroot red in the face, with sweat pouring down; his hands jerked on the reins as he bobbed up and down like a cork on water. Pride jiggled and danced and fought him. He turned Pride to stand in the usual waiting position. Pride trotted on the spot, jiggling and throwing his head up and down.

The hooter blew. The race was on. Away raced the horses. Away raced Pride.

Into the back straight flew the horses, whips whistling. On the other side of the rail, in the middle of the pack, came Pride in full pace, the Clerk of the Course's bum high in the air, his arms wrapped around Pride's neck.

The crowd went wild with laughter, whistling and yelling.

'Go, boy, go!'

'Give 'em curry.'

'Put a bet on the guy with his arms around that horse's neck.'

'For Christsake, someone take a bet; that bloody horse might get a place!'

Down the straight they thundered.

Last in the dust, still happily pacing and thoroughly enjoying himself, came Pride. The crowd roared and cheered. Pride stopped. The Clerk of the Course slid to the ground. Ambulance officers carried him off. It was as if he had won.

We didn't see the Clerk of the Course or any money!

Finally a job. A real job. In a motorbike shop.

I knew a little about motorbikes as my old BSA kept breaking down and Bill would help me to fix it. He had a passion for motorbikes and never stopped telling the story about the time he was on his bike with Doris riding pillion. She was carrying a cake. Over a hump-backed bridge they flew. 'I thought I'd gone deaf. I couldn't 'ear 'er. I looked back and there she was sittin' in the middle of that bridge with the cake.' He'd laugh and laugh.

I lasted two weeks in the job.

On the Friday of the second week the old man who owned the shop turned up. I was employed by his sons and this was the first time I'd met the old, bent man. I had no trouble at all as a female working with the sons. So long as I did my job and the customers didn't complain, they left me alone. Not the old man. He followed me around the shop all day, breathing down my neck. Towards closing time I went out into the stockroom to return an exhaust pipe. As I bent down to place it on the rack a pair of hands went up my dress and grabbed my arse.

I swung around, the pipe still in my hand, and brought it crashing down on the side of the old man's head. Down he went, out like a light!

The two sons came running.

'He grabbed my bum,' I yelled at them.

They sat the old man up. He opened his eyes, focused on me and screamed, 'You're sacked!' I spat at his feet.

I found a job in a photography studio. I learnt to develop black-and-white film and to print photographs. Then I was taught how to do sepia prints and how to tint them. Hour after hour I hand-tinted wedding photos for 'Goldwyn Studios'. We were extremely busy as Max, the photographer, rushed from wedding to wedding. I kept my distance from him and managed to keep our relationship formal.

Max was sitting on his stool one day when I walked past. He pulled me to his lap and banged me down on his erect penis, trying to kiss me. I gave him one hell of a shove and over he went. He backed me into the darkroom. I picked up a tray of developer and threatened to throw it at him. He backed off. When I reached the door I threw it. I think I missed him.

'Comes from not having enough women in the town,' commented Doris. 'You belt them, love. Or I'll go and belt the daylights outa them for you.'

I returned to dreaming and breathing horses. Riding and betting. I told Doris I was being paid — it seemed easier.

On Saturday nights when Bill was free, he and Doris would go out to the clubs. Whyalla had many workers' clubs where the men and their wives could socialise, drink and dance.

My mother also went to the clubs and so Doris kept me up on the latest about my mother.

'She was with that big ugly Greek fella …'

'Saw her with that Weston bloke …'

'Saw your mum with those Croat blokes …'

My mother still lived in the same house a street away from Doris and Bill. Two houses away lived Olga and Pat and all the fostered children. I'd often ride Pride over to visit and give the children rides.

Olga had been a bar maid in her youth — in men's pubs in Sydney. She enjoyed men and men hung around her voluptuous warmth. She met men on their own ground. Honest. No flirting, no pretensions and always with her love of Pat, her husband, shining from her eyes. She was compassionate but firm; the bar life had left her with few illusions. 'I've heard every story a bloke has to tell and then some,' she'd say, lighting a cigarette or lifting a glass of red wine to her ruby lips. She was loved by all the people in the street. A friend to them all and a loving mother to every child she fostered. Pat was a tiny quiet man with a head of bushy hair. Gentle and kind, he lived between worlds and liked to just sit, a beer in his hand, a child or a dog at his side. My brother was wild and happy there.

Olga defended my mother. 'It's just the way she is. Some women are like that. You'll never be what she wants and she'll never be what you want.'

I kept my distance from my mother, but still the stories came: 'Your mother's not been home for days …'

'Westons's wife has been down arguing like bloody hell with your mother …'

'There was a big punch-up on the lawn. Your mother hit a fellow over the head with a flagon …'

'The police are always being called …'

I decided to sign on as a jillaroo and work the sheep-shearing season at Yudnapinna. They needed all the hands they could employ. Peter came to collect me, towing a float behind his battered ute. Pride came too.

'Well-meaning' complaints about my mother followed me to the station. Finally came a call that I could not ignore.

'She's in Adelaide. In a pub. You'd better go see because there's going to be trouble.'

I packed my bags and organised a lift into Port Augusta. One of the jackaroos bought Pride from me. I cleaned myself up at the bus station when I arrived in Adelaide, then caught a taxi to where my mother was staying.

I arrived at her room. The door pushed easily open.

She lay half on the bed, her head hanging over the edge. She was dishevelled, beaten up, covered in blood, dressed in a nightie and unconscious. Blood was splattered everywhere — on walls, furniture and carpet. Bottles of alcohol were leaking into the carpet and ashtrays littered the room. Holes were burnt in the carpet and the room stank. Someone had had a wild old party and my mother was the only one left.

I rolled her over. Her face was bruised and blood ran from

her nose. As I turned to get help, the door banged open and a huge man entered and began to abuse me.

'Get an ambulance,' I said.

'I'll get the fucking cops.'

'Just get an ambulance quickly before she dies.'

The thought of a dead body in his hotel spurred him into action. He was out of that door in seconds. Other faces peered in. I shut the door. Suitcases were open against a wall. I closed them and found my mother's handbag. Her purse held quite a lot of money. I placed it back in her handbag and, laying it on her chest, I wrapped her arms around it. I covered her with a blanket. I cleaned up anything that could have been hers and dumped it all in a suitcase. I placed the suitcases outside the door and asked someone who was hanging around if he could please call a taxi. I watched while the taxi pulled in and asked him to put the suitcases in the boot and then to wait.

The big manager returned. 'Ambulance is on its way. Look at my room! Look at my bloody room! Who's going to pay for all this? Shit. Fuck and shit. Just look at it. I've also called the police. Someone will pay for this.'

He glared at me. 'Who are you?'

At that moment the ambulance arrived. The men picked up my mother, blanket and all, placing her on a stretcher.

One of them said, 'Drunk. Jesus, what a mess.'

'What about my room?' asked the big bloke.

'Who is she?' asked one of the ambulance officers.

'I dunno, they registered as Mr and Mrs. Where the hell is the Mr?'

A crowd had gathered. I melted into it, headed for the taxi and climbed in. In the confusion I left. I deposited my mother's cases in a locker at the railway station then I delivered the chit to the hospital in an envelope with her name on the outside.

I slept at the bus station on a bench and early next morning caught the bus back to Whyalla.

I went to see Mr Walker to ask if there was any possibility of a job. Mrs Smoker was on leave and I was employed until she returned. I had three months work and I'd offered to babysit for the Walkers so they could socialise. They took up my offer and I spent some quiet evenings in their home, listening to the children sleep while being kept company by a beautiful, plump and friendly golden Labrador dog. Supper was always left out under a white cloth. Gracious and kind people.

My mother's rented commission home was painted and re-let. I visited my happy brother and life looked good.

I headed over to my beloved horses, anxious to see old Mr Reynolds. The stables were empty. The paddocks were empty. No horses. Nothing. Everything was gone! The tack room, feed room, hay shed, all empty.

I discovered that old Mr Reynolds had died of a sudden heart attack.

My next need was transport. David had pulled my bike apart and it was in pieces. I bought a small step-through Honda 'put-put' bike. It was not fast but it was reliable. I borrowed my friend Nancy's little green Morris Minor and went for my driver's licence. I drove to collect the inspector's dry cleaning, returned to the police station and parked.

I explained 'I want a bike licence too.'

'Can you ride one.'

'Yes. I have a bike.'

'Okay. Well I should really see you ride; I should follow you, but you seem to have been riding and driving for a while and only experience will improve you. You drive as well as anyone who's had a licence for years.'

'I've been living on a station,' I explained.

We went inside and the inspector okayed my bike and car licences.

I was independent, legal and free. I spent the afternoon with Nancy, walking the shoreline and telling her of my dreams.

A dream, a death, a betrayal

I worked in the drapery store and longed for horses.

For a few weeks I took myself to work, came home and spent the time reading or socialising with friends. I'd ride my bike and walk in the bush.

But after a few weeks of not having my life revolve around horses the pull became too great and down to the racetrack I went. I began to brush horses and hang around. Then I began to ride track work each Sunday morning. I loved the feel of a racing horse under me, the sense of freedom and flight. The feel of my eyes streaming water, the wind on my face and that big heart under me. Life. Warmth. Motorbikes can be fun but to ride a living being is a joy indeed.

My friend Peter from Yudnapinna Station came to visit. He had come to tell me of a horse that was for sale.

'She's a five-year-old chestnut mare with a touch of Arab in her. She's a quiet, solid beauty. Fifty quid.'

'Fifty pounds!'

I didn't have that amount saved. I told Peter I would think about her.

Old Mr Reynolds had a brother, known as Young Mr Reynolds. He was a butcher and kept several trotting horses at the track. A short round man like his brother, he was not sentimental about his horses. His son drove the horses on race days but he wasn't interested in caring for them. He was the party boy, enjoying all the glory and the slaps on the back in the members' stands.

Young Mr Reynolds asked me if I would like to work for him. I could have a stable and winnings if I said yes.

I said yes, thinking of the chestnut mare — my dream, but I promised Doris that my horse work would not interfere with my employment.

Once again I was up before dawn and down at the race track as the galahs began their early-morning vocalising. I'd clean stables, brush horses, prepare feeds and work any horse that Mr Reynolds allocated to me. My favourite was Smile-a-While, or Smiley, a former champion with a roomful of trophies. He was breathtakingly beautiful and held himself with pride and dignity; he was so black he was blue. Smiley had a big, big, heart and I loved him. He was no longer young but he was a favourite of Mr Reynolds who had decided to 'give him a final season before we retire him'.

We began to take Smiley to the beach and I began to ride him. The other trainers smiled and shook their heads. Smiley loved the water. One morning Mr Reynolds went off to get something, leaving Smiley and me trotting up the beach. I was bouncing along on his back when suddenly I felt his spirit come alive; he neighed and lifted his body into the most glorious canter I've ever experienced.

'Never, never canter a working pacer or a trotting horse,' Old Mr Reynolds used to warn me. 'Or they'll "break" in a race.'

I'd seen many horses break while racing. They'd be hauled back unmercifully, the bit sawing at their mouth. Breaking in a race brought disqualification.

What a canter that big horse had — poetry! We turned and cantered up the beach, Smiley loving the freedom and exploring that movement. For me it was bliss — the mirror-blue sea, the kiss of early morning and a time of unity with another soul not of my species. We halted beside Mr Reynolds.

'Now that was a sight', he said, tears glistening in his eyes.

'I know he shouldn't canter but does it really matter now that he's so close to being retired?'

'You can canter him, girl, if that's what he wants. This is his last racing season — let him enjoy himself. It doesn't matter now.'

Sunday mornings became heaven!

Peter came to visit.

'The chestnut mare is still for sale.'

'She is my Dream,' I told him. 'That horse would be a dream come true for me.'

Peter drove us the hundred miles to 'have a look at her'. I fell in love.

'Look,' said Peter. 'I'll lend you the fifty quid for her and you can pay me back when you've got it.' I gave him a big hug of thanks and bought my Dream. We organised to collect her the following month. I arranged with Mr Reynolds to rent a stable and yard. I bought a second-hand saddle, bridle, halter and brushes. I bought a rug and feed. I was ecstatic.

The race meeting that weekend was set for Whyalla. Smile-a-While was to race — his first for the season. He was ten years of age and as he went onto the track trainers smiled and nodded their heads. They viewed him as a brave horse but on his last legs!

I had brushed him until his black coat rippled with rainbows. His white harness was spotless and his black sulky like a gleaming chariot.

I raced over to a bookie I knew and placed a bet. He looked at me. 'Smile-a-While to win? You've got to be kidding but it's your money. What do you know that we don't?'

'Nothing. I just have faith in the old horse.'

I screamed my lungs raw as the horses raced. Mr Reynolds was beetroot-red in the face, slapping the rail and yelling. Then he was banging me on the back.

Smiley had come in first! The crowd cheered. The officials frowned. The horse was swabbed for drugs. Negative.

I bought a celebratory bottle of Benedictine liqueur. Bill was on night shift. Doris and I had a drink to celebrate. Then another. And another. I lay on the floor of the lounge unable to move. Doris was on the couch.

'I think I'm drunk.'

'I know I am,' said Doris.

I crawled up the passage and onto my bed. All night the room spun. In the early hours I managed to make it to the bathroom where I was 'as sick as a dog'. I crawled back to bed. I've never been able even to sniff Benedictine since. It was evening before Doris surfaced from the couch. Bill teased us for days. We'd both groan at his teasing, our queasy stomachs remembering the alcohol.

Smiley won the next four races.

Peter arrived, towing a float behind his battered ute. My Dream had arrived.

We took her to her new home where she was dutifully admired and patted. She was stabled next to Smiley and my heart overflowed as I gazed at them both. Mr Reynolds laughed at me. 'Some blokes would kill for a woman who looked at them with all the love you bestow on those horses.'

'One day she will,' said Peter.

Mr Reynolds laughed. 'Well if she does he's going to be one very lucky bugger, I can tell you. I've never seen a woman love a man like she does those nags.'

I couldn't stop breathing and talking horses.

'What you need is a place of your own,' said Peter.

That stopped me talking to listen. Living with my mother had taught me many a lesson. I looked at Peter. 'I'm happy here. I have all I want from life.'

'But I could make you happier.'

'Peter, I'm really glad to be your friend but I'm not interested in anything else. I thought we had sorted that out.'

'I know you are still young, but you're growing fast and I want first shot. I can make you happy. You make me happy. Don't you want a boyfriend?'

'No.'

Peter returned to the station and in my mind I thought his romantic interest in me had been well and truly quashed.

Doris encouraged me to 'go out' with 'fellas'.

I went to the 'drive-in' with a male friend of my own age.

Drive-in cinemas were very popular at that time — especially in Whyalla. It was a place where families went, the children all dressed in their night wear. Couples went to smooch and teenagers to have a little passion in the back seat. Many a child was conceived at the Whyalla drive-in.

We went to meet friends and watch the film. On the way home my friend's car ran out of petrol. I stayed with the vehicle while he walked to get fuel. Once mobile again we made for an all-night diner and tanked up on food and Coke. Then we sat within the warm cloak of the night and talked. I arrived home in the early hours of the morning.

Doris was waiting up. I tried to explain the situation.

'That is the oldest story in the book,' she raged. She went going on about boys and pregnancy and 'getting into trouble'. She didn't hear a word I said. She believed what she had pictured in her mind.

'He's religious,' I yelled at her. 'He wouldn't do anything like that. We just talked!'

'Talked my arse!' and away she went again.

I didn't see that young man again. I felt if that was the experience of having a boyfriend, it was one I could do without.

My life revolved around Dream. I went to work, but was distracted within my soul all day and chafed to be with horses.

I trained Smiley and occasionally worked another horse on the track, but I couldn't get enough time with my beloved Dream. I rode her through the scrub, along dirt tracks and spent hours with her on the beach. I set up an arena where I practised dressage from books and tried to ride in the English manner, the Olympics ever on the horizon. I built jumps and discovered

Dream could clear them easily. We began to jump more and more, the dream of the show-ring in my eyes.

Peter came to visit. I was wary and watchful, but he seemed the same old Peter — friendly and not pressuring me about more than friendship.

That weekend, Smile-a-While won his last race. It was announced over the loudspeaker system at the track and he was cheered by the crowd as he gave his last trot-by. I washed the sweat from him and left him to roll and cool in the sand pit. I went for his rug and brushes but stopped outside the Reynolds tack room door.

Father and son were arguing.

'You're a fool not to keep him racing. Why retire him while we're winning?'

'Because he won't keep on winning and I want to retire him while I can proudly say that he won his last race. No. He's still got heart and I will not break that through greed. He's done us proud.'

'Jesus Christ, you're getting as soft as that girl you've got working for you. Mad bitch, that one, thinks more of horses than she does of people. She's not right in the head.'

'You leave her out of it. If it wasn't for her, that horse would not have won this season.'

'What bullshit. She's crazy, old man. Everyone here thinks so. She's not normal.'

'You just shut up. She's had a gutful of being told she's not normal and she doesn't need you to keep repeating that drivel. She's the best worker we've ever had. That horse is retired.'

'I think you are an old fool. You're living in the past, old man. That horse could easily win another season — maybe two, with the stuff I've got.'

'I don't want to know. You keep that damn stuff out of my stables. When you have your own horses you can do what you like, but not under my roof.'

'You're a stupid old man.'

'Get out!'

Pushing me out of the way, the son made his exit. He knew I had overheard.

Mr Reynolds looked old and tired.

'Well, that's that,' he said. 'A great race won.'

'He went out winning.'

The old man hung his head, I grabbed the brushes and left.

During that week I rode Smiley, brought him little treats and fed him all the food he really loved. Then a young girl and her parents arrived to collect him and I said a very teary farewell.

I brushed and worked Mr Reynolds' other horses — all characters with large personalities, but my heart was with Dream and my special times were with her. I also rode track work again on Sunday mornings. The fast rides cleaned out all my cobwebs.

Then, at the next home-town race meeting, one of Mr Reynolds' horses was swabbed positive. All his horses tested positive.

The old man took the blame and the horses were placed in the son's name. Mr Reynolds suffered a heart attack. His son took over. A male strapper with rough hands and heart was employed. I rented another stable and yard in another section of the stables, well away from the Reynolds' lane.

The old man never returned to the stables. The young man was cocky and full of himself. He was not liked. The men at the racetrack had patience. 'He'll get his comeuppance.'

He did, when taking a young woman out on a date just before he was to have a 'society wedding' to a wealthy Whyallaite! So anxious to 'talk' to this date, he parked the car far too close to the railway tracks. The train caught the small car, spinning it around and causing a great deal of damage though neither person inside was injured. The teasing was loud.

'I say sport. When can't you hear an ore train coming?'

'When you're too busy telling the young bit about your impending marriage.'

The men would laugh and laugh. The butt of their jokes would fume but say nothing.

One Sunday morning I was asked if I'd ride track work on a big seventeen-hand thoroughbred. He was a lanky horse of great power. I hadn't ridden him before but I had ridden others from that stable. He was very strong and feisty but so were many other racers; that didn't bother me. He was anxious to run.

I pulled on the fibreglass riding helmet and, with a leg up, was on the mountain. He was so high! He felt like a storm about to break.

Out on the track we went and there was no warm-up. We shot like a bullet from a gun into a gallop. I leant down into the gallop and went with him. There was no slowing this horse down. I thought, 'I'll let him run it out.' I sat tight and felt for him. No response. I pulled on the reins. He had the bit between his teeth and only flight on his mind.

I realised I had no control and neither did he. We were bolting. Flat out. I expected him to tire and I knew I was reasonably safe on the open track. He didn't tire. We were still racing. As we came around the track towards the starting line the big horse swerved and galloped through the open gates. People scattered as we thundered through.

I sat tight.

I thought he'd stop at the stables. We galloped down the length of the stables. Horses neighed and bucked in their fright. The big horse was reaching the dead end. We had to turn. Too late. Too fast. The big horse couldn't make it and fell as he tried to turn the corner.

I rocketed from his back, crashing into the wall head- and hands-first.

Silence. Peace. Absolute peace.

I looked down at my body.

All seemed to be in slow motion. My body lay crumpled up against the brick wall. I looked at it with awareness. I thought, 'I'm not going back to that. When that body wakes up it will be in pain. I'm not going back.'

I kept looking down at myself, watching the horse struggle to its feet, breathing hard but uninjured — no longer scared but exhausted. His head hung low and his sides heaved. People were shouting and running — all so slowly.

I drifted. I was not scared because as a child I'd often

experienced astral travelling and this was the feeling I now had. Floating from my body, being aware of leaving it behind. I floated above when suddenly it felt as if I were being grabbed. A feeling of being sucked along through colour. Colour that is indescribable because I've never seen or experienced such colour and words cannot describe it. As a writer I am unable to offer an adequate description of the light, the sucking and the peace. I sensed music — some sound of a great harmony yet it drifted and would not register within my thoughts. It was just there.

I felt myself no longer being sucked, just drifting, within nothing. Like air or a fine mist. Peace. Then a feeling of joy. Sheer joy. The spirit people appeared. I cannot describe the spirit people. I could see them — shapes within the mist.

Voices filled my being.

'It is not your time yet.'

'You cannot join us yet.'

'You must go back.'

'No, no,' I heard my voice arguing. Yet my voice was not my voice. There was no voice. I heard myself but there were no words. 'No. I don't want to go back.'

'You must. Your journey is far from finished.'

A feeling of great peace and warmth enveloped me. I wanted to cry. Then I was full of colour and light. I allowed that feeling to be me. Again there are no words to describe what I experienced.

Death.

I floated. I experienced a beauty of being that has never ceased to amaze me when I recall that moment in space and time we call death.

Then the going home! The feeling of sucking again — like a giant mouth pulling me into it. I felt myself spinning, the sucking feeling so strong, almost painful, as I felt my soul re-enter my body. I came crashing back into my flesh with a shock that shook every part of me. I awoke.

People were standing around me and over me. Someone was kneeling beside me with a glass of brandy. The fumes filled my head and their voice was telling me to 'just take a sip'.

'She's conscious,' a voice said.

I tried to say, 'I've been dead,' but I felt the black cloak of unconsciousness enfold me and I welcomed it. I awoke again unable to move. I was strapped into a bed, my body held tight. A woman's face peered down into mine, angry and distorted. I blinked to clear my vision. The woman leaned back saying, 'Good. You're awake.' It was the matron of the hospital.

'I was dead.'

A kind young doctor appeared and sat beside me. 'Can you remember anything?'

'Yes. I couldn't stop the horse. He fell and I crashed into the wall.' I swallowed down the rest of the story. I knew what had happened. Who would believe me, that I had died? I looked at the doctor. He placed his hand on my cheek and the tears slid down my face as he spoke. 'You have a broken neck. You are very, very lucky to be alive. In fact, we are all amazed that you are alive and that all your responses seem to be working. You are going to go through a great deal of pain but we will keep you as free from that as possible. It doesn't look good. You will have to have surgery. For now you are in traction and then we'll put you in a brace. You will have limited movement and should face the possibility that you may be confined to a wheelchair. Your hands and wrists are shattered and we are going to repair them as best we can. Do you understand?'

I tried to nod but I couldn't move my neck.

'Good.' He removed his hand from my face. I was crying freely. All I could think of was, 'What about my riding?'

He wheeled the bed into the X-ray unit where several men stood waiting.

'We are going to set your hands. I'm going to give you some-thing to relax you.' I lay groggy half in, half out of the world as I watched the surgeons move my hands and wrists about. I drifted in and out of sleep. Warm soft sleep. When I awoke my hands and wrists were encased in plaster.

Over the next few days I was tested and re-tested; tapped and pricked; wheeled from room to room, doctor to doctor. No one spoke to me directly.

'She shows all the normal nerve responses.'

'She shouldn't.' They'd shake their heads.

I had a broken neck, yet all systems worked.

'She can walk.'

'I don't believe this.'

More tests and more tests.

Doris came every day to visit. 'Don't worry. Just get better. Dream is fine. Mr Bear has taken care of her and everything is okay.'

Only at night was I left alone. Someone was forever prodding at me, poking me, administering X-rays, needles and pills.

'Wake up, wake up, here's Doctor so-and-so to see you.'

'We need a sample of blood, urine, saliva.'

'We are going to sit you up. It's time for you to go on solids.' I had to be fed. I hated it. The nurses were always too busy to feed me slowly. They shoved the food into my mouth and spoke to me as if I were a baby. 'Now open up. Just a teeny, weenie bit more. Now you'll like this dessert. Eat up.'

My vision and hearing were normal and I had not lost my sense of smell. I hated the smell of food being boiled, of antiseptic, sickness and decay. The various gels and creams they used on my body left me giddy with overload. I was forever itchy, needing to scratch. In a few days I was restless and wanting to go home.

The doctors finally decided they could do no more for me unless I agreed to major surgery in Adelaide. Some doctors wanted to proceed with an operation immediately; others wanted me to recover further before they operated; one just wanted to 'see what would happen'. Opinions, opinions. Doris and I were both overwhelmed by all the different expert opinions.

Finally they decided I could be left to heal naturally; my neck would fuse itself into place. I'd have limited mobility but there was nothing else they could do. I would have to wear the neckbrace for at least two years and have continual physiotherapy. They were happy with the way my broken hands and wrists were healing. They congratulated themselves time and time again over the 'marvellous' job they had done. But they told me, 'You will have big problems in old age. Arthritis. Your hands and fingers may distort. Your wrists will never be the same.' I was told to think about all my options.

Doris just wanted to get me 'out of their clutches'. When the doctors told her I could go home only if there was someone to care for me she gave them 'a mouthful'. I don't know what she said but she had a look of victory and satisfaction on her face. 'I told them where to get off,' was all she said.

Doris hated to be bossed but she provided a wall of loyal support for me as I struggled back to some sort of independence. She cooked, helped me eat by cutting up all my food, helped me to wash and dress, pulled on my boots and did up my buttons. She understood my frustration and, rather than taking over, she gave me the space to do things very slowly for myself. Not once did she speak of the accident as my fault. A bond of love developed between us.

I could not come to terms with what I had been told — that I would never ride again! I shed buckets of tears.

Bill drove me out to the stables to visit Dream three times a week. At weekends I'd just sit and be together with her. The trainers were concerned, and offered all sorts of advice. They had lost friends in horse accidents and many wore broken bones and scars from accidents they themselves had experienced. They scoffed at the doctors.

'Don't you bloody well listen to those quacks. You'll ride again.'

'You don't need to ride to train trotters!'

'You'll be right, mate. Just give it time.'

They joked.

'Jesus, I thought you was dead.'

'Christ Almighty, I heard the bloody crash as you hit the wall.'

'Pity that big bugger couldn't fly down the track like that on race day.'

'Bejesus, Ted, what the hell did you put in that horse's feed? He flew.'

Dream was happy and well cared for. I'd sit in the wheelbarrow and watch the day's activities. I gouged out some plaster from around my fingers so I could begin to use my hands. I managed to free enough fingers to hold a brush, a fork and drive my motorbike. I could just manage to pull the gear lever in! I was mobile. I could spend the days at the stables as I healed.

The doctor and specialist followed my progress. They were furious to find I had removed plaster so I could be independent. They re-plastered my hands to keep my fingers still. I dug the plaster out again.

Peter came to visit with a horse box, suggesting that while I was recovering Dream could be 'turned out'. He had bought ten acres just outside the small township of Melrose and he was planning to build stables and yards and 'do up' an old home he had bought and placed on the site. He had big plans to break in stock horses and work the shearing sheds during the season to bring in some money. His ten acres were flat and treeless, with plenty of potential. I farewelled my beautiful Dream, telling her she was going for a rest until I recovered.

One hand and arm of plaster came off. A white, skinny arm greeted me.

The doctors were amazed and congratulations were in order. 'Look at that. Beautifully mended'; 'Look how she has movement.'

My hand and wrist seemed okay — sore but working. I used a squash ball to exercise my fingers.

My neck was another story. 'You are healing remarkably well. You neck is fusing, but with limited movement'; 'You will need a major operation. Your neck is holding but it's temporary.' Doctors, nurses and specialists all examined me. I was prodded and tested ad nauseam!

After several chiropractic treatments on my neck I decided enough was enough. I hated the manipulations. They made me vomit and faint; after each treatment I was in pain for days and I swallowed pain-killers as if they were lollies. After an argument with the therapist, I decided not to return. I hated his 'No pain, no gain' ethos. 'What dill thought up that piece of wisdom?' I asked Doris.

'Hitler.' She looked at me. 'Some bastard who wants power

by seeing you suffer. Don't go back.' I didn't and the pain-killers continued.

The other lot of plaster was removed. The doctors beamed. My hands worked, my wrists worked and there was no pain.

The metal neck-brace was driving me crazy. It chafed and rubbed my skin raw. Doris wrapped the metal with sheepskin to try to lessen the pressure. The heat of Whyalla, the brace and the wool finally frustrated me so much that I removed the brace forever. It was a relief, but migraine headaches began. I wore a soft rubber collar. It irritated me but I persevered.

I fretted about not being able to ride again.

'No, no, no,' said the doctors. 'No riding. Your neck needs to heal. Maybe in a couple of years after your operation. If it's successful.' They explained over and over about the damage and the healing process. I was not to ride. 'If you have another fall then that's it! You can't afford to have another fall. Not even from a bike... Do you understand? Do you understand?'

I understood them. They didn't understand me!

Doris and Bill drove me to visit Dream. My beloved horse was fat and well. I brushed her and promised that it wouldn't be long before we were back together.

Peter talked of getting her in foal. 'While you're recovering. Put her in, then you'll have a bay to train. You won't ride again but you can still handle horses and train them. I'll ride them. We could make a great team.'

I started to get excited. Yes! Yes! To work with horses again. Maybe in time I could ride again. A placid horse was not likely to throw me.

What an idea. Old Mr Reynolds' stables are empty. I could rent them and work the young horses from there. Peter and I were walking his block while Doris made a 'cuppa' and Bill fiddled with a water pump. I was excited about the idea and babbled cheerfully.

Finally Peter managed to get a word in. 'That's not quite what I mean.'

I stopped and turned to face him. 'What do you mean?'

'Us. You and me. You're old enough now and I've waited long enough. I'm a patient man, but — well — girls are married at your age with babies.'

My heart stopped. I knew where this was leading and I didn't want it.

Peter faced me. 'I want to marry you. We can live here and you can work with horses. We will have a great life. Kids and horses — what more could you want? I knew when we met that you were for me.'

'Just because you think I'm for you doesn't mean that I think I am.'

'I can wait. It's only a matter of time.'

'Do you really think you'll wear me down?'

'Of course. All women want to get married. All women want a man — we all know that. It's only natural!'

I was fuming by now. Red rage. Trying to keep it under control, I said, 'I don't want to marry you.'

'So what has all this been about?' asked Peter angrily.

'Friendship. It's about friendship.'

'But I want more.'

'I don't.'

'Of course you do. Men belong with women and women with men, and you won't do any better than the offer I'm giving you. You'll have everything.'

'I don't want everything. You are a friend and that's all you'll ever be.'

'Okay. I'll give you time to think about it.'

I was exasperated. 'I don't need time to think about it. Why is it that with men "no" always means "yes" or "maybe"?'

I exploded, shouting, 'I'll just take Dream home and we can forget about this whole stupid idea.'

'You won't be taking Dream anywhere.'

'Dream is mine and I'll do what I want with her. Whether or not I ride again, she is my friend. I can enjoy being with her, living with her, having her in my life.'

'Horses have to be used; to work. What a stupid thing to say, that you can just live with horses and not use them. You won't ride again. All the doctors have told you that. I'm offering you the best deal you'll ever get.'

'I don't want your bloody deals. I hate people who offer me deals!' I stormed away.

His words stopped me. 'You either marry me or lose Dream.'

I turned. 'What the hell are you talking about? How can I lose Dream. She's my horse.'

'No, she's not your horse. You still owe me fifty quid for her and the receipt is in my name.'

I stood and stared at him. Betrayal. 'What are you saying?'

'You haven't paid me back for the horse. She belongs to me.'

'That's not true. I've paid you thirty quid of the money.'

'Show me the receipt then.'

'You know there was no receipt — it was all done in good faith.'

'What's that?'

'I've nearly paid you back.'

'Marry me.'

'No.'

We left. Doris and Bill knew something had happened. The only comment Doris made was, 'You shouldn't have strung him along.'

I never had any contact ever again with Peter or Dream. Three months later he married a woman with several kids.

I cried at night for the loss of my Dream. I cried at the change the accident had brought to my life. The future looked bleak. There was no work in Whyalla. The city was growing fast and married couples were like mushrooms. Suddenly there were plenty of women to fill the service jobs. I needed to work and I needed a change. I burnt the neck-brace and packed my bags. I said goodbye to Olga, Pat and Ronald. Doris and Bill promised to keep in touch and to visit when they could. I caught the bus to Adelaide.

Independence

I arrived in Adelaide with very little heart, no job and nowhere to stay.

I went into the botanical gardens and sat in the arms of a big Moreton Bay fig. No family, no dogs, no horses and a broken neck. I felt miserable. I cried away my pain, gathered myself together and hugged as many trees as I could find. Tree-hugging has become a catchphrase; I hugged trees when it wasn't fashionable. They are solid to hug with that deep inner strength of the earth. Old, old trees have a marvellous strength that comes of being alive for hundreds of years.

I left the beautiful gardens in a happier mood and headed for the YWCA. Within a week I had a job in a large city store as a clerical-cashier. I entered figures in ledgers and relieved cashiers in different departments so they could have their meal and tea breaks.

At that time I had no head mobility at all and had to turn from the waist. It was an effort to look down. I preferred to lift things up to eye level rather than bend my head. I worked with my ledger propped up in front of me.

'You need glasses, girl, working on the books like that,' my boss would say.

I never told them about my injuries. I knew employers shied away from anyone with a neck or back injury.

The YWCA was busy and impersonal. Women came and went constantly, the sound of singing voices and laughter filled the corridors. Meal times were loud and women smiled and chatted. Paths crossed and stories were told. Breakfast and dinner time were gossip times and I heard so many stories of travel, romance and heartbreak that I could have written several books without leaving the dining area! But it was far too noisy and busy for me. It was exciting at first, but then lonely; I missed the companionship of animals and I was heart-sore for a dog.

I went to board with Mr and Mrs Coombes in their home in a suburb called Dry Creek, at the end of the train and bus line, north of Adelaide. Signs along the highway read, 'Last stop before the desert', 'The cheapest petrol you'll get' and 'Welcome to the North'. The signs were riddled with bullet holes until only slivers of metal held it all together, the rust acting like glue. I read those signs every day as I passed.

The homes at Dry Creek were railway-owned and of painted timber — white and green. They stood in military formation, facing the railway tracks and stockyards, which were continually packed. Sheep and cattle mainly. They went from paddock to truck and from truck to rail to the butcher. Some days there would be yards full of brumbies or donkeys or camels. The day the yards were crammed with Clydesdale horses I cried and cried.

'Jap meat market,' said the small bloke giving them water. 'They pay big money over there for horse meat. The "Froggies" eat horse too. They have butcher shops selling only horse — imagine that. It's a pity all those buggers don't eat donkeys too. The donkeys go to the zoo. Now the camel — that's another matter. They don't end up in someone's gut. No sir-ee. The Arabs buy them for racin' and breedin'.'

'The Arabs?'

'Yeah, the bloody Arabs. Don't that just beat it all! We got the buggers from them in the beginning and they bred like wildfire in the bush. Used to shoot them. Now we sell them back to the Arabs and make a packet.'

'Why do we export camels?'

'Good, big, tough stock. Good for racing. And another thing, we ain't got no foot-and-mouth disease in this country, so all the stock that comes from here is real clean.'

When the camels were in quarantine at Dry Creek I smiled. They were not destined for the dead-meat market. They always looked regal even though they were usually a wild and nasty bunch. They showed their outrage at being caught. I could not pat them like the horses. They looked down on humans, fully knowing that we are not to be trusted. They had a genetic distrust of humankind.

The week when the Clydesdales waited in the yards I would help feed and water them. They were all human-friendly and I sang songs to them and told them stories of how great they were. Mighty warrior horses. The men who fed them looked at me as if I were moonstruck and made what they thought were amusing comments.

'Do you treat your boyfriend like that?'

'Lucky fellow.'

'Keep them happy, girl, it makes the meat stay soft.'

I'd shake my head and refuse to bite back.

The day the beautiful horses were to leave I took a 'sickie' from work and I brushed each horse and fed them sugar and carrots. As they were loaded I leaned over the rails to pat each head as it passed. I sang to them a song of farewell.

'Mad kid!' said the men loading the horses.

I decided I had to move from the comfortable home in which I was boarding to get away from the sight of so many animals waiting to be slaughtered. I was reluctant to leave as I was working two beautiful trotting horses belonging to Mr Coombes and it was a joy to be on the track at dawn, pounding the earth awake, the sound of snorting horses and the cold air freezing my ears.

I moved into a shared flat with a wonderful friend, Tigger (called after the tiger in the Winnie-the-Pooh stories). She was a vivacious, intelligent person with a big heart, laugh and smile who dreamed of finding a rich husband. Taking three-quarters of an hour each morning just to paint her face, she was a work of art. She was one of those rare people whom everyone immediately likes.

I was once again without horses. Living across the road from the beach, I would often see the gallopers in training in the grey mornings, the sand flying from their hooves. Riding had become too painful and even the couple of rides I took on quiet riding-school horses hurt my back. I lived with the pain and fear, scared of ending up in a wheelchair as the doctors had predicted.

I decided to work with dogs and for the next eighteen months every weekend I worked voluntarily in a big, lost-dogs' home. There were rewarding stories and heartbreaking stories every weekend but I needed change.

I said farewell to Tig and my job and travelled with a friend to Darwin. We shared a flat there and both found work. For me Darwin was dominated by men, alcohol, violence, racism and humidity. The highlight of my time there was the arrival of Shelly who stayed with me until she died fourteen years later. I saw her in the window of a pet shop — no bigger than a large drinking mug. Black and white, with ears that resembled open doors on a car. She was gorgeous. But being mauled by the other bigger pups.

I entered the store. A skinny woman in a smock was smoking and talking on the phone. The cigarette was all ash. I waited for it to drop and the conversation to stop. The ash dropped, the woman ground it into the floor and lit another cigarette from the glowing stub of the completed smoke.

'Hang on a tick, Josie. Yeah? Can I help you?'

I explained that the small pup in the window was being mauled.

'She's two dollars.' The woman went back to her conversation. I was furious. I slammed down two dollars and gave her one of my father's colourful insults; picked up the puppy and took her straight to the vet. The vet sewed up the bites and tears, rinsed out her mouth and gave me antibiotic for her.

I bathed Shelly in the hand basin at my flat. Under all the shit and grime she also had a beautiful, spotted belly. She became a loyal friend and companion — a foxie cross, possibly part-heeler, she won everyone's heart with her winning ways. Never pushy but always there.

Back in Adelaide I decided that I finally needed to consult a specialist about my neck and constant migraines, followed by spells of blindness. The endless tests began.

I spent hours in waiting rooms looking at fish and listening to muzak. I was told, 'You will never ride again and you will have limited mobility... You need an operation. We have a fifty–fifty chance of keeping you out of a wheelchair... It is for your own good, this operation... We must do it as quickly as possible... In three months.' The date was set.

I returned to work and explained to my boss that I would be leaving and why. My boss was an elderly woman caught in a time warp. She belonged in a genteel English society of good manners, the vapours and women who did as they were told. She kindly promised that a position would be available for me after my operation. If it were successful.

Working in a large department store brought me in contact with many people.

Work was never dull.

There was the time when I went to remove excess money from a cash register only to find it empty.

'Where's all the money?' I asked an assistant.

'Oh, the register mechanics said they'd pass it on. They took the register for service.'

I looked at the register closely. It had the label of another store on the front. It turned out that the 'register mechanics' had swapped registers in four stores!

Once, during late-night shopping, just before Christmas when everyone was in a rush, I caught the old lift up to the second floor. There were four models, a crate of champagne and me. The lift jammed between floors. We were stuck for over an hour. When the lift finally moved and came to rest at an open door out we all fell. Pissed and singing.

We had sat on the floor of the lift and cracked open a couple of bottles while I listened to the models' life stories. They decided I would make good modelling material and so I let them paint and powder me, dress me in clothes I would never dream of buying and walk the catwalk. I looked at myself in the mirror and laughed. Tig photographed this stranger.

As I removed the make-up, powder and paint, my new friends told me, 'You come up real well.'

'But it's not me. I feel false.'

'Think of it as a piece of theatre.'

I refused further offers.

I had become involved in the protests over the coming Springbok tour of Australia. I was reading and questioning. I became involved in the anti-Vietnam-war movement, convinced that women did not give birth to sons to have them injured or killed in war. I became outspoken in my beliefs and was warned that I would be sacked if politics interfered with my work. Store policy would not allow staff to wear a peace sign to work.

Meanwhile I had purchased a beautiful seven-year-old ex-trotting horse, Bluey. A gentle, willing animal, he did all I asked of him but he preferred his solitude and was very much his own horse. He was friendly when called, but had been 'over-handled' due to the rigours of the racing industry and he liked just to 'be'.

I bought the last working horse-drawn bread van from Nailsworth Bakery. It was in excellent condition with the original lettering on each side with the name of the bakery and 'Bakers and Pastrycooks' scrolled underneath. With the help of six friends, the van and its shafts were sanded, scrubbed and painted. We pulled the turntable apart, greased and replaced worn bolts. I bought a beautiful set of harness.

Where the baker usually stood to drive the horse, inside the cart between the doors, I placed a sliding board. I could pull this across the space to form a bed base. I had canvas cut and sewn to clip over the windows and doors at night, giving me a cosy private space to sleep in. I could climb in and out of the back door. I planned to recover from my operation. I was determined that I would not end up in a wheelchair. If I couldn't ride I'd drive!

As work on the cart progressed I decided to travel in it to Victoria, to start a new life. I had a horse and cart, no car and an open future. I started to make plans. My friends all thought I was mad, then brave, then said, 'It's something I'd love to do.' I made lists of things I had to take. I planned to cook outside, or if caught in the rain I had a one-burner gas stove. I added a kero lamp, candles and torch to my list.

In the front of the van would be my food and cooking utensils; a first-aid kit for me and the horse; dog food. Buckets, ropes, brushes, spare clips for the blinds, shoes, a rasp, nails, horse food and water. I added wet-weather gear, a clothesline, books and personal stuff. I had lists and lists that I slowly pared down until I took only what I needed. I read maps and planned the quietest route to Melbourne, avoiding main roads. I planned to head off as soon as I had recovered from the operation. If I was going to end up in a wheelchair then I was going to live my life the way I wanted until that had happened. I was having bad dreams about the operation, asleep and awake. I was scared, unsure and definitely wary of all the expert opinions I was receiving. I was tired of being talked at and talked over.

I went to a local doctor about my asthma and he suggested that I should see a local chiropractor who could give me lessons in breathing. She might also help with my neck, the pain and mobility.

The chiropractor was a tall, elderly woman of great compassion. She was also a Buddhist. It was from her I learnt about meditation and yoga and to care for my body — what I did with it, how I maintained it and what food I put into it. She started to work with massage on my neck and talked to me about my diet. She asked why I still ate meat when I had such compassion and love for animals. I heard her. She challenged me, opened up a new belief system for me and gave me reading matter to help me understand that 'true healing' was in my own hands.

I read about my body, about health and diet; I questioned the specialists who told me it was all nonsense or a 'fad'. I remembered my nana and started to grow vegetables; to bottle, preserve and dry. I learnt about herbs, spices and sauces. I began an exciting life-adventure with food. My nana would tell me, 'Never, never cook when you are angry. Buy fish and chips, but don't cook or your anger will go straight into that food. Never cry over food, it makes it all bitter. Always cook with a song in your heart.' My nana always 'thanked the Lord' for each meal. My father always thanked the earth. Friends either said grace or, 'Two, four, six, eight, bog in, don't wait!'

Visits to specialists continued. It seemed they all wanted to examine my neck and back and marvel that I was still walking and not already in a wheelchair.

At the same time I regularly visited my healer and she managed to improve mobility and reduce the pain.

I felt locked in at work. The big department store had been fun for a while, but eight hours a day shut inside an artificially lit and aired building began to tell on me. I wanted to be out-of-doors.

My ageing boss was prone to weeping; a large bombastic co-worker wanted her position and things were not pleasant in the office where all the book-keeping was done. Dorothy was a nasty piece of work, deeply unhappy and bitter, and when gentle Alice retired, she became acting head. Work was hell. She ranted and raged at my 'peace movement phase', as she called it, and threatened that I'd be sacked for 'going against the grain of our country. All those poor, poor men...' Then a new woman came to be our boss — innovative, charming and efficient, and as long as we 'did our job' she left us alone. Dorothy declared war! The office became a battle zone.

Hair was the 'shocking' play that everyone wanted to see; Joan Baez was singing anti-war songs and Janis Joplin gave us a new role model.

I exploded. Dorothy had been really obnoxious all week. The tension in the office was horrific. My friend Nancy was telling me to 'have some understanding' but I came to work with a peace badge on my collar and refused to take it off. We had an altercation. Dorothy went straight to the top and I was sacked. I was told it was because I would not keep my politics where they belonged. Three fat suited men explained that I had a bad attitude and that I had verbally attacked a sensitive member of staff who had been with the store since she left school.

I spent the next two weeks finishing off all I needed to do on my cart and organised my life around my coming recovery. I was shit scared of the operation and the consequences.

Five days before the operation I made many decisions. I took control of my own health. I knew I had to shift the energy surrounding me. I said goodbye to friends, hitched up Bluey into the cart and headed for Melbourne, the open road and a new life. From fright to flight. I forgot to cancel my appointment with the doctors and the hospital. I hit the open road with joy in my heart, a song in my soul and the friendship and companionship of my dog and horse.

On the drom

I began my journey at the side of the Murray River. There I hitched Bluey to the cart, said goodbye to the friends who had helped transport us, and boarded the ferry. Bluey was excellent. He pulled the cart onto the hollow-sounding metal floor and stood quietly as cars were loaded, the ferry engines started and we crossed the water. We clattered off the ferry, amusing those waiting to cross and those following us. Then on to the beginning of what is known as 'the Coorong' — a stretch of straight road some ninety miles long. Bitumen with dirt verges. The Coorong is an ancient seabed, one side of the road dry, though capable of sustaining sheep; the other side a world apart from the farm country, with salt pans, sand blows and coastal vegetation which in places during the wet season becomes lush, green and full of bird life and animals. The ocean, some half an hour's walk from the road, pounds the shore into huge waves of sand which, viewed from a distance, create the illusion of huge moving waves.

The beauty and solitude of the Coorong captured me in its spell. The spirits are very ancient there. Timeless. The Aboriginal people knew — know — this Dreamtime place; a paradise for them before the white invasion. Rich in wildlife, fishing, medicines and food; the land is dotted with Aboriginal middens.

There is a sense of abundance in the Coorong despite the apparent lack of fresh water. Dig down, and fresh water can be found — enough to drink and use with care. The Coorong has been grazed. Farmers have run sheep, horses and cattle on the fragile land, houses and huts reminders of that past. The settled side of the road had no water to spare. Dams held muddy water and the earth was cracking, opening her mouth for moisture. Rain teases the Coorong. Coming in from over the ocean, it begins with the smell — the smell of coming rain. Nostrils sniff the air expectantly. The rain teases with a few drops, then passes on to the rich dairy land beyond.

I visited 'Chinamen's Well'. A tax was levied from ship owners, requiring them to pay ten pounds for each Chinese person they were carrying on their ship. Rather than pay the money, the ship owners dropped the people off at the Coorong. From there they walked overland to the goldfields of Bendigo, Ballarat and further on. The well, dug by the Chinese, held fresh clean water. It was lined with blocks of compressed shells, and sand footholds were carved into the inner wall. The surrounding wall was of hard stone. I sat thinking about all those thousands of Chinese men abandoned in this place. What must they have thought and how on earth did they find their way? So many questions in my mind. I looked down and there lay three old Chinese coins. I picked them up, thanked the ancestors and kept them for many years before passing them on to a friend who read the *I Ching*. Years later I returned to the well to find it surrounded by a thick metal grille. Vandals had destroyed so much that after restoration it was imprisoned.

I was very conscious of the need to carry water. I had two large plastic containers that I kept full, but I did not mix water as quality varied. I could last several days, or less, according to Bluey's needs. I knew how to be frugal with water — how to wash, wash up, wash clothes and water plants all with very little water. And water is very easy to heat with wood or even in the sun using a plastic covering. It's always cool when hung in a hessian water bag and I had two on the back of the cart.

The other essential item was a shovel — used to dig a fire pit, to release wheels from a bog and, most important of all, to cover human shit! Nothing is worse, when out camping or walking, than to come across a pile of human shit, the nearby bushes and scrub decorated with flying toilet paper. 'No bloody self-respect at all,' my father would have said. Many a time I've collected and buried other people's shit, paper, bloodied pads and soiled nappies! I'm always amazed that humans can leave such garbage.

I was surprised by the number of fishing shacks and homes hidden in the scrub or sitting beside the road surrounded by white-painted stones. Baskets, nets and boats all telling the story of a life lived with the sea. Some were holiday shacks; others were sinking slowly back into the earth, a mass of rusted metal and flapping tin. Many were lived in and dogs barked as we passed. Some homes were decorated with driftwood, huge bleached bones, hanging baskets or tin drums gloriously alive with the colour of geraniums.

My dog Shelly rode in the cart with me. She stood in the door looking out or perched up on my bed roll watching the world. She was 'on guard' and would bark whenever we had a visitor.

Towards evening I would begin to look for a camping spot for the night. I consulted rough maps to see if there was a hope of water but mostly I just had to take whatever came along — a paddock, or a camp somewhere off the road. I often pulled into a farmhouse and asked if I could stay in one of their paddocks for the night. I only had one refusal. That was a very modern, new farmhouse where the woman just said, 'No' and slammed the door in my face.

Everyone else was friendly and curious. Some people invited me in to share a meal, or have a shower, or both. Some invited me to spend the evening with them, offered me a bed, or came to my campfire in the evening to talk. Each place was different and special. Most people asked me why I was 'doing it'. Then they'd tell me: 'I would have really loved to have done so-and-so in my life.' I touched the wanderer and adventurer in them and they remembered.

In one place I camped in the front paddock, ate with the family and went out spotlight-shooting for rabbits with the two sons. Like most farm boys they drove and shot well. I left next morning with two rabbits. The dog and I lived well on stew for the next few days. I was not a vegetarian then. When travelling, I would shoot a rabbit or hare to feed my dogs.

To park on the route was not always easy. Fences would soldier beside the road for miles. I'd start looking for a suitable spot mid-afternoon. I'd think, 'Oh well, if it comes to that, the side of the road or a dirt track will have to do.' It never came to that. Bush spots would reveal themselves, often with water or trees.

I experienced velvet nights of watching the moon on her dance of waxing and waning, to reappear again, a silver sliver of light — the light and the dark moon, for so long worshipped as a manifestation of the Goddess. I've never been able to see 'the man in the moon'. She has always been a woman to me, perhaps it was so for my father too; he never spoke of the moon as anything but 'she'.

Mornings of grey and purple, or pink and blue dawns. Early-morning washes that wake the body like no other wash can. The shock of cold water! I splashed myself awake in the mornings, saving the hot, relaxing wash for night-time. Breakfast outside is a special time. Tea is brewed and bread toasted over hot coals. The smell of toast and tea! The smell of the morning — hot and heavy or crisp and clear, sweet and washed dry, humid and threatening, windy and malevolent — each morning is a mirror for the day to come; each opening a new scene, another weather story. When the sky blazed, the day shimmered and the flies settled, I settled too. I'd camp or rest. Bluey was far more relaxed and comfortable if asked not to work in heat. Then a good book, a cup of tea and a shady tree were in order. When the rain trickled down my neck and my hands froze I'd also make camp until the storm left to play in another area.

I kept a routine with Bluey each day. Up in the morning, a few sticks into the fire as I raced past to pee. A few small logs on the fire, on with the billy. A cold splash and a big yell. Feed Bluey. (I carried mixed hard feed, oats, molasses and carrots. I carried a bale of hay or bought hay from where I camped.) Breakfast. Wash up. Make another billy of tea. While it brews roll up my bed, tidy up, wash any clothes, hang them in the doorway or out the back, tea into thermos, fire out and all signs of my stay cleared away. Lay out harness. Unrug Bluey and brush him. Harness up, into the cart and away.

In the evening. Pull in. Brake on. Take Bluey from the shafts, unharness him. Wash him down. Turn him out or walk with him so he can roll. Let him drink and then brush him. Water, feed and hay accessible. If the night was cold, I'd rug him before I retired for the night. I'd also check his body and feet each night; I'd oil his hooves. Then, set up camp fire, feed Shelly, make a cup of tea, prepare a meal. After that, the evening was mine. Or I might spend it with the host family or a guest or two.

One evening, as I was sitting watching my food cooking, Shelly started a low growl. I put my hand on her head, looked up in the direction she was intent on and waited. An old woman and a young man came into the firelight. The old Aboriginal elder slowly sat down, sinking her large body into the ground. We looked at each other. The beauty of her soul, pain and a deep happiness flowed from her eyes. We held out our hands and touched with greeting. The young man sat, his hands reaching out, too much sadness in the depths of his eyes. I handed him the tobacco. He rolled a thick smoke and took extra papers. I smiled, thinking, 'One fat smoke and extra papers makes several "race horse" smokes.'

I poured us each a mug of tea, handed over the tobacco again and told them why I was travelling to Melbourne this way. After the tea the young man stood, nodded and melted into the dark. I shared my meal, made another billy of tea and added logs to the fire. The elder spoke to me of her people, the people of the Coorong. Once a proud people, thousands strong. They lived in paradise. Then came the white man. Then came the diseases — epidemics, killing thousands. Then came the farmers, the Christians, the businessmen, the Welfare. Then came men who loved the sport of fox hunting, complete with horse and hounds, gung-ho and guns. The fox? The Aboriginal people were the fox.

She talked of the spirit of the land, the song of the land. Her dream was to keep her language alive and her people proud. We talked about women and she spoke of the beautiful pelican-feather cloaks the women used to make. I talked openly to this wise elder about the spirits I saw — how many seemed to be from other places.

'Like the rats that came with the ship,' she replied and laughed until the tears ran. We made more tea.

For years I had chosen who I spoke to about seeing spirits, the colours around all living things and living with magic.

This elder understood and we talked until the light turned. The young man returned, bringing with him a loaf of bread. I scrambled eggs and made tea while he browned the bread.

After breakfast I followed the elder down a path to a large stone homestead. The owners were away on holiday. I followed her into the house, through the beautifully appointed kitchen into a formal dining room — long polished table, heavy chairs, thick carpet, velvet drapes, artwork on the walls.

The elder stopped and waited. I looked at the artwork. Horror hit me. A series of paintings of 'The Fox Hunt'. I burst into tears. The elder led me from the house and we sat in the grass. 'They painted it.' I let the tears run down my face.

We walked slowly back to camp where we drank more tea. The young man shook my hand, mumbled a thank you and walked away to wait. The elder and I talked a little, then hugged. She gave me a headband which I wore until it fell to pieces; then I sewed those pieces onto a pair of pants.

I watched her walk away, turn, wave and become one with her beloved land. I realised how little I knew.

I caused interest when I passed through towns.

But the best incident happened one day when I stopped at a roadhouse for a burger. I wasn't sure how Bluey would react to the pumps and traffic but he was fine. I pulled in and waited. A tourist bus drove in, all the people looking at us, pointing and laughing. The pump attendant came over, grinning. 'Super or standard?'

'I don't need petrol but I'd kill for a burger and a soft drink.'

He laughed and came back with my order, telling me the people on the bus had paid.

'Good on them and thank you,' I replied. As each person on the bus had passed us on their way into the roadhouse, they all made the same joke. Yep. Same as the attendant. But they made up for it with my free lunch.

Once I was trying to take a good look at the fishing shacks beside the road when out of one popped an old man, small and ropy.

'Hey, you, stop!' he yelled. I did. 'Watcha doin'?'

'Going to Melbourne to live.'

'I'll be buggered. In that?'

'Yes.'

'Bejesus. Now I've seen everything. I haven't seen the likes of you on the road for years. Why you goin' to Melbourne?'

'I hope to get work. To earn some money to travel.'

'Don't go. Big cities kill you people.'

'I'll go down the coast, out of the city.'

'By Christ, girl, you've made my day. Whatcha eatin'?'

'Stew.'

He laughed. 'Wait a mo.' He returned with a newspaper parcel. 'Here, this'll give you a decent feed.'

'Thanks, thanks a lot.' I shook a hand that told stories of the sea. I looked at him. 'Would you be of the MacNamaras?'

'Now how did you know that? How did you know me mother's name?'

'You feel like the sea.'

He bent over double, laughing and saying, 'Bejesus, bejesus.'

When I unwrapped the parcel I found fresh fish and a small cooked crayfish. I dined in style for the next few nights and laughed aloud thinking of the delightful old man and his sense of humour.

Bluey did really well on the journey. Never went lame or became sore. We took it slow. I never pushed him. He trotted twice on me. Once was on a tarred road. I was dozing in the sun, reins slack. Bluey was nodding away to himself and snorting at flies. A rail line ran beside the road. Suddenly one of those little put-put machines that travel the line came along. Startled, Bluey took off. I awoke with a start, still holding the reins and, speaking to reassure him, I brought him back to a walk. 'Is your heart thumping as much as mine?' I asked him.

The second time was on a dirt road. We were both dreaming, when suddenly we were away in the chariot race! Pots and pans clanged and clattered. I pulled him back. 'Did you dream you were racing?' I asked him. He flicked his tail, refusing to talk about the incident.

'Embarrassed?' I queried.

He kept his condition well. He was my first concern, the dog my second. I studied our route, other possible ways; talked to locals about roads, creeks and hills, and always listened to my horse. One way might be a little longer but with fewer hills. Traffic did not bother Bluey as much as it bothered me. He was a gem. I kept a close eye on his shoes and organised farriers as I needed them.

Only one farrier was a 'real bummer'. He was older than me but not yet forty, cynical and with no manners or patience. He grabbed the horse's foot and yanked it sideways in temper. Bluey jumped to get balance. 'Stand bloody still!' yelled the man and hit Bluey in the side with his rasp.

I grabbed the rasp from his hand. 'How dare you hit my horse.' I advanced with fire in my eyes and the rasp held out in front of me. He grabbed his bag and ran, into his car and away in a cloud of dust! I stood holding the rasp, my mouth open. I still have that rasp!

When it poured for two days I stayed with a hospitable aged widow who loved to cook. I was driving through her small town as the first drops of rain began to fall.

'Hello, hello,' came a friendly call from behind a fence. 'I'm on the lookout for you. Read about you in the paper I did. Knew it was going to rain. It's going to rain you know. For a couple of days. Bert said he saw you yesterday on the road so I'm watching for you. It's going to pour.' Out through the gate she came, small and white-haired, covered by a large flowered apron. 'You go down that lane there and put your horse and wagon in the paddock, then come inside. You and the dog. I'll put on the kettle.'

By the time I had tended to Bluey it was pouring. I removed my wet clothing and changed into warm, dry clothes. By the time I entered that fire-warm kitchen I could hear my stomach growling from all the baking smells. The kettle was singing, hot scones were steaming under a tea towel and small pancakes frying golden on the range.

The sky poured rivers of water for the next two days. I ate and read, ate and talked, ate and read. The kitchen was cosy, the bath deep and the bed heated with a hot-water bottle.

As I was driving from a large country town a black Rolls Royce cruised up beside me. The driver invited me to camp for the night on a nearby property owned by his employer. I drove along a tree-lined drive, passed an elegant mansion surrounded by a well-kept garden, and found myself parked in a yard of blue-stones. Bluestone stables and sheds made the area feel heavy, like a prison. I put Bluey in one of the yards, fed and watered him. A young man invited me to spend the night in his home. He was the owner's son and he lived in a separate home with his wife and children, a portable home squashed into a section at the back, probably the mansion's original large vegetable garden. I later regretted not sleeping in my van as that was not a happy house-hold — too many undercurrents.

I was invited to a sherry with the owner. At six the chauffeur came to collect me. I followed him into the bluestone mansion. It was elegant inside and cold. No laughter or joy had been in that house for years. The matriarch was as elegant as the house. Local history was her speciality. As I sipped my sherry she said, 'You look at history now. Look at all the big mansions — where are they situated? In wealth, along the trail the Chinese walked on their way to the goldfields. So many mansions, all because of the wool boom. Beautifully built, many three storeys high. Many rival the very best of British manor houses. South Australia didn't have convicts so there was lots of money but not enough labour. Until the Chinese arrived. They weren't convicts but they were certainly labour. As they walked to the goldfields they were captured and used as forced labour. It was their blood and sweat that built these tombs of grandeur for people with pretentious ideas about the glory of the old country and the queen. We built these shows of wealth with the blood and bones of a captured slave force. These places sing of death.'

'No wonder there is no joy here,' I thought.

'My son will show you the stables in the morning. Ask him to remove the bricks and show you the body that was bricked up in the wall. We've found several over the years. Rather than bury people who died, they bricked them into the wall. The bodies' companions must have wondered at such madness, or did they brick up their dead companions' bodies in the hope they would be found some day to reveal the truth of how these mansions were built? What forebears we truly had. Good upright Christian men who ruled councils and governments. How many are bricked up in walls all along this trail?'

I couldn't sleep that night. I kept thinking that maybe the bodies had been alive when bricked up, to teach others a lesson? The place was alive with disturbed spirits and I was pleased when dawn came and I could leave.

Every town had a local historian. People talked history and were interested in their locality. Several were fascinating in their knowledge of history but it was all male 'white-fella' history. A few knew something of the history of the Chinese or Aboriginal people but it was only a little of what they could have known if they had asked or searched. No one mentioned women unless asked.

I stayed on a sheep farm where every half-hour a gun would go off. The farmer patrolled his fence line all night, shooting every half-hour to scare away the foxes. His paddock was full of newborn lambs. They must have been as terrified as I was! One evening I drove into a farmhouse and a young boy answered my call. He said I could use the front paddock to camp in. As I was setting up for the night I heard the roar of an engine and looked up. Coming down the road was an old flatbacked buckboard with wooden-spoked steering wheel. I stood up to watch. The largest woman I have ever seen was driving behind that huge wooden wheel, filling all the cabin. The back was packed with kids and dogs.

'There's gypsies in our paddock, there's gypsies in our pad-dock,' I heard the kids singing.

The buckboard swung up the drive and shuddered to a halt. Kids and dogs came screaming over, followed by Mum.

That was one of the happiest nights I ever spent with people. Thirteen kids, lots of dogs and Mum.

It was a dairy farm. Mum and the kids were farmers, and gen-erous, happy farmers at that. Dinner was mountains of food. Mashed potatoes, meat, gravy and veg., followed by pudding and thick, sweet, fresh cream. The table bounced with food, elbows and laughter. After dinner Mum told me the local stories. Her history was that of the bushrangers and she was a storyteller indeed. The stories were of robberies and tough, bearded men who rode wild horses. Banks, booty and stagecoaches were their business. Her pride in these colourful stories made me feel that one such character with a great deal of panache was proudly related.

I spent an evening singing around a fire with another woman and her seven musically talented children. They were 'piss-poor' in money but rich in spirit.

All too soon I found myself coming closer to the city of Geelong, a satellite city of sprawling Melbourne. All the roads beyond Geelong seemed to be freeways. I was advised to end my journey at Geelong.

Camping on the outskirts of Geelong was like being in a light show all night — no darkness. Friends found me next morning. We loaded Bluey into a float, placed my wagon on a trailer and 'hit the freeway'. Melbourne was so big, so polluted, so noisy! My friends knew how I would feel. They found me a quiet house beside the sea, an hour from Melbourne city. I could breathe!

Bluey was put in a paddock of thick grass. I brushed him, checked him over. He carried weight but was not fat. He was fit and healthy. His eye and coat shone. It was time for him to rest. He needed a spell and as I watched him roll and eat I thanked him for our journey together.

Soft eyes
and velvet lips

I settled down to living in a house. I spent a great deal of time walking on the beach and I was working as a 'kennel maid', caring for three boisterous Afghan hounds until permanent homes could be found for them. Shelly was not at all pleased. The job was consistent, physically hard and very underpaid — no regulation and certainly no union. So many young girls wanted to work with animals that they were exploited, and still are in many animal-care industries.

A young girl of eleven came to talk with me about Bluey. She had fallen in love with him and wanted him for pony club. I agreed. He couldn't have gone to a more loving home. I had begun to have an active social life in Melbourne which placed any travel plans on the back-burner. Eventually I also sold the cart and harness to a collector.

I shared my heart, my life and a period of time with Jo, laughing, singing, generous Jo. She was fluent in many languages and would sing or talk to dogs, horses and myself as we ambled along. She would sing in whatever language was drifting through her mind but she always swore in Dutch. 'God verdomme!' she'd yell with passion. Jo convinced me to try acupuncture for my neck pain and continual migraines.

The only acupuncturist was a two-hour drive away. Jo drove me there twice a week for nine months. Four hours in the car, two with me asleep on the journey home. I will always thank Jo for that suggestion and all the support she gave me as I began the healing process.

The acupuncturist was Frank, a short Hungarian. He had gentle hands and was forever studying his healing arts. He looked at x-rays of my neck and shook his head, talking in Hungarian. He then explained to me that I had two breaks.

'Two breaks!'

'It seems so. One from the fall and another.'

'The helmet. I had cracked the helmet in half.'

He smiled. 'So this is so. What a mess. All tight like rope. Acupuncture will help you. You must watch your diet, your weight and have massage and saunas. I will teach you exercises you must do each day. It will be a long one this, yes. You should be a quadriplegic. You defy the gods.'

'I don't think so. I think I argued with them.'

I told him about my experience.

'You died. You have been to the place we will all go. So you did defy them, yes.' He laughed and gave me a book by Elizabeth Kubler-Ross to read.

I told him what the specialists had said and advised.

'Sometimes they are wrong. Acupuncture is ancient and old. It will be used by all doctors one day. You will see, yes? No wheelchair for you. You will never have full neck rotation. Your neck muscles will support you, but you must use massage and these herbal creams I make for you, yes?'

'Yes. The migraines?'

'No more migraines, just headache now. Migraines maybe, if you neglect yourself. They will remind you.'

He was right. The migraines were the first to cease. Then the intense pain. Frank was correct about neck rotation too for I still have to turn at the waist to see behind me and my neck mobility also varies with strain and the weather. The pain is always at low level but when it becomes intense it will settle with rest or pain-killers or acupuncture.

After nine months of treatment by Frank, I knew enough to

manage my own health and since he was taking an interest in my personal life it was time for us to part.

I knew I would ride again. I have stayed with the methods that work for me, and have used acupuncture regularly now for nearly thirty years. It keeps me mobile. I still ride and I know I owe my mobility and dance in life to that ancient healing art.

We moved into a large, rambling farmhouse on five acres on the edge of a small town on the Mornington Peninsula. The surrounding paddocks were full of horses. People rode.

I bought on a whim, and in a moment when such beauty filled my gaze that I simply had to have her, a pure white, fine-boned, big-eyed, fairy-touched Arabian. Missy met Jo and they fell in love. Missy danced, her head and tail high, hooves flashing. She was a show-off and loved an audience. With a coat of silk and flame inside her nostrils, she was sensitive and shy with a beauty that was truly winning.

A well respected German couple gave dressage and riding lessons in a large covered arena. Jo rode there and back once a week; she was a superb rider. Her lessons in dressage were advanced and formal. The riding was no challenge for her; the art was in persuading Missy to conform to the complexity required in dressage.

It was a challenge Jo loved and Missy enjoyed the learning, but retained her self-respect by 'throwing wobblies', just to let Jo know that she was humouring her.

Not being very practical, I bought Midnight. I was desperate for a horse to ride. She was jet-black with a white star — a sturdy barrel of a horse, very friendly and very pushy. Midnight was indulged! She was ideal for me to ride around the country. She was like a block of dark earth beside the ethereal Missy and behaved well in all situations.

All but one. She had absolutely no manners. No regard for fences, gates or human space. She walked through and over fences and gates and barrelled into feed sheds which created a circus when we tried to move her! Midnight was impossible to budge if she chose to root herself into the ground. Only food would work. But have a cup of tea and a piece of cake, or a picnic in the backyard, and Midnight would barrel through the fence to join the party! She broke halters and ropes, stood on everyone's feet, trampled over me and my friends and simply 'loved' everyone. Even after she stood on a person's foot they would like her. She had one of those big-baby, 'I-know-I-done-wrong-but-I-just-love-you' personalities. As we fixed gates and fences, sheds and feed bins, there she'd be, cuddling up and whispering in our ears.

Both Jo and Missy loved flight while Midnight liked to plod along, which suited me just fine. Midnight did not conform to Jo's ideal of a well trained horse. I just tried to work with Midnight's idiosyncrasies. Mending gates and fences became second nature. We tried an electric fence worked from a small battery. It tickled Missy and sent her into hysterics even if she were six feet from the wire. I kept patching and mending. Jo worked with Midnight, trying to teach her manners. Midnight took no notice of the lessons. Jo became frustrated! 'She's impossible. A brick wall would learn more. She has no concept of *no*.' The world revolved around Midnight. She knew she could get away with anything.

Jo was still riding Missy but was itchy for another challenge, one that would stretch all her formal skills — a horse so precision-trained that Jo would have to pay strict attention and be highly disciplined. Big Cedar came into our life. A seventeen-hand chestnut of magnificent stature with white socks and a full blaze, his coat was velvet. Big of eye and alert to all around him, he followed commands. A fifteen-year-old, he had recently retired from A-grade showing but his list of impressive wins and superb manners won Jo. Cedar was still able to win at every local show, outclassing many other superb horses; his Olympic training made him a true athlete. He challenged Jo and she perfected her skills. She planned to show him, then changed her mind. Her heart was with Missy. Cedar didn't give of himself; he remained a cool customer, aloof and watching. The gentle giant went to another home. On show all his life, he remained untouched by the love Jo and I gave him.

Midnight kept crashing out. We sent her to a friend whose place had strong fences and was surrounded by electric fencing which was bow-tight and run from the mains. Midnight definitely felt those shocks and for the first time since we'd known her did not crash out! Our friend asked if she could buy Midnight as she wanted to learn to ride and old plod-along-barge-through was perfect.

I said yes. Midnight was once again an 'only horse'. Just her cup of tea. Horse heaven — no other horse and a person who adored her, indulged her and didn't give a fig about manners.

At the same time a British pointer dog was about to give birth. I watched the event.

'That one. I will be that dog's person,' I said. I watched the puppy grow. Jessie was beautiful. What with liver patches and spots, she was a dog of great joy, humour and personality. At nine months old she was hit by a car and the accident broke her pelvis. The vet strapped her together and for six weeks I carried her everywhere, nursing her with great love and care. When all the bandages were removed she wobbled a little. She wobbled all her life which was a full fourteen years. She came out riding with us a few times but it was too hard on her so I left her home. She had a personality that could wheedle biscuits out of the most hardened heart.

Jo decided to move to Canberra to live. Missy went to another home. The young woman who bought her fell in love at first sight and Missy seemed happy to go with her, so, many tears later, we waved her farewell.

I started working in a riding school, teaching young people the basics of riding. The young riders learnt on a big, beautiful, aged mare called Jingles. This horse was a gem — full of personality yet steady as rock. Gentle and kind, she had been born into the circus life. Raised on the road with the smell of sawdust in her nose and on her feet, she was the horse the young women used to ride bareback. I was besotted with her. Sold from the circus to pay a gambling debt, Jingles arrived in the riding school where she was adored but overworked. It must have been a huge debt indeed to have caused anyone to part with such a horse. Children loved her. I bought her. Way overpriced but I paid out of love.

I had a friend, Helen, who had once worked in the same riding school with Jingles. One day she said to me, 'If you can't catch Jingles run at her full pelt and she'll stop dead. Rock still.'

'Why is that?'

'In the circus she was the horse the girls in the tutus rode — you know, looking all pretty, standing up on her back.'

'You're kidding.'

'No. You run at her and she waits for you to spring up on her back.'

'I can't do that. I can't bounce up that high!'

'Watch.'

Helen took off. Double my weight, she moved faster than I and she was very fit. Jingles saw her coming and stood, on alert, upright and waiting. Helen reached Jingles, her hands went onto the rump and she sprang. She landed on Jingles' back, crouching. Jingles went into her rock canter in a perfect circle. Helen stood. One full circle was completed. Still she stood; Jingles never faulted. No saddle, no bridle, just years of repetition. Helen swayed, toppled, somersaulted and landed on her feet. Jingles halted. I clapped and clapped. Jingles took a bow. I raced inside the feed shed for a bucket of carrots.

'We used to do that all the time at the riding school. We had bets on who could stay upright the longest.'

Jingles would also lie down on command. She loved to be cuddled. I'd lie against her belly inside her legs and talk to her. What stories we shared! She could also undo any lock, bolt or door. Locks were to be played with. Unlike Midnight, Jingles stayed put, bits of lock strewn around. She loved a padlock. No human could take it apart in so many pieces. The furthest she'd wander was to the kitchen window or door, begging for food. She would bang for attention and I'd look up, startled. There she would be, laughing from her eyes. I could never be angry with her and of course she would receive apples and bread, carrots and ice-cream. Jingles loved ice-cream. And chocolate. Probably popcorn and fairy floss too!

Then Helen's horse Connie gave birth to a beautiful foal — the pride of Helen's heart. To wean him away from his mum when that time came, Helen placed him in our stable. He tried to scale the door, breaking his leg and Helen's heart. The vet was called. We all cried.

Helen and Connie had many friends. One of Helen's friends, Viv, a tall thin woman who constantly smoked, joined us on our ride. She rode a big gangly thoroughbred. Viv rolled her own and could do so with ease as she rode along. I watched as she rolled her smoke, not one-handed like the skilled bushmen did, but with two hands, the reins draped over her arms. The rollie went into her mouth, she struck a match and her horse put his head down between his legs and gave the biggest buck I've ever seen. Viv flew into the air and a shower of matches rained down on us. We roared laughing.

Viv picked herself up, and someone said, 'That's him telling you that he's sick of you smoking!'

Suddenly I ended up with four rescued horses, two of which were in foal! I tended to their physical and mental needs and fed them a balanced diet. Like humans, horses are what they eat. Both the mares bloomed. They put on weight, their coats became shiny and two healthy foals were born. All went to good loving homes.

I always seemed to have a donkey too. Rescued, no longer wanted. I love donkeys — their looks, their forward personalities, their strength of character and will, and the 'honk' they make. I always want to cuddle a donkey; they have that place in my heart where the child of wonder and joy sits. Such an ancient animal. Pepita came into my life. A Jerusalem donkey, grey with a dark line down the back and across the shoulders — so named because of the cross and the Biblical tale that such a donkey carried Mary and later Jesus.

Pepita loved a good barbecue. Sausages were her favourite. If a barbecue was lit or a picnic began then over would trot Pepita.

If we paid no attention to her she'd bray loud and long, dancing the fenceline. That always worked and goodies went her way!

One balmy evening while I was sharing a barbecue with friends, Pepita was trying to mug everyone over the fence. She looked down and there was Tamara, all of three years of age, holding a sausage and gazing up at the donkey. Quick as a flash, Pepita snatched at the sausage in her greed and temporary lapse of manners. She took Tamara's hand with the meat! Tamara yelled, Pepita released her hand and the poor little girl's fingers were black and blue. After she recovered, there she was, patting the donkey and telling her, 'I forgive you for biting me. You are very naughty to be so greedy.'

Another time I was washing the lunch dishes when I looked through the window and saw Tamara, not quite four, toddling across the paddock towards Jingles. I knew Jingles would not hurt her so I just watched. Over to Jingles she burbled and stood under her head. Down came the big head to sniff and talk. Tamara patted her on the nose; I was too far away to catch the conversation. Then she walked around to Jingles' tail, grabbed two handfuls and began to climb!

My mouth hit the floor. I recovered enough to yell for Ree, the child's mother. 'Quickly, quickly,' I called.

We both watched amazed. Up the tail went Tamara, along the back, then she sat up. That's where she sat all day, ambling along singing, as Jingles wandered and ate. Ree and I sat all afternoon, moving with the shade and making big pots of tea; quietly talking as topics arose, enjoying that moment of seeing a friendship born between a child and a horse. It was one of those rare and precious afternoons.

Jean came to share my heart, my life and a period of time living together. Born in Calcutta, her family came to Australia when Jean was fourteen, and she has the richness and texture of the many stories that colour her life.

Loving animals but not knowing horses, Jean decided to learn to ride. We purchased Pebbles — an old, reliable, chestnut mare, solid earth. She was sold to us by a young man who had 'outgrown' horses after fifteen years with her. She was probably twenty, a good-natured horse who liked to go slow and this suited Jean, who liked to amble along, looking, talking, and stopping to listen to the birds. She was a delight to ride with if I ever wanted to have a slow, easy afternoon. I had some neck pain and the occasional bout of soreness but I was managing my injuries, my health and, most importantly, I was riding! I was very careful what horse I would ride; my wild riding was well over. The threat of the wheelchair made me cautious.

Jean learned to trot. 'It's too bouncy for me. I can't look at the day because I have to concentrate to stay on!'

I tried to get her to canter, saying, 'It's more comfortable.'

'Walking's comfortable,' she replied, 'and I'm not in a hurry to get anywhere.' I decided that Jean knew what she liked best and I'd canter away to return after Jingles and I were 'puffed'.

One day I was riding beside Jean in a trot. She was bouncing up and down and I was trying to be encouraging. 'Keep going, keep going, you're doing really well.'

'I'm losing it. I feel I'm going to bounce off.'

'Grip with your legs. Hold on. Keep it up.'

'I am. I am.'

'You're doing really well.'

'No, I'm not. Help.' Jean dropped the reins and reached out for me. Off she came. Thump! We stopped. She sat on the earth stunned. 'I fell off.'

'Why were you reaching for me?'

'So you could catch me!'

I brushed her down and that night she soaked away the fall in a hot, salted bath.

From then on when we rode I let Jean and Pebbles set the pace.

Into my world of horses intruded that other world, the world of my family.

My Auntie Hilda had died of a brain haemorrhage; my brother

was living with my mother and her boozing partner, and my nana was in a home with only her body living in this world.

My mother had settled in a hot, northern country town, a place of community, with all the racism, ockerism and local power fighting that comes in insular communities. My mother was anxious to appear 'good'. She craved conformity, to seem no different from anybody else and to have access to drink. Easy — for years she was the cook in the local pub. She built a house with her alcoholic partner and seemed 'settled'.

Then Bob, the partner, rang me. 'I'm fed up with her. She's coming down to stay with you. We need a break before I end up killing her!' He hung up. No argument. I had no idea what state she was in.

The next day I waited with trepidation at the airport terminal. Everyone came off the plane except my mother. I waited. And waited. Out came the hostess pushing a wheelchair. In it sat my mother, too drunk to walk.

I said an embarrassed thank you, poured my mother into my car and looked at her.

She was a wreck. Another nervous breakdown. I knew she was being beaten too.

She sat in the kitchen drinking her stout and smoking. We didn't talk. After three days all the spirits she had been consuming seemed to leave her kidneys and body and she reassembled herself. I'd thrown out all the brandy in her case. She was trying to make peace with her demons and I suggested she kept away from the hard grog. During that time she refused to eat, just drank her stout. It was then I realised that I'd never seen my mother eat; never seen her sit down and eat a meal. I'd seen her sit at the Christmas table, laden with food. She'd just pick at things.

After three days she wanted to return to her home. I waved her goodbye at the airport, hoping they would not offer her alcohol on the plane. Impossible, but at least she would return home 'tight' rather than roaring drunk!

We avoided each other over the next few years, allowing the passage of time to flow between us. My brother came to spend a couple of school holiday periods with me but once puberty hit I didn't see him again until he was a man beginning a family.

I had begun my personal healing about my mother, and I began to understand her life and pain.

I had returned to school to study. I attended the local college, completed Year 12, and headed for higher education. I was tired of factory work. A flirtation with journalism left me disillusioned, and the hard physical jobs that were available to me no longer appealed. I supported myself by working weekends in a local hospital, delivering linen to the wards, and believed an education would offer me another kind of freedom.

I was at university and swamped with essays when Pepita the donkey decided not to get up. No amount of coaxing would make her rise. She ate, drank and defecated lying down. She seemed happy enough. The vet was called. He could find nothing wrong. Still she would not get up. We rolled her onto a horse rug and with the help of friends dragged her into a stable lined with straw.

Two weeks went by with me caring for Pepita and there had been no change in her health. The vet could find nothing wrong, and Pepita seemed happy enough. We borrowed a sling and pulled her to her feet. Her legs would not take any weight. For the next week we pulled her up in the morning and lowered her at night. We rubbed oil and creams into her legs and gave her massage and love in big quantities. She still ate and drank well.

Then she stopped eating and drinking and became depressed. Her ears drooped; her eyes became dull. The blood test came back positive. Rapid cancer of the blood. She died a few days later. I returned to university to find I was the butt of my lecturers' jokes. They could not conceive that I had taken time out of my studies to care for a dying donkey.

'I'll give you an extension on your essay,' one lecturer laughingly said, 'because you've got the most outrageous excuse I've ever heard.'

Jingles was starting to become slow and to look old. We'd tried her in cart and harness with hysterical results. Jingles was resigned. She sighed as we harnessed her up as if saying, 'What are those fools up to now?' I drove her around a couple of times, then placed her in the shafts. I had great confidence in her. She stamped her foot, turned to look at me and lifted her lip as if to say, 'Let's stop this nonsense.' For the first time she refused to respond to the reins, turned and headed for two pine trees.

'Whoa, whoa,' I shouted. Jingles was deaf and determined. Bang! In between the pine trees we jammed. If a horse could have laughed it was then. Jingles was laughing at us! We unharnessed her and decided that Jingles would definitely win this one. She knew too many tricks and she was too wise to be conned into more work when she had decided that retirement was definitely 'the go'.

I decided to listen to her and she was retired except for the odd ride or the occasional walk with children. She had started to lose weight in winter so I began to hard-feed her and to use double rugs. She picked up with all the care, attention and special foods and the light shone in her eyes. I rubbed her legs with lotions and potions to ease her arthritis.

A sale of Arabian horses was advertised. Jean and I decided to attend. It was the liquidation sale of a big commercial stud. All horses had papers.

We sat ourselves up on the rail next to a goddess-bodied wild woman who introduced herself as Nancy. Friendly, with a happy-go-lucky attitude to life, Nancy shone like a sun. She had the passion for horses, for horse sales and for watching the dealers work their stuff. Horse after horse went through the ring. The prices ridiculously cheap. Then came the brood mares in foal.

'Look at those poor creatures,' cried Nancy. 'Foal after foal, like a factory, year after year. Always pregnant. Handled from the back of a motor bike, a stallion bunged in with them to keep them pregnant and every foal ripped away in early weaning. It disgusts me.'

The mares became older and thinner. 'Look at that chestnut mare that's coming up. She's been a beauty. A bit stocky for an Arab, lots of strong bone there. I bet she drops that foal within forty-eight hours. A bit wild of eye though. She's had a bloody rough life, poor old thing. If I had the money I'd buy her and just turn her out on our 300 acres.'

Up came the mare for sale. Her hooves were long and cracked and broken. She had whip marks on her rump and her head hung low; she was afraid and her eyes were terrified.

'Lot number so and so,' called the auctioneer. 'In foal, sixteen years of age, with papers. A good proven brood mare with many good foals in her yet. Good blood lines and easy to handle. You get two horses here and this mare will foal in the next couple of days. Never a moment's trouble foaling either. Let's open this bid shall we? Say, at three thousand dollars.'

No one moved. Down came the price.

'Now come on, ladies and gentlemen. You know we have to sell all the stock today. Now this mare is going for a ridiculous price. Next it will be for dog's meat. Come on! This proven brood mare is too good for this. Nine hundred dollars. Come on now, what am I bid?'

'I wish I could afford her,' muttered Nancy. 'That's gunna be a great foal, I can feel it in me bones. Then she could run free. Our block is up bush and has a big Clydie retired on it so she'd have company.'

I bought her for eight hundred dollars. Nancy nearly fell off the fence.

'Great. I can help you train the foal and she can have her retirement.'

We all grinned at each other.

Her name was Annabel. Stroppy, unfriendly, difficult and always on the brink of flight. A horse of air and scare. Annabel delivered a chestnut colt to us in the early dawn when the breath of frost was hazing the grass. He was friendly from the first moment he spotted us. He remained so, always curious and wanting to be in things. He was a delight and a puzzle to his mother who would try to whinny him away from us.

We had a neighbour we named Spartacus because of her short, stocky, strong body and her determination in life. She rented a small house on a few acres, living there with her children and an assortment of animals. She was tough with her children and soft-hearted with all animals. She preferred animals to people. 'Animals are honest; you can't say that about people,' she used to say. 'They'll always let you down.' She was 'piss-poor' yet all her children were clothed and all were fed and warm. She sat with us as Annabel gave birth. The foal captured her heart. She was in love. 'I want to buy him.'

The foal loved Spartacus and would call, trotting over to her when he spotted her coming.

'I want to buy him.'

'He's not for sale.'

Her face fell.

I looked at that stocky, tough woman whose road had been so hard; at those stained and worked hands. I looked at her colours. That foal would have a truly loving home.

'He's yours,' I said. 'He's not for sale. He's yours as a gift.'

Spartacus looked at me as if I'd gone mad. Or she had. I repeated what I'd said. She went white and sat down with a bang. 'I don't know what to say.'

'Just "thank you" is enough.'

'Thank you. You'll never regret it. Never. He'll be with me until the day he dies.' I knew that.

We had friends, Betty and Stan, who ran an Arabian horse stud. They had a magnificent liver-chestnut stallion called Ramah — fire on fire. Betty and Stan came to see Annabel and the new foal. Jean told them what I had done.

'Well, well,' said Stan. 'I'll tell you what. That's a nice mare, just been treated bad. That's a pity. She's not stupid and she's not what she could be because of mistreatment. She's going to come into foal heat so we'll take her and the little fellow home and put Ramah over her. You love him so much you can have a piece of him for a Christmas present.'

I was astounded. What a wonderful, generous gift. It was my turn to say thank you.

I watched Ramah talk to Annabel. Dance beside her, lick and nip her, mount her and begin the life that became Espirit. The morning she came into the world Jean and I were watching. With the dawn Annabel lay down and began to labour. As the foal's hooves came into view she suddenly stood up. The foal came halfway out and hung there. I jumped up and placed my arms around the slimy mass. Annabel felt the weight lift and she heaved. I collapsed, holding the foal, the wet birth membrane plastered all over me and Jean laughing.

Spluttering, I placed the foal gently on the grass. She was perfect. I cleaned her mouth and eyes with a soft cloth. I found myself not breathing. Annabel passed the last of the afterbirth and turned. She nickered at the foal and began to clean her. As she licked, the foal's colours came to life. Long-lashed eyes opened, the mouth sucked and she tried to stand. The feet shed their soft covering and, like a drunk, the foal staggered around. We watched every movement. The first drink. A fire horse. An ancient horse with kind eyes and a big trusting heart.

'Espirit,' I whispered.

'Espirit? Is that her name?'

'Spirit. What a beautiful spirit.' I cried, my heart so full that it could only overflow in tears. I was besotted.

I spent hours with Espirit. Talking to her, brushing her, singing to her, reading in her paddock. She loved fruit, especially pears. The bond between us deepened and I've always loved her with great respect and honour, feeling blessed to have her sharing my life.

Meanwhile poor old Pebbles developed a stomach tumour. It grew very fast.

'Cancer,' said the vet.

'Again!'

'Again. Cancer is the result of a polluted environment and the animals suffer too. More and more rapid cancers are being diagnosed.'

We stabled her and kept her warm. She lost weight rapidly.

One morning the light had gone from her eyes. I called the vet. Jean's grief was intense. We both missed that old horse and for a long time talking about her brought tears.

Playing with Espirit one morning, I suddenly realised that our haven was being surrounded by suburbia. Brick 'venerials' were eating up the horse paddocks. I could hear music, voices, noise. One fenceline now backed onto houses. Within that year we became five acres surrounded by concrete and fumes. The primary school up the road suddenly seemed quiet. Dirt roads were being tarred. Antique shops were bringing the tourists and every shed was becoming a junk-hunter's delight.

We moved. To a place called Moorooduc! A singing name. Moorooduc was a tiny place. A store-cum-post office, a telephone box, primary school, fire brigade and a huge undercover antique market that had great afternoon teas served in front of an open fire.

We rented fourteen acres and a run-down cottage that belonged to the local council and was sublet to a wealthy businessman. He had several of these council properties. He came for his rent each week, driving his yellow Mercedes, and he always said the same thing, 'You girls have made the place pretty. I am a fair man. I will keep the rent at the sum we agreed but you must understand that I am a poor man.' He was — a poor spirit in an overfed body.

The cottage was in such a mess that I had insisted on a lease, knowing that in a few months it would not look the same and that our 'poor' landlord would surely increase the rent.

After removing eleven ute-loads of rubbish, two ute-loads of bottles and all the dead fridges and washing machines that sat like mushrooms across the paddock, we were ready to begin. We scrubbed and whitewashed the place — inside and out. We painted the windowsills and door blue. We pulled out rotting carpet and stained the floorboards. We peeled the greasy lino from the kitchen floor and covered the concrete with matting. We threw out the fat-encrusted stove and replaced it with a clean second-hand model. We bought a cheap water heater for the bathroom and threw out the immersion-heater that resembled an instrument from a torture chamber. Behind the oil heater in the lounge we discovered a useable, large, open fireplace. (When I told my farmer neighbour that I'd uncovered the original fireplace, had cleaned it and was using it he said, 'Do you know how to tell if it's got a good draw? Well, you build the fire up real high and get it roaring. Then you chuck the cat in front of the fire. If the cat's hangin' on to the carpet with its claws to resist being sucked up the chimney then you've got a real strong draw!') We replaced broken windows, a smashed door and cleaned out the rainwater tanks; one had a dead possum floating in it!

From the carport through the back door into a long thin kitchen, a small cosy lounge was a step up; then there was a tacked-on, breezy bathroom and a long, leaky sunroom.

Stairs in the lounge led up through a hatch to a room under the roof. A-framed, with windows at each end, guests repeatedly complained of hitting their heads. It was a room full of light and song. There were trees at each window filled with birds, different kinds at different times of the day. On full-moon nights there was an orchestra of sound.

What we cleaned from the old tin stables and poultry sheds we used as compost to begin a wonderful vegetable garden. We planted herbs around the house and the water tanks. I planted roses and lavender under the windows.

Horror of a different kind awaited us when I opened a feed bin one night to find a rat inside. I ran for the cat. Jean and a friend Belinda followed me back to the feed shed.

'You lift the lid, Catherine! You chuck the cat in, Belinda, and I'll hold the torch,' said Jean. We did this. The bin lid shot off with a bang and out flew the cat with the rat close behind. They went up Belinda's arm, over her head and onto the rafters where the cat turned and headed for the rat. The rat went to jump. We all screamed and there we were, jammed in the doorway trying to get out!

Rats took over the chook house like muscle-bound terrorists. The neighbourhood 'boys' (men in their thirties) came with their guns and Jack Russell dogs. It was clean-up time. The chooks sat like stone as shots whizzed past them and rats dropped like flies. What the bullets missed was killed by the small, fast and furious dogs.

Rats stole the chook eggs. Rats left their droppings all along a new saddle blanket and chewed holes in a new bridle that was hanging 'rat-safe' on its hook!

Big tarantulas lived in stables and buckets. Spiders in rugs and boots. We always placed our boots upside down and shook them before putting our feet inside. I've had millipedes, centipedes, spiders and a mouse in my boots!

Then there were the snake encounters.

Snakes have killed three of my cats and tried to kill another. Vita (the 'fortunate' one) dragged her half-paralysed body up the path miaowing in pain. I recognised her symptoms and could see the poison in her aura. We saved her by using an antivenom injection. It was at the end of the snake season when their venom does not seem as powerful. The other pussies were not so lucky.

Snakes are part of our life and I prefer to leave them be, so far as possible. But there are limits. The house area is out of bounds to snakes and so far they have accepted that. Not so in our tepee. A friend was sitting meditating in the tepee one warm summer's day. She opened her eyes, feeling an intense gaze upon her. Sitting in the doorway watching her was a very large brown snake. She held her breath and mentally asked it to please leave. It did. But she was terrified and that was the end of her tepee meditations.

The time came for Espirit to be weaned. Nancy arrived with a horse float. We loaded Annabel on board and wished her a long and lazy life. Espirit neighed and neighed for her mother. I felt really upset. As I prepared dinner I could hear her calling. At dusk, when I locked away the poultry, she was still distraught. Before I went to bed I took a torch and went to check her. She was no longer calling. Jingles was lying down. Folded into her was Espirit. This continued for the next couple of years until

Jingles became ill; then Espirit lay beside her, no longer a big bundle pressed against her.

Shelly became old and ill. She barely left her chair. We would carry her outside to go for a wee or poo. Then her eyes faded and the light dimmed. We cried and buried her in the garden.

I was telling a group of young students that my best friend had died. One of the young girls said, 'My father's a vet and he had a dog brought in to be put down because the owners don't want her any more. She's a beauty. My dad wants to find a home for her.'

Off to the vet I went for a look. Heidi was just over a year old and she was gorgeous — part Irish wolfhound. She had a wiry grey-black coat and huge gentle eyes of great wisdom and compassion; a big head, beard, paws and heart. I fell in love. She was a dog that laughed.

'She's a beautiful dog,' said the vet. 'I hate to put down a healthy, happy dog like this. She was bought as a cute Christmas present and she grew too big for the family's lifestyle. Also they think she's ugly.' Heidi was far from ugly. She was so beautiful that she attracted attention wherever we went. Home she came. She rode in the back of the ute, happy in the wind. We arrived home; she leapt from the back, spied our colourful, proud rooster and within seconds he was minus a tail. I reprimanded her and that was the only time she molested any poultry.

Heidi never chased other animals, with one exception. Cows. She loved to play with cows — to chase them and have them chase her. I never broke her of this habit but was always vigilant.

One morning I awoke to a great hullabaloo. I looked out the window to see Jean in her pyjamas and gumboots, wielding a great lump of four-by-two, running around the paddock next-door, yelling. Black and white cows were going in all directions, bucking and kicking. Having the time of her life, playing chasey, was Heidi.

Whenever we had to leave her at home it was on a running chain or in the house. She adored to come riding. The moment we walked towards the stables she would begin to bark. When the saddles came out she'd dance and spin in excitement and when we mounted she'd run to the gate and back, barking frantically. No amount of 'Shut up, Heidi, calm down!' had any effect. Heidi was happy and the world knew.

We also discovered she had a passion for children's slides. Up the ladder she'd go, then sit at the top and slide down, a big grin on her face. We use to cheer her. This was Heidi's party trick!

We also shared our lives with cats and goats (goats' cheese and milk is simply the best!) and rescued injured wildlife. I toyed with the idea of breeding Arabians but I knew I'd never want to sell those beautiful horses who would become pieces of my heart.

I had my Arabian. Espirit was so easy to teach and willing to learn.

Jingles was now old and slow. We fed her mash and a grain mixture, lucerne and love. Her spirit was often not in this world as she stretched out in the sun. Many a time I thought she was dead. One morning she had blood coming from her nostrils and her breath rattled. I called the vet. It was time. More tears and more tears. I still don't like to make the death decision.

Espirit watched Jingles die from the injection. She saw her sink to her knees; the big head touched the ground and she rolled over — still. We let her in the yard. She sniffed Jingles and lay down beside her. After Jingles' body was removed Espirit stayed in that place. There she slept the night. The next morning she joined the other horses we had agisting with us.

I entered the teaching profession. Espirit became an adolescent, and Jean went to live by the sea, remaining my heart-sister.

Espirit

I began to share my heart and my life for a period of time with Lynne. With her came four new friends. Jindi was a tubby Labrador cross, a seal of a dog with big brown eyes and a winning manner. She had epileptic fits. Lynne would sit and hold her until they passed. She needed a great deal of reassurance after each one. George, a black-and-white border collie and spaniel mix, was dependent on Lynne and shadowed her everywhere.

George would shut doors on command.

'Shut the door please, George,' Lynne would say and out would come the paw and the door would bang shut. As he grew old and blind he banged the doors the wrong way. They still seemed to shut; they bounced back off the walls! He could also climb ladders. One day when Lynne was up on the roof cleaning the gutters, she heard a sound and found George up beside her, but he didn't know how to climb down. So she hung him around her neck, swore and cursed, came carefully down the ladder, then collapsed into fits of laughter.

Sijan and Cija were Lynne's two beauties — mother and daughter, dark bay thoroughbreds. Cija was water and earth with a little air. Her face and nose would screw up and she'd mutter.

She wasn't unhappy or depressed, just grumbly. Her eyes would laugh back when I talked to her; it was all a big joke. She had a beautiful temperament, willing and aware of people. Sijan was fire on fire. She had no respect for people or other animals — only the faintest regard for me and Lynne. She was her own horse, proud and closed. She'd take a pat or a hug, give back when she felt like it but always made humans feel they were in the presence of royalty.

When I first met Lynne she was hobbling around with two bandaged ankles, both sprained. Sijan had thrown her twice. The next time we met she was repairing the back of a float. Sijan had objected to being taken to a show and had reduced the back door to firewood.

When Sijan and Cija were brought to Moorooduc and placed in the big paddock all seemed well. Two days later they were in our top paddock.

'Must have left the gate open,' said Lynne.

We went to have a look. It was as if a Mack truck had driven through our top fence. The closed gate was the only thing left standing. The fence was scattered across the paddock, metal posts bent in half. The horses were not injured, not even a scratch. Must have been a UFO we decided!

Sijan gave Lynne some wild rides, but, if she decided she wanted to go out, then Lynne was given a treat — the ride would be delightful. Sijan liked to go on rides with her mother nearby so I began to ride Cija. Espirit was not quite ready for a saddle. Cija was a comfortable and easy ride, though she had a habit of tripping, which kept me alert.

I was secure enough to jump Cija over small logs but I longed for those days when I soared high on the back of a jumping horse, feeling that life, muscle and power under me. My balance certainly improved because of Cija.

But one day at a walk Cija tripped and fell. I felt her feet slipping in the wet, her body swayed and I thought, 'Oh, no, not again.' She came crashing down on me. All the way home I was falling in and out of consciousness and pain. I was back with a rubber collar, acupuncture and rest, the latter being the hardest to do. 'No more accidents,' repeated the doctors angrily. I was determined to keep on riding. Pain-killers were resorted to once again.

Sijan became comfortable enough to canter away with Lynne, sometimes coming back into a gallop. Her energy was high and it needed expression. It was a joy to watch horse and rider when they were in harmony. Lynne would work her in the arena and the standard was superb. Try to do the same on show day, and Sijan would explode. That horse could throw a great 'wobbly.' She could spin, twist, rear, pig-root, buck, prop and dance circles.

Lynne adored her. She learnt to give in and go with the flow of Sijan's life. It was easier. Sijan was the stronger character of the two of them. She had a grudging respect for humans but no respect for dogs. They were a target and she'd chase them and strike out with her front or back legs if they came too close. The dogs gave her a wide berth.

Espirit began her training to be ridden. She was used to being led with and without a halter, would tie up, lift her hooves and stand for the farrier, and stand without any restraint to be brushed. She listened to our voices, knew how to back, turn and whoa, all with no constraints. If she began to push through a gate a few spoken words had her stop, walk a few paces back and wait. Once through the gate she might prance and dance but she had respect for humans.

Lynne taught Espirit to lunge. She took time. She used a gentle voice. With skill and patience she introduced the bridle and bit.

'I really don't think Espirit needs a bit,' she told me, 'but we don't know the future, so it's best she gets accustomed to it.'

Every step was taken with patience. She'd explain to Espirit, talking to her all the time. Then I would copy her. Lunging Espirit is fun. There is no other word for it. It's never a chore because she's never boring. She lunges out on a full rein, in a full circle. Only twice in the twenty years that followed her training has she broken and galloped away, taking the lunging rein with her. When this has happened she surprised herself. She came to a sudden halt, then looked behind her with those big eyes wide and surprised. 'Whoops, I threw a wobbly,' she seemed to say.

Full of pride and spirit and beauty Espirit has only ever known love. She calls out when she hears my voice or sees me and she will nicker softly in response to talk. She loves to be hugged.

The saddle lessons were also slow, walking Espirit first with the saddle, then with weight. Then lunging with the saddle and bridle. Lynne sat in the saddle. She taught her all the lessons of responding to the hands and legs — gently and with respect, both enjoying the lessons. Espirit was a willing learner.

Then I rode Espirit and that was a monumental moment for me. I had to stop crying to see where I was going. What a joy to be part of the horse I loved so much, to smell her and feel her — that life, that warmth. Espirit has a small, tight movement until she warms up and relaxes. Then she is an Arabian ride.

It was time to leave Moorooduc. We moved to a six-acre property just out of the small town of Tyabb. We had a small, red brick cottage, a car shed and an overgrown garden of tall, old roses. The old man who had owned the place had lived his last few years in the kitchen. We scrubbed and painted. We planted fruit trees and shrubs, herbs and a vegetable garden. There were open paddocks around us, a five-acre bush ride with many tracks, farmland and dirt roads.

The horse-riding people were being pushed further and further out into the country; it was becoming a necessity to float your horses to somewhere quiet and scenic for an enjoyable ride, if the motorbike riders had not claimed the place first. Motorbikes, trail bikes, cross-country cycles, and horses — all looking for the same space. Walkers and campers too! But before 'progress' caught up with us, we had a great deal of fun on the horses.

I went to meet a young woman who liked Espirit and decided that if she took care of her for a year the experience would widen Espirit's horizons and familiarise her with traffic and noise. Espirt had green paddocks, a well aired loosebox, and she was groomed daily. She had day rugs, night rugs, travelling rugs and shower rugs. She also had the best in feed and someone with a gentle touch when teaching. She loved the shows and came home with many ribbons. Chestnut in winter, Espirit is a liver colour in summer with dapples on her back and rump. She is stunning and the show judges never failed to notice her. She was happy and learning all sorts of new ways in the world.

I went back to riding Cija and the bush rides we shared have left me with images of trolls in the creek, fat rabbits that watched us and the smell of bush perfumes. The spirits in that bush were contained and shy. Their habitat was being eroded by housing, inch by inch. Drains were appearing and we began to see rubbish dumped under trees. The area sang with running water and the overgrown creek held long shadows and fingers of slime. All the children who visited the creek with me knew immediately that they were in troll territory.

Espirit was always afraid of trolls. Not only were they in creeks and under bridges but they were also in farm mailboxes! She never liked getting her feet wet and would go to any extreme to avoid water. Water was only for drinking, according to Espirit. I tried to get her to walk through water, even small puddles, but it was a major drama. Her neck would arch, her eyes pop out, the tail go up and, snorting, she would dance the 'I do not want to do this' act. If we really had to cross water she would spring across it in her version of a jump — most uncomfortable. On one ride we came to a small drain that someone had dug across the track. Espirit saw it as she was about to step into it. She leapt into the air. I knocked my head on a low branch and tumbled straight over her rump! Espirit stopped and turned, a shocked expression on her face. I sat and laughed.

The only other time I fell from Espirit was when we were cantering along a dirt road with Lynne and Sijan right behind us, Lynne hoping that this tactic would calm Sijan down. It didn't; it was stirring Espirit up! Around the corner we went, slap bang into a paddock of pigs! Espirit stopped dead. I banged down and fell from the saddle. Sijan and Lynne shot past me sideways, Sijan's eyes bulging and her nostrils snorting like a dragon. Then they were off. I hobbled along, leading Espirit until my circulation came back and I remounted. Only dust was left of Lynne.

Time accelerated once again. Espirit had been home for a couple of years after her show period. I was riding her and Cija; Lynne would ride all three horses.

I had the opportunity at this time to go to China. At one point the officials asked each woman if there was something special she would like to do or see while we were in China. I wondered if it would be possible to ride a horse? The other women on the tour and the Chinese officials looked at me strangely.

I did get a chance to ride a pony around a lake in Nanjing — a thickset pony, perhaps of Mongolian heritage. He was stocky and hairy, had no bit in the bridle and was still a stallion. In fact, most of the male horses were stallions and I saw very few bits used. Those I did see were rusty. Horses worked hard in China pulling heavy loads. I did not see a skinny horse but none were fat or indulged.

I brought back from this trip a beautiful dragon teapot and small cups in dark clay. When tea is poured from the pot a small dragon's head pops out from the lid, steam coming from her nostrils! Each of the delicate cups has a carved dragon encircling it and each cup is shaped as pieces of a lotus leaf.

I had been following the tour through the old part of Shanghai, along narrow, winding streets that trapped smell and conversation into a roar of living humanity. The guide was rushing us through and telling us that during the time of the British, following the Opium Wars, this area was for Chinese only.

It felt as if they raced us past shops and people. When I spied the small shop selling teas I stopped and smelt. All those open bags of tea! I glued myself to the window and saw a dragon teapot and cups.

The guide pulled me away from the tea store reminding me that the shop was not for tourists but for Chinese and that if we didn't hurry we would be late for our pre-booked lunch at a very famous teashop. Grumbling, I trailed after the tour, noting our route. The guide seated and counted us. Out came a magnificent spread. All the dishes were meat and I was a vegetarian. I left the table and went outside to watch the water fountain. The young guide joined me.

'Can I go for a walk?' The guide looked at me blankly. 'I just want to wander around the street.' She nodded. I raced back to the tea shop. The Chinese all smiled when I entered. I walked around the inside of the shop smelling the open bags of tea. Eyes watched and faces grinned. An old lady held out a handful of tea. I smelt it. She rubbed her back and I pointed to her kidneys and feet. In signals I told her to sit, put up her feet and drink tea. Everyone laughed and resumed talking. I pointed to the teapot. Heads nodded. Each piece of the set was wrapped in newspaper and tied with string. Then it was all wrapped in newspaper and tied again. The shopkeeper wrote down the cost. I opened my wallet. He grinned, took some money and gave me change. I thanked him and left.

Returning to Australia, we often went to the high country camping with friends, dogs, horses, people. It was magic to wake in the misty morning to the smell of woodsmoke and the beauty of the sun playing kiss-chasey on the water. So much of the high country is still beautiful, with spirits of air and earth. It is a world within worlds. Until I came across all the logging. The destruction of fallen and torn trees, the wailing of the spirits; desolation, pain and destruction. A wilderness destroyed.

I began to miss South Australia and started to talk about returning to live in that State. I missed the spirits of that place, the smell, the gum trees, the birds and the pace of life which is not as frenetic as in the larger States. Wherever I settled, my country life seemed to be invaded by crawling suburbia.

I drove back to South Australia with a goat, a dog and a cat. My ute was loaded high and all my belongings were packed into a truck. Espirit was floated to South Australia by a large racehorse company.

I was elated at returning 'home'. I took pleasure in the femininity of the hills surrounding Adelaide — so many female giants! The gentility of another time still lingered in Adelaide and in the old stone buildings, their history still alive and breathing.

With my friend, Chris, I rented five acres and a stone farmhouse about forty-five minutes from the city — close enough to enjoy the city delights but far enough to be 'out in the country'. Ten minutes from Adelaide and one is 'out in the country'. We were considered far enough out to constitute 'an overnight stay'! Unlike Victoria, where a two-hour drive for dinner in the city with friends was considered quite normal.

The house was of soft apricot and yellow stone. The owner had removed all the doors and this eliminated any feeling of being 'shut in'. The acreage was set behind the house, which unfortunately faced a main road. The compensation was the miles and miles of pine forest across the road, known as 'Kuitpo Forest' in various stages of growth and with pockets of eucalypts alive with kangaroos and birds. The forest was crisscrossed with dirt tracks and roads, ideal for riding. The motorbike riders thought so too, although the motor bikes, being extremely loud, gave us sufficient warning to clear out of the way. The riders were often surprised to come across horses!

The three paddocks behind the house were in reasonable condition but neglected. The owners had attempted to plant a plantation of nut trees in one paddock and the black plastic watering system ran everywhere; 'like a bloody dog's hind leg,' as my father would have commented. I tried to water the gasping, stunted trees in summer but the watering system was beyond use. Broken and cracked, it could not take the pressure of the bore. Many a time, walking through that paddock, I thought I spotted a snake — it was black plastic!

Living on and with the land is often seen as idyllic by city people. It's hard work. The land never lets you rest. There is always something to do. The incessant job of digging out weeds. The beautiful purple-flowered Salvation Jane that leaves an itchy prickly rash on my arms and as I itch and scratch at it I try to have compassion for this despised plant of great beauty that gives a delicous honey from its flowers. I wrestle with marshmallow, dock, daisy, nut-weed, blackberry, gorse and wild roses. I mend fences, gates, and mow over water lines, those snaky long black plastic hoses that hide in tall grass and as the mower masticates the plastic I chalk up another dead line and chant, 'bugger, bugger, bugger!'

Then there are troughs, saddles and harness to clean and the never-ending saga of repairing and replacing rugs. All this physical work comes with great excitement as I find spiders, lizards, rats and snakes just waiting to surprise me. It can bring about uncontrollable hysterics, as on the day Keith pulled the canvas off the horse-float and a snake dropped into his lap!

I waited on tenterhooks for Espirit to arrive from Victoria. They were late. Twelve hours. Fourteen, fifteen. I was on the telephone to the company. 'Where is my horse?' Sixteen hours later she arrived. I was frantic. I heard the truck arrive and my feet didn't touch the ground as I rushed out, calling, 'Have you got my baby in there?' A huge neigh answered me. Then another and another.

'I think I might,' the man said. 'I think she knows your voice.'

Espirit staggered out.

'Sea legs,' said the man.

'Float legs,' I replied. 'I thought you'd detoured to Sydney!'

Very soon I began to ride with Espirit through the forest.

When the heat of summer baked the earth the pine scent filled the air. Riding was an aromatherapy delight. Forest edges were bordered with wildflowers. Fungus and mushrooms grew in abundance. We both enjoyed the rides until Espirit came face to face with a kangaroo.

We were cantering along a track deep in shadow. Espirit came to a skidding halt. Up on the ears I went, then banged down in the saddle. She was shaking. Every muscle was quivering and her eyes stood out startled. Her tail was up on her back, her nostrils wide open and she held her breath. The kangaroo bounced away. Espirit did a pirouette and we were away. Not down the track but into the bush. Branches banged against me and I kept ducking and weaving. Then I yelled, 'Espirit, stop, stop! I'm going to come off.'

She stopped. Shaking. I dismounted and talked to her, patting her and trying to calm her. I was scratched on the face, arms and hands. She danced and pranced, swung her head around, seeming to imagine kangaroos everywhere. I talked and talked to her. I'd just get her walking quietly when she'd 'throw a wobbly', swing around, dance and snort.

The next few rides were along dirt roads away from the forest. We only had to watch for farm dogs and cars.

Coming back at sunset one evening we turned the last bend towards home and I brought Espirit to a walk. There, opposite our home, was a huge grey kangaroo, grooming herself. This time Espirit didn't bother to shake. She spun around and away we went! This time on the road. The fairy blood was in control, in full force. I had to laugh.

Living with the forest

It was a stormy winter's night and I was snuggled down warm and content, knowing that all the horses were safe, when the doorbell rang. I answered it. Two very wet men stood there. They reeked of alcohol.

'Hello,' said the bearded one. 'We've had a bit of a car accident and it's rolled. Could you drive us to the local pub?'

'The local pub?' I repeated in astonishment, looking at them. They were both white-faced and the other bloke was in shock. 'Are you sure? You both need a doctor, by the look of you. I'll take you to the nearest hospital.'

'Please,' croaked the one in shock. 'The local pub.'

I looked at them. 'A car accident?'

'Yeah, we rolled it.'

'Are you guys okay? Look, you do need a doctor.'

'We're okay. Not too bad. Yeah, we just need to get to the local pub.'

I brought them inside. The smell of alcohol filled the house.

'They must have been drinking when they rolled their car,' I thought. 'It's all over them.' In fact they were soaked. These two were dripping wet — not rain but alcohol dripping wet.

The bearded one had a broken arm and the other a broken shoulder and collarbone.

'You guys really should get to a hospital.'

They still insisted on the local pub. That's where I dropped them. The one in shock had fainted.

I drove up and down that road looking for a rolled car. None. It was as I thought. Their still had blown up! I found the remains months later in a hidden grove in the forest.

A friend of a friend decided to stop riding and was looking for a good home for his horse, Humphrey. Humphrey was 'pretty as a picture', a big brown carthorse type, stocky and with character. A full white blaze complete with moustache, white-feathered legs and a big barrel of a chest. He was around ten years of age. He was friendly to the point of being pushy and trying to stand on humans' feet. He liked to go his own way and if he decided not to obey then he'd just barge on and take the human too. He was very strong. Humphrey did humans a favour by doing as we asked, and we had that message loud and clear from him.

He was a guts and pushed over gates and fences to reach whatever he desired. He was not like Midnight who used to barrel through the fences; he just leant on them until they bent. He seemed ideal as a beginner's horse for Chris to learn with.

One evening he bent the star dropper fence to the ground and found himself knee-deep in the lush green grass that grew around the sewerage outlet. Late that evening as I was washing the dishes I heard groaning — very loud. Taking the torch, I went to investigate. There was Humphrey lying in the garden very off-colour. Colic. Out came the vet. Humphrey, the guts, saw the vet several times while he lived with me, all because he managed to force his way into somewhere lush. One morning I discovered him caught across a fence — one half in his paddock, the other over the wire. Goodness knows how long he had stood there.

Then one day he came across three kangaroos sitting in our path. They bounced away from us. Humphrey did a U-turn and we were off, thundering down the track. No slow old Humphrey now. He wouldn't respond or listen. We stopped eventually. He heaved and heaved. I thought he was going to have a heart attack and so I dismounted and led him gently home. Sweat ran down him in rivers. His head hung low. Poor old Humphrey.

The next time we rode in the forest he was wary but willing. He saw a kangaroo. Chris managed to stop him bolting. We began to see more and more kangaroos.

I thought, 'This is too stressful for him.' He looked the part of a light-delivery carthorse so I began to consider putting him in harness. He was good in traffic and I thought it might settle him into new patterns.

I bought a jinker and harness, with a set of harrows thrown in, from a local woman who had used the jinker to take her son to school. I began to introduce Humphrey very gradually to the harness. He didn't seem at all fazed.

I was happy and busy — riding and working in paid employment as a lecturer.

Jessie, my British pointer dog, was now old and slow.

Meanwhile, my friends Helen and Clara lived a stone's throw away in a tumbledown cottage with their dog Mabby. I arrived to visit the day Mabby was giving birth. We three sat with her as labour began and life entered the world inside a membrane sac.

Out came the first pup. It was big.

'Look at the size of that pup,' I exclaimed. Mabby licked the pup into a warm ball of fur. Black and gold came alive under that tongue.

'It's a girl!'

I put my fingers on her. 'She's beautiful. She speaks to me.' They both looked at me and nodded. I was hers.

Out came two more pups, then another — blue-black with a white chest. I touched her. 'She speaks to me too!' Helen and Clara grinned and we made a huge pot of tea. Two puppies!

I visited them frequently and watched them grow into two fat round butterballs full of mischief. Heeler-cross, kelpie pups with a dash of this and that added. The first born is Morrigan. She is solid and boofy with a large head and big, soft brown eyes. She is black and gold with some white; she wears eye make-up and has fluffy gold breeches. Her sister is black with a blue chest and paws. Her name is Maeve and she has bright eyes and pointed ears, all of which are continually moving. She is not as friendly as her sister, but likes to be the guard dog; is bossy and slightly overweight. For years the two would brawl in some ear-tearing fights that caused blood to flow and the fight area to look as if something had been slaughtered there. Finally the brawls turned into stiff-legged growling sessions.

They came riding with us. At first they stayed near me, but after they met their first kangaroo all their training went out the window! No amount of yelling would bring them back. I'd have to ride to find them. It is not always fun trying to follow the sounds of howling dogs, their voices wind-whipped into different directions.

While cutting sage one day in my herb garden I first smelt fire — always my biggest worry, especially living next to a huge pine forest. Helicopters patrolled the forest and every motorbike rider was suspect. Summer heat burnt the community into fire consciousness.

Fire! I couldn't see any smoke but the smell was there. I can smell fire for miles. I pushed on the switch to the bore hoping the electricity was still on. It was. The sprinkler system was set up, and it worked! I thanked the Goddess and raced inside. I turned on the radio to get the news and rang the fire hotline. The fire was in a section of forest some miles away.

I brought all the stock up to the house and caught the cats, poultry and ducks. By then the smell filled the air and smoke blotted out the sun. I bundled up photo albums, clothes, favourite possessions and bathroom necessities. Outside hot ash began to fall.

The fire truck arrived — brave, brave men and women.

'It's five miles from here, on farmland and in the forest. We'll let you know very soon what to do.' I waited. Hot ash hit the water tank and sizzled. A wind lifted my hair.

'Is this what they were waiting for?' I thought.

There was a wind — well, a breeze. 'Blow, bugger you,

blow!' I yelled, for this wind would take the fire back on itself.

The pump was still working and the trees dripped water onto hot pavement.

Three paddocks away, a neighbour's small haystack started to smoulder. I ran for the phone. By the time I returned the stack was alight.

A fire truck screamed towards the blaze. Water poured forth; other trucks arrived — farmers and local people.

The wind lifted. The fire truck roared out of the way and the stack suddenly fell in on itself, sparks blackening as water hit. The fire truck roared away. The farmers pumped water into the smouldering mass. Sparks flew in the air, screeching as the water ended their life. The spirits of the land were hysterical. All fear the power of wildfire.

The fire truck came in the yard. 'No need to panic, missus. It's turned.' Away they went. They had hours of work ahead before they brought that fire under control. It had been deliberately lit.

I sat in the water with the dogs. We still couldn't breathe clean air. I thought, 'I can't go on living here beside this forest, not with my fear of fire.' I knew while I lived there I would always worry and summer would be a time of continuous anxiety.

We talked about buying a small property. We were paying a high rent so why not pay that amount from a mortgage? We began to visit real estate offices, read the papers and talk to people. Buying property is an amazing adventure, especially in communication.

I said to the real estate agent, 'This is what I require.'

He said, 'This is what I'll show you. I know what you like.'

We had different perspectives and expectations about the ownership of land. I did visit some beautiful neat and modern farms but they didn't open my heart to storytelling.

Home of the enchanted dragon

I found my home: eight and a half acres with a small stone cottage built at the turn of the century, and sheds of great character situated in courtyards on the south side of the house.

'I'd put a bulldozer through all those sheds,' said the land agent.

'The house will fall down before the sheds,' I commented. Iron sheds and stone sheds, all built with character and built to last of thick tree trunks, heavy wood, railway sleepers, and thick wooden doors with long, hand-forged hinges. I turned some of these sheds into rooms of light and charm. There was a huge dairy. We replaced the wood stove with a slow-combustion stove that also heats the water.

It was a very neglected holding, bare of trees and garden; all the water tanks were rusty and leaking. Water would be needed, though we had a dam. Now thousands of native trees ring the property and many have grown in the paddocks and around the nearer dam. Another dam is surrounded by bush, and there are two substantial orchards, with other fruit trees dotted in the garden and the courtyards. I have opened the old well and it is bricked and stoned, offering water and a peaceful place to sit. Equally peaceful are the jetty on the dam, the iris gardens and the meditation area with water and fish. The house garden has native plants as well as fruit trees and roses, flowers, vines, herbs and lilies.

The vegetable garden is abundant, the herb gardens rich, and I've built verandahs on sheds. The spirits have returned and this home sings with peace, laughter and joy. The holding did not have a name, so I have called it 'Teach Dragún Dráiocht' — the home of the enchanted dragon. It is a home that sings.

The property is long and narrow with a slight rise and dip. A rail line runs down one side of the holding and every Sunday a steam train thunders along the line, singing of travel and romance. Other trains occasionally use the line and numerous little put-put machines clang past.

The dogs 'have a session' whenever anything is on the line but they adore the steam train. They bark and yodel and run from area to area. The train whistles just behind the house as it reaches a crossing, which excites the horses. The train rushes past in the morning but chugs back again more slowly at night, puffing thick smoke that lingers in the air, smelling of coal, romance and adventure. The train reminds me of riding in trains and baggage trucks with my father. Sometimes he'd throw me up into a truck and we'd rock along, the scenery a moving picture to watch. My job was to keep the dogs quiet. Sometimes he'd buy tickets and we'd ride in a carriage.

My father used to say, 'Hear that noise — clack, clack, clack. It's saying: Going to get a haircut, going to get a haircut.' He'd laugh.

With the help of friends, I built internal fences to help manage the paddocks. Humphrey proceeded to rearrange all the fencing. It depended which way he'd lean!

I had him working well in harness. I had added chains and a log. He pulled it with ease. I added tyres. He looked at them at first, pranced a few steps, then settled down — no problems. I was pleased with his progress even though he seemed to be getting very bossy with the other horses and very pushy with humans. Then a young friend came to spend the weekend with me. We decided to go out with Humphrey. Away we drove.

Instead of coming back along the wide road, we came back along a narrow dirt track. We were walking quietly, talking. A Jersey cow came thundering down a paddock to have a better look at us. Humphrey startled and jumped, thinking 'Kangaroo!'

We were off! We were away, like Ben Hur, galloping down the road with me yelling, 'Whoa, whoa!' I stood up, slammed down the brakes and worked with the reins.

The smell of burnt brakes went up my nose. Gone!

We thundered towards the bitumen road.

'Stop, Humphrey, bloody well stop! Whoa, whoa.' The side of the cart hit a branch, whacking out a piece of the seat. I let out a blood-curdling yell. 'Stop, Humphrey, stop!' And he stopped! Bits of cart were loose and broken. Humphrey was sweating and snorting. The chariot-horse looked as if he was going to have a heart attack. I led him slowly home.

The next few times he was placed in the cart he acted in the same way. He'd jump and jitter and try to bolt. I decided to go back to basics. Humphrey decided that cart work was not his cup of tea.

I was telling his story to my friend Nicki, a young woman who has the courage of an Amazon on horseback. Her husband, Brad, wanted to learn to ride. She thought Humphrey would be ideal. We went over to Humphrey. It had been raining and the ground was wet and muddy. We caught Humphrey and I handed the lead rope to Nicki. Humphrey walked away. She tried to get him to stop. He bulldozed on. Down in the mud fell Nicki, still holding Humphrey's rope. He pulled her through the mud, not stopping until he reached the gate.

Nicki stood, covered in water and mud. Grinning, she said, 'I'll take him!'

One night I had a dream. I dreamed that there was a dog for me and it was in the weekend paper. I awoke, showered, and went to buy the paper. I didn't get to read the section on 'Dogs' until the late afternoon. An ad said, 'Scottish deerhound pup to give away. Eleven weeks old. Phone.'

I phoned. A voice answered, 'Oh dear, you are far too late. She went early this morning. You are about the hundredth caller I've had today. I'm afraid she's gone.'

'That's funny because, you see, I had this dream.' I went on to tell the woman about the dream, my loss of all those much loved dogs, of Jessie, and of Maeve and Morrigan.

'Oh dear,' she said, 'and you sound so nice. Look, I'll take your number. If she comes back or something, I'll let you know.' I thanked the woman.

That night I asked the Goddess what she was up to. Some people talk to God. My God is a woman — the old ancient goddess known by many names all leading to the triple Goddess of the Maiden, the Mother and the Crone.

I heard my dog's name — Macushla, meaning 'my darling heart' or 'the heart of my mother' — a beautiful Irish name for a beautiful Scottish deerhound.

At seven o'clock the next morning the phone rang. A voice said, 'Look, you don't know me but yesterday I took the Scottish deerhound puppy. Well, I've got four kids and three dogs already and my husband did a berko so I rang the woman to ask her if she could take the pup back and she said to ring you. Do you want her?'

'I'll pick her up in an hour.'

We met at the Green Dragon Hotel and I returned home with Macushla, thanking the Goddess all the way. I promised to plant her many, many trees.

Macushla is still with me, a loyal and devoted companion. She gives big toothy grins and is often mistaken for a wolfhound. She is tall and hairy like the wolfhound but is slender with long legs. She goes with me everywhere.

After Macushla arrived, Sinead came into my life.

I was walking across the parkland when music and the smell of Guinness caught my attention. It was the St Patrick's Day celebration and there, under the trees, lay seven Irish wolfhounds. I fell in love. A week later Sinead came home. It's like sharing a home with a lion. I watch other dogs as they meet 'the happy hedge' and am always amused at their amazed expression. They look incredulous as they observe just how big she is. The reaction of most humans is also one of amazement, and a ten-minute walk can take up to two hours as people come to talk and pat her.

Maeve and Morrigan had just recovered from the size of Macushla in their home — then came Sinead; the pup they bossed around but they very quickly had to learn to mind their manners as, to their amazement, she grew! Eighty-two centimetres at the shoulder and weighing around eighty-seven kilos, she is a big girl.

One day she was with me in our local town. I was sitting having a coffee in an outside cafe. A car pulled up, a woman got out, unstrapped a little boy from his seat and turned to lock the car. The little fellow looked at Sinead. His eyes opened wide, he grinned and he was off! He ran towards us and threw himself at the dog. He wrapped his arms around her neck and, rocking, began to sing. His mother was pasty pale and seemed about to faint. 'It's all right, it's all right,' I called to reassure her. 'This dog will not hurt your little boy.'

She came over and sat down, tears running down her face.

'No, no. You don't understand,' she said. 'My little boy is autistic; he does not relate to us. He will not communicate gently at all. I've never seen this before. He's singing!'

She was sobbing.

'You will have to get a dog,' I said gently.

'We have a dog.'

'Then I guess you'll have to get a wolfhound.'

People always ask, 'What were such dogs used for?'

I reply, 'Have you ever been in a castle in winter? These were the hot-water bottles!' These ancient dogs are truly the dogs of magic.

Horses are like all species. They have humour and moods, good days and bad days. Missy can be hit or miss on any day. Called Missy (my second Missy), her full name is really Missed Out. A big thoroughbred mare, she was the only foal in her year to miss out on being coloured, thus her name. A rich bay with a touch of white on her face, she was elegant and now as she ages it's still with dignity and elegance. Of air with a touch of water and earth, the fairies fascinate her. Some stop her dead in her tracks and render her unable to do anything but stand and stare. Others put her into flight mode. She hates being tied up and has busted rope after rope. She is also scared of gates. It seems as if she's been tied to a gate, taken fright and pulled the gate from its hinges. Her phobias and fears, her visions and her strong will I'm still learning to work with. And I'm learning how to relate to her and keep her reassured. She is a wonderful ride, with a dream of a canter.

Occasionally, when out on a ride, she will suddenly see her fairies. Chris, who was still learning to ride, was shocked when Missy suddenly stopped and stared. She kicked Missy into action. Missy spun in circles and dumped Chris in a ditch. She went back to staring! An inexperienced rider does not have the knowledge to deal with Missy's fairy fits. Chris, determined to learn, again came riding with Missy. We were riding the picturesque fire track, up and down the hills, through gates and over creeks. Unfortunately, one section of the track was polluted with rotting cattle, dumped by a city farmer. There was no way we could avoid his stinking graveyard. Blowflies accompanied us on that section in thick black clouds.

Missy shot past, Chris up on her neck. The gate ahead stopped her. I dismounted and opened the gate. Missy danced through. Then she stopped and stared. Chris urged her on. Upset at the death she'd been past, she spun up on the verge and began to back towards the fence. Chris lost control and panicked. Missy shied and Chris fell off over the fence. Missy danced back onto the track and stopped staring. I caught her. We walked the horses home. That ended Chris's riding career; she became an observer of horses.

Wanting to acquire a quiet harness horse, I placed an ad in the local harness shop. Snowy, an owner, phoned. 'Yeah, I've got a four-year-old mare off to the knackers. Quiet as a mouse, well behaved and pretty as a picture but no good at winning on the track.'

Ebony was 'broken in' at six months of age and raced when she was a yearling. At the age of four she had broken down. She has been described as 'sour' from being over-handled — never left alone. She will not bite, kick or hurt me but her ears are always laid back and she grumbles. She's nice when carrots or apples appear and she bangs on a post if her mineral lick is finished.

I placed her in the small paddock. She ran into the fence and split her chest open. She had only ever lived in a stable and small holding yard. The vet was called and stitched her up.

A rich red-brown in colour, Ebony is quiet to handle, alert and willing in harness, and very traffic-wise. She was raced along the sides of busy roads. She takes me to my local town, shopping, and the street activity does not faze her.

I had Ebony checked out by the chiropractor. 'She's had a fall,' that brilliant young woman said. 'A very bad fall. You will never ride her but she's okay to use in harness.'

I asked Snowy about a fall. I told him what the chiropractor had said.

'Well, that's right,' said Snowy. 'She did have a bit of a fall. Quite spectacular really.' He had the race and fall on video. It was horrific. She had fallen in a race and other horses and carts had crashed into her and over her. It was not just a bit of a fall. I am amazed she trusts humans and this shows me the depth and beauty of this horse's heart.

Ebony's fence injury was right where the breastplate should sit. So I had her measured for a collar by a master craftsman, a beautiful hand-tooled collar stuffed with organic wheat.

She is a friend, and takes me and our friends on wonderful picnics, wildflower spotting and local shopping. Always travelling with a thermos, a blanket and a bag of apples means we can share cuppa time together while out exploring the country.

The bravery of horses astounds me. My friend Trish has a beautiful black cob named Ruffy who works well under saddle and in harness. Intelligent and alert, Ruffy saved Joe's life.

Joe, the father of Trish's daughter, was visiting the farm. A short, nuggety, practical man, Joe was out in a paddock picking up the horse droppings. At the time Ruffy was sharing the paddock with a few ewes, and visiting them was a large black ram with a mean disposition. The ram's owners had warned, 'He gives beautiful lambs with silver wool but watch him, he's a mean bugger.' The ram had done his job and was due to go home.

Joe had turned his back on the ram and was bending down. Trish's mother saw the ram from the kitchen window, lining up Joe's bum with his horns.

The ram charged. The mother screamed. Joe went head first into the ground. The ram jumped on him and began butting him in the back and neck.

Trish exploded from the house. Grabbing a pitchfork she charged at the ram, and he turned and charged back. Joe was unconscious. The ram crashed into Trish, bending the pitchfork in half. They eyeballed each other. Trish knew he was going to charge again. Suddenly Ruffy came between them. With flying hooves and feet he bullied the ram into a corner of the paddock and held him there.

Joe was airlifted to a hospital in the city where he had major surgery. Joe owes his life to that brave horse, for Ruffy is a hero.

I built a small jetty on the edge of the dam. I can sit over the water and watch the fairies skip, forming rings of waves as their toes touch the water. Dragonflies and swallows, bats and water birds share the space, and an odd snake or two. Sinead loves water and will play in it, splashing and swimming with joy. Macushla will occasionally surprise me by having a swim. Maeve chases the dragonflies into the water and Morrigan will swim for hours following a ball.

I sit on the jetty at twilight watching as the reflections double the number of animals. At such times the blessings are great. The horses remind me it's growing dark. I open the gates and they thunder past, sending the summer dust up in red clouds. While the heat of the day is still in the air, I strip and swim with the dogs. As I walk back in the dusk I hear the sound of the horses eating their hay and I stop to listen. Horse-hearted people listen to the sounds of horses as a lover of music listens to a symphony.

Irish magic

Planning a journey to Ireland with Chris, I discovered that one could hire a horse and 'gypsy wagon'. The only true vardos I saw were in museums and, although I did see a few horse-and-jinkers, the only 'travelling people' I saw had cars and caravans. Gypsy wagon trips may be romantic but the reality for the Romany is very different.

There was only one trip on offer around the Dingle Peninsula. I was planning to search out places of interest with horses attached, to find Irish wolfhound kennels, and visit bookshops. It was the opportunity to visit the land of our parents and grand-parents.

Eire. The island of the Goddess, rich in poetry, magic and history. A land of gossips, storytellers.

Arriving at the horse-drawn holiday establishment, we were shown to a tarred-roof vardo. Painted red and yellow, it looked like a gypsy vardo with a Celtic C, in the shape of a bird, on the front and back. With rubber tyres and brakes, it was definitely romantic! The table inside dropped down to a hard bed. There was a cupboard, a sink and a two-burner gas stove which leaked.

We stored away our possessions and food and went to meet the horse who was to pull us, Jimmy — a beautiful wide carthorse; black and white, beautifully painted, an aged, wise horse who took care of himself. He was a gypsy's dream.

The next morning I was fretting to get going. The harness was old and needed attention. The reins were sensible — rope. All the saddlery needed attention and oiling. In Australia we would have considered it borderline useful, perhaps because here in Australia we can still purchase new or very good second-hand harness while in Ireland harness is extremely hard to get.

Out of the yard we clopped, down the narrow lane and into Ireland at my pace. Grinning with happiness, looking over hedgerows and into paddocks. Watching the life around me. Being greeted by people and barking dogs. We wound down through small hills towards the sea. Every car and truck slowed down, some crawled past, the occupants waving and photographing us. We clopped past pretty, whitewashed cottages, their front gardens blooming with flowers and bumble bees. Under a crumbling Roman aqueduct, past a groaning stone mill, around a corner and the view of the sea — still, like reflecting blue glass.

Into a small village and behind the two-hundred-year-old inn we trotted. This was our first stop, at which we were to park for the night. We intended to cook our own meals and to sleep in the wagon but we went into the pub for a drink or two. A pub of great character; we sat drinking the dark liquid, sighing with pleasure. Over came Paddy. Just like a little, round, happy gnome. Over he trotted and sat down, talking. 'Pissed as a fart', he loved and talked horses. He told us about his racing days, about how he bred and raced winners. His wife had show horses. She was recovering from a fall. 'Bloody silly woman shouldn't be jumping at her age. She's seventy-four.' He told story after story and drank pint after pint.

American tourists filled the little room. They ordered loudly. A man and woman arrived to play music, he the squeezebox, she the fiddle. We sang along to 'Goodnight Irene' and all the favourites.

As the musicians began 'Danny Boy', Paddy lurched to his feet. He pushed his way to the front of the musicians, grabbed a post and hung on. Swaying, he sang. He had the voice of an angel!

In the morning, I opened the half-door of the wagon to let long fingers of blue-grey mist inside. The light danced silver magic into the landscape. We ate breakfast as the sun cleared away the morning of water-colour softness. We walked to the beach. I sat on round rocks and watched the water. I felt the spirits of Ireland all around me.

I wandered slowly back along a lane. Two women passed me with a donkey, its baskets heavy with turf. The women had shawls over their shoulders, long skirts and boots. We greeted each other.

I harnessed Jimmy into the shafts and we set off on the next lap of our journey. I had not expected such a volume of tourist traffic. 'This is nothing,' I was told. 'Ireland is only at the beginning of the tourist season.'

For me, our journey was not just a holiday adventure. It was certainly a holiday, but for me it represented far more than being a tourist.

Tourists would ask me, 'What's it like in winter? Going far? Have you been doing this long?' It was often assumed that we were gypsies. The only time the roads were quiet was on a Sunday morning. It was wonderful. We were following a steep and rugged shoreline — mile after mile of peace. We entered small quiet villages where not even a dog stirred.

'It's like everyone is dead,' I commented.

Then through a small town. The explanation soon became clear. Everyone was in church. The church building was hugged deep by cars. Cars were parked at crazy angles indicating hurry. Running late for mass. We wove around parked cars, some with their doors open. (Those people were definitely late.) Organ music and voices raised to Mother Mary filled the air. The congregation sang us out of town and the music lingered with us in the air until the last faint amen.

Along the winding, country road with fencing that was worse than ours at home. Not one gate was hung and held by a chain. Wire, rope and leather bound gates to fences and fences to wobbly posts.

'I thought my home had character fencing,' I commented. 'My old fencer must have been taught in Ireland. Come to think of it, he never visited Ireland, so it must be genetic!'

The next town was asleep in church.

Church was coming out in the town after that. Girls in short, black, tight dresses with coloured satin blouses in lime green, fluoro blue and bright yellow. They looked like exotic flowers amid the dark colours of their fellow worshippers. Their God would have been pleased by the colour, for he has great humour. It's just that so many of his worshippers lack the same grace and sense of fun. The young girls made me smile, just as their God would be doing, to see such vibrancy of life. The roads came alive again.

Lunch and then the pub. Or ... the pub, lunch, the pub. For miles we had smelt the odour of Sunday roasts in the air. It was heavy with tradition.

I couldn't resist a postcard to my mother. Her favourite beverage being stout I sent her a postcard of a glass of Guinness and wrote on the back, 'I've found heaven for you and it has 52 pubs!'

I found my first *sheela-na-gig* in Dingle. For years I've been fascinated by *sheela-na-gigs* and the truth of their representation. As soon as I showed an interest people opened up and talked about them beyond the commonly-held view that they are rude or dirty women. They can certainly appear to be rude with their wide open vulvas. Christianity tore the *sheela-na-gigs* from the buildings and churches but some still survive. Many are in private collections or museums. To the Christians they are evil, to others rude or ridiculed. To the people of the ancient goddess they were respected and held great meaning.

Travelling from Dingle was a scenic dream through small villages, hamlets and towns. B&Bs were everywhere! No shortage of places to stay, all near pubs. Or maybe pubs are near everything else, as the community and tourism certainly revolve around the thousands of watering holes.

We camped next to a double-storeyed pub where the landlord was friendly but very surprised that we were not going to stay in his inn. 'Everyone does,' he said.

I then came to the conclusion that most 'gypsy wagon' holiday-makers not only travel from pub to pub but they eat and sleep in them. The wagon provided the adventure, but not the comfort!

Returning to our wagon one evening we were surprised to find another wagon parked beside ours with a delightful American woman, her worn-out husband and two bored children.

'Hello, hello,' she greeted us. 'We're staying at the pub; which is your room? Maybe you could join us for dinner? The rooms have been so comfortable and the breakfasts fabulous, don't you agree?'

After we explained our preferences, she continued, 'What do you mean you are staying in the wagon? It's just terrible on the road. We hate all this traffic and we've been scared so many times. We are so worn out, my poor husband just has to sleep. It's quite stressful, and that dreadful little man said we'd be okay. We haven't seen him or anyone else. All these people want to do is talk, talk, talk. It's so tiring.'

(Ireland for me was a storyteller's dream because everyone does want to talk! Plus they don't weigh one up; they are just people who love communication, even in everyday conversation.) In Australia and America to be called a talker is somehow derogatory and to say, 'You do talk,' is a put-down. We also have the idea that talking is a waste of time and money.

'So business makes millions from self-help books and courses on communication,' I told her.

'Oh yes, we're big on communication, and relating too. But these people talk!' she replied.

'Well, think of it this way,' I said; 'you get an interesting holiday and a communications course all wrapped in one!'

'But it makes my poor husband so tired. It's a dreadfully stressful holiday. We're worn out. So much walking up and down all those hills. And the traffic is a nightmare. It's horrific, like being in a big city all day. We're not enjoying this.'

'Never mind, you will,' I consoled her. 'I suspect, for most people, it's one of those holidays you enjoy in retrospect. At least it hasn't rained and we were told that's quite unusual here.'

'If it rains then I'll leave this where it is and fly home,' she commented.

I laughed and invited her to join me for a warming whisky.

So into the pub we went and spent a tipsy evening talking with Gaelic-speaking farmers who could not speak English. I cannot speak Gaelic and they wanted to know all about Australian sheep! The pantomime was so funny that my body ached with laughter for days!

Mountains of teeth, valleys of green and a startling drop to the ocean on one side of the road. We hugged the rock wall on the other side. The road was narrow and winding. Cars stopped as we passed. Wild spirits danced the waves and brought song in the wind. I was captivated, lost in stories. We plodded along, the turns became tighter, the road seemed to narrow. I began to pay attention and hoped we wouldn't encounter a bus. We didn't — it was a large petrol tanker. We stopped. The tanker stopped. There was not room for us to pass. The tanker driver reversed until the road widened slightly.

Jimmy walked on, hugging the stone wall. A hair's breath between stone and moving wood. Gently and slowly we passed the tanker. Two fingers separated us. I winked at the driver; he winked back. I held my breath as we passed into safety. The truck's brake system hissed. Jimmy jumped.

'Steady, boy, steady,' my shaky voice croaked out.

I kept talking and thanking Jimmy; I walked with him to stop my legs shaking.

'You are worth more than your weight in gold,' I told him. We plodded on. I breathed in and out slowly. My heart returned to normal.

We wound down from the heights with the spectacular view before us, purple and blue haze over a silver sea; white curving sand forever. The beach scene from 'Ryan's Daughter'.

We walked the water's edge and, although Jimmy was a special horse and a delight to be with, I missed my dog companions. I knew they would have adored this adventure. I patted and talked to dogs and rang home frequently to ask after all my companions, but right at that moment the tears ran freely. It was not only missing my companions, but the sheer beauty and tranquillity of such a place opened my heart and touched my soul. I stood in a washed blue twilight, watching the whispering mist roll in across the sea.

Then the next day I walked beside the sea, over rocks, and explored rock-pools alive with water life. I sat on the sand and read of Maude Gonne, the poetry of Irish women's voices and pieces from Ella Young.

That night we had a small campfire of wood and peat. We delighted in the smell that only peat as it burns gives to the air; the stars, the sound of water talking to earth, the billy singing and the sound of Jimmy's presence in the dark. No traffic and no lights. Just us and the moment.

The journey ended far too soon. Jimmy knew the way home as up and down the lanes we plodded. Chased by ten border collie puppies through one lane, we were asked to join a party for a 'whisky bridge' in another lane, and passing an Irish busker playing his banjo, his voice singing to the Green Goddess, our wagon journey came to an end.

Before leaving Ireland we visited the Irish horse stud. Deep green paddocks held horses from paintings and dreams. The pregnant mares were so breathtakingly beautiful, I gazed at them in love and wonder.

We entered the grounds and had the opportunity to visit the superb Japanese water garden but I declined — I was there for the horses. The grounds were immaculate — lawn, white pebbles, smooth paths and gardens of flowers. Fountains and stables out of a dream. Big beautiful loose boxes, and every mare's box with its own clinic. Stallion boxes that looked like fancy motel units, with baskets of coloured flowers hanging from the covered walkway. All heated, all with a skylight.

I had the privilege to be shown one of the stallions. I stopped breathing. I heard how many millions he was worth but that made no sense to me at all. No price tag could be placed on such magnificence. I felt I could die happy! I never wanted to wash my hand again!

We saw long-legged foals, newly born, asleep in deep beds of hay.

'All the water given to these horses comes from the same source as the Holy Well,' we were told. Bridget's Well. The waters of the Goddess who was sainted but not converted.

The museum was also fascinating. The original owner and breeder of these horses bred and raced all his stock according to their astrological calendars. That's why all the stables have a sky-light — so the horses can see the night sky and be influenced by the stars. Magical, and it must have worked for some time, for the place has an imposing history. There is a castle in the grounds, supposedly that of the Black Knight. He must have loved horses.

To travel by horse and wagon in Ireland filled me with stories which have nourished my soul. To be in the land of my grandmother, the people of her blood, my blood and to be in the land of so many storytellers is an experience in living the magic.

Clydesdale kisses

I had another dream and bought the paper. Sure enough there it was: *Clydesdale horse, cart and harness for sale.*

Over to a small country town in Victoria I went — to the blacksmith's shop. Tied out the front, harnessed into a heavy tourist cart, stood two Clydesdales.

Inside I met Jim. Outside I met Tigger. Nearly seventeen hands and way underweight he looked sad, dull of coat and eye, with cracked and broken hooves, only one shoe, and a docked tail.

I went for a ride. Tigger continually tried to trot and hurry. 'That's his problem,' said Jim. 'Too fast. Wants to trot all the time and ends up doing all the work. He's okay and well-behaved but just too fast.' Tigger came from a farm where he was used in machinery but never on the road. Recently he had been working in the tourist industry. He was not suitable to use in a pair.

His eyes did not sparkle. He was branded on both shoulders and looked as if a brush had never touched him; probably one seldom had, as he suffered from a skin itch due to being left sweaty and unbrushed. He seemed scared yet wanting to trust.

Back at Jim's place, Jim harnessed Tigger into a worn set of harness with a rusty bit. 'This is his.' I made no comment but lifted my eyebrows. He swapped the tattered collar for one that was reasonable. A rubber-tyred, flat wooden cart that needed a seat and attention was dragged out and Tigger placed into it.

Away we went — at a trot around a big, bumpy paddock. I was not sure about this horse or any of this.

'He'll go all day for you,' Jim had said, 'and if he gives you any trouble just starve him down.'

I looked at Jim. 'Starve him down!' I thought. Tigger was underweight now! We arrived back with Tigger sweating.

'Don't you brush him?' I asked.

'I put a high pressure hose over him. I taught him to tolerate that and to stand still.'

'Oh yes?'

'Yep. I put a heavy rope with a slip-knot around his neck and let him pull back until he fell on the ground and his tongue hung out of his mouth blue. He's never pulled back since.'

I caught Tigger and tried to lift his feet. He wouldn't let me. Nails hung at all angles from his hooves. I didn't push the issue, I knew those feet would need work and patience. This big fellow had been hurt.

I went back to a friend's place to stay the night.

I had thought about Tigger all night and kept seeing his white-feathered legs, spotty belly, bay with white colouring, black mane and scrubby docked tail, big white face that is beautifully marked and the most kissable lips in creation.

I returned the next morning. I looked at Tigger through the eyes of love and saw the horse he would become.

Two weeks later Jim delivered him. He arrived in an open stock crate and staggered down the ramp. Jim laughed. 'Travel sickness.'

I settled Tigger into his paddock, brushed him, fed him carrots and talked with him.

He stared at the hay net and couldn't believe his luck.

So Tigger came into my life.

He has changed. He is now a big, heavy (fat) Clydesdale. 'He'll change,' said old Bill. 'I know these fellows. It'll be love that transforms him.' The first time I washed him he nearly fainted! I used warm water and washed him with care. He loved it.

Then I set to work on his feet. He would not allow me to pick up his feet and when I managed to lift a foot he'd throw his front feet out and plant them firmly in the earth, narrowly missing me. He responded to all the loving attention he was receiving but his feet were a no-go zone. I suspected he had been dropped to the ground to be shod. He was terrified.

Bill Brooks arrived to measure Tigger for his new rug. A kind, gentle man who is very skilled with horses, he persevered in lifting Tigger's feet. He knocked out all the rusty nails, removed the last shoe and cut Tigger's feet back while the horse held them on the ground.

'That will help until you are ready for the farrier,' he said, straightening his back. 'He's a big boy!'

Tigger loved the attention and has come into his own. He has a passion for bread. Once, my friend Jayne went through his paddock carrying a picnic lunch. Tigger heard the rattle of plastic and within seconds was mugging her.

'Help, Catherine, help!' I heard. I ran over. Tigger had Jayne up against the fence, bossing her for the bread she held.

'Give him the bread,' I yelled. She threw the bread to me and Tigger followed. He ate our lunch!

I borrowed a sled and began to work Tigger. I had great plans for him: harrowing, bringing in the hay and wood, seeding and working when necessary.

I went to an auction where there was a great deal of horse-drawn farm equipment for sale — most of it for two horses or big-team work. But there sat a single-horse, super spreader. I checked it out. An old boy watched me. 'You know what it is?' he said.

'Yes, I do,' I replied.

'Then you and I must be the only buggers here who do.'

'It looks like a coffin on wheels,' I commented. The old boy wheezed laughing.

The spreader was knocked down to me for twenty dollars! I'd been offered the same thing, though not in working order, for two hundred dollars!

I love attending farm auctions. I can come home with wood,

wire, gates and all sorts of bits and pieces for the cost of a few dollars. Our local clearing sales and auctions are a social event. Neighbours meet and talk, locals catch up, and the 'Ladies' Something-or-another-Society' provides tea, scones, cakes and sandwiches.

A retired farrier rang me about an 'old man' who had a wooden cart for sale. I rang the number he gave me.

'Yeah, I've got a couple of old wooden carts for sale. Big wooden wheels. What do you want one for?' the gruff voice said.

'For my Clydesdale horse. I want one with a brake and seat.'

'Yeah, well, one of them is like that, the other not in such good nick. You sure you got a horse?'

'The last time I looked out the front door my Clydesdale was still in the front paddock.'

'You sure about that?'

'I am. Why?'

'I won't sell it to you unless you've got a horse for it. I'm gettin' all these bloody phonecalls from people who want me carts for their bloody garden. Not bloody likely,' he snorted.

The following day, Joshua, my moon-child, now twenty years of age, was visiting. We drove my big ute up north to have a look at the cart. A big, old, wooden-spoked cart stood in the paddock. It needed a new floor and lots of attention.

The 'old man' was around my age. He kept sitting down to talk with us. 'Me legs are buggered,' he explained. He had ridden brumbies, had fallen in rodeos and worked as a stockman all his life. Too many falls had taken their toll. He was no longer able to use the heavy horse; his injuries made life painful for him.

We talked horses and I decided to buy the cart.

'Now to get it up on the back of my ute!' I said.

'Ahh yes,' said the man, looking at Joshua. 'No problem there, eh mate? You see this young buck? Well, he should be able to lift it on board with his dick!'

I backed the ute into a verge and we rolled the cart on board.

That cart is like the train — it brings dreams of other times!

I have turned fifty!

Each season I have acupuncture and I have learnt to listen to my body. I check it out, grizzle about being tired and forgetful with this time of menopause and enjoy being the age I am now.

It had been some years since I had last seen my mother. The last face-to-face visit was when I was forty. Right, time to visit, I thought, to heal the past. I had named my past and healed the hurt so I felt confident about reaching out to her. We lasted a day before the argument. She exploded, and facing me said, 'I hope you get killed.' I left.

I cried it out and away. We are oil and water and we can never relate. We can only look at each other in amazement that we once shared a body.

But at fifty I gave her another try. I phoned.

'Hello, Mum, it's me. I'm fifty today, I just thought I'd contact you.'

'Who are you? I don't remember having you.'

I put the phone down gently. No tears this time.

I sighed. I looked at the phone. 'Well, Mum, you did give me life, reluctant as you may have been, and for that I thank you.'

I embraced our intertwined lives and with an open heart finally released our bond. I rang my heart-sisters for love, hugged the dogs and went for a ride, singing to the spirits about the joy of life.

It was Tigger's feet time again. I'd been lifting the big feet up and rewarding with carrots. It was a slow process. Fred, the farrier who cares for my girls' feet, refused to work with Tigger. 'Get a Clydesdale man,' he said. 'I don't ever do these big fellows.'

Fred is a small, wiry man, strong, and a very skilled rider. He rises at dawn to excercise his polo and race horses. My horses and dogs really like him because he always greets them with pats and kind words. A great storyteller and gossip, Fred brings me up-to-date on local horse news.

'I haven't lost a lamb all year,' Fred told me proudly. 'I bought an alpaca. He works like a charm and keeps the foxes away.'

'Have you seen any foxes?' I asked.

'Funny you should ask that,' Fred replied. 'The dog woke me up just before dawn last week. Barking and carrying on. That night when it was bitter and frosty. I went into the kitchen and looked out the window. There was a bloody fox in the yard. I grabbed the torch and the gun and tore outside. The cold hit me like a sledgehammer and I was frozen to the spot. I suddenly realised — there I was out in the yard, stark naked except for my ugg boots, torch and gun. I can still hear that fox laughing!'

Barry, the farrier I found to care for Tigger's feet, is a delightful, tall Australian who uses all the old colloquialisms in his speech — 'bonzer', 'cobber', and 'beauty', pronounced 'buudy'. Patiently he's persevered with Tigger and now can work on the feet while holding them between his legs.

Tigger is still bribed with carrots. 'When I can put shoes on him like this I'm gunna buy him a bag full of carrotts,' Barry tells me. He calls Tigger 'The Quince'!

I'm forever kissing and hugging all my horses. Tigger has just started to call and to kiss me back!

This autumn finds me preparing for winter. There is wood to cut, a vegetable garden to plant, paddocks to harrow, and rugs to clean and mend.

Chris left the country experience for another life and although I am the only human here I am surrounded by rescued wildlife and chooks, ducks, geese, a donkey, goat, horses, dogs and four cats.

I am riding Tigger every day. Half a click to his paddock, back by night. Bareback. He is excellent with most traffic and the road is very quiet most of the time. A friend, Jen, and I enjoy a country ride once a week, taking Tigger or Missy and Espirit. Ebony is driven once a week to the local town for the shopping, and occasionally for a picnic. The local Irish pub and post office have promised to erect hitching rails. Jen and I are using Tigger for farm work and we plan to put him in his cart by winter. I'm saving up for his shoeing (it's an arm and a leg).

The spirits of the land I caretake (for how can anyone ever really *own* land?) sing and dance; it is the time of the falling leaves, and the cold season is only a few weeks away. The horses' coats are changing colour with the passage of the season.

I am dreaming of a vardo, a bow-top wagon. My dream is that Tigger, the dogs and I will hit the road for a few months every year, to travel this beautiful country, to meet people and share a cup of tea and our stories. My story continues.